Catch the Bird but Watch the Wave

A Pacific Sociorhetorical Reading of Luke 18:18–30

FATILUA FATILUA

Foreword by Vernon K. Robbins

◠PICKWICK *Publications* • Eugene, Oregon

CATCH THE BIRD BUT WATCH THE WAVE
A Pacific Sociorhetorical Reading of Luke 18:18–30

Copyright © 2024 Fatilua Fatilua. All rights reserved. Except for brief quotations in critical publications or reviews, no part of this book may be reproduced in any manner without prior written permission from the publisher. Write: Permissions, Wipf and Stock Publishers, 199 W. 8th Ave., Suite 3, Eugene, OR 97401.

Pickwick Publications
An Imprint of Wipf and Stock Publishers
199 W. 8th Ave., Suite 3
Eugene, OR 97401

www.wipfandstock.com

PAPERBACK ISBN: 978-1-6667-8835-8
HARDCOVER ISBN: 978-1-6667-8836-5
EBOOK ISBN: 978-1-6667-8837-2

Cataloguing-in-Publication data:

Names: Fatilua, Fatilua, author. | Robbins, Vernon K. (Vernon K.) 1939–, foreword.

Title: Catch the bird but watch the wave : a Pacific sociorhetorical reading of Luke 18:18–30 / Fatilua Fatilua ; foreword by Vernon K. Robbins.

Description: Eugene, OR: Pickwick Publications, 2024. | Includes bibliographical references and indexes.

Identifiers: ISBN 978-1-6667-8835-8 (paperback). | ISBN 978-1-6667-8836-5 (hardcover). | ISBN 978-1-6667-8837-2 (ebook)

Subjects: LCSH: LSCH: Bible. Luke XVIII, 18–30—Criticism, interpretation, etc. | Bible. Luke—Criticism, interpretation, etc. | Bible. Luke—Socio-rhetorical criticism. | Poverty.

Classification: BS2595.52 F37 2024 (print). | BS2595.52 (epub).

VERSION NUMBER 02/16/24

Scripture quotations are from New Revised Standard Version Bible, copyright © 1989 National Council of the Churches of Christ in the United States of America. Used by permission. All rights reserved worldwide.

Catch the Bird but Watch the Wave

This is dedicated to my wife, Vaituutuu, and our children:
Alexander, Portia, Karis, Dauvunau, Selene, and Letaeaomanino;
And in remembrance of my parents:
Satiu Fatilua and Faatuaiitaua Silafau Fatilua

Contents

Foreword by Vernon K. Robbins | ix
Acknowledgments | xiii

Introduction | 1

Part One: *Tautai Seu*

1. Scoping the Land/Sea-scape of Biblical Hermeneutics in the Pacific Island Region | 13
2. Engaging *Tautai* (Steersperson) in Other Context | 43
3. Political-Economic Context, Poverty, and Institutional Constraints in Samoa | 78
4. Steering and Situating the Lukan Narrative | 111

Part Two: *Tautai Ama*

5. Social, Cultural, and Ideological Texture | 135
6. The Political-Economic Context and the Institutional Environment of the Household | 168

Part Three: *Tautai A'e*

7. The Mooring Point: *Aiga*, Church, and the Island of Hope | 199

Glossary | 219
Bibliography | 223

Foreword

IN THE CONTEXT OF the international spread of sociorhetorical interpretation (SRI),[1] it has been especially exciting to see its presence and use in the Pacific Islands, with special prominence in Fiji and Samoa. Fatilua Fatilua's book follows a pattern, introduced by Vaitusi Nofoaiga, of selecting a word or phrase in Samoan language that has special significance for the people who live there.[2] It is common for people who live on a major continent to use the metaphor of a journey to describe the adventure of discovery the author presents in a book. Instead of a journey, Fatilua uses a Samoan proverb that I am tempted to translate as, "Catch the bird but keep an eye on the wave" (56). The proverb comes, as Fatilua explains, from the Pacific Island experience of riding the waves to catch a low-flying bird that will serve as bait for catching fish. One must be careful not to succumb to the wave that rides one high enough to catch the bird in the net. But for Fatilua, the proverb describes the nature of his adult life traversing the oceans to gain international knowledge, credentials, and insights to guide and nurture him as he tries to become the leader he should be among Pacific Islanders. He must keep his eye on the goal of helping his people live among the chaotic waters of today's world.

What aspects of biblical criticism should Fatilua use as he answers a call to study the Bible, teach the Bible, become a professional interpreter of the Bible, and live in the biblical tradition of *following in the way he should go*? What aspects of classic literary-historical criticism should he use? What aspects of liberation interpretation should he use? What aspects of the social sciences should he use? Should he use aspects of rhetorical

1. Robbins and Jeal, eds., *Welcoming the Nations*.
2. Nofoaiga, *Samoan Reading of Discipleship*.

interpretation and post-colonial interpretation? If so, who will guide him? How will he know if he is being too Pacific-Islander oriented? Or if he is being too international? Or too North American? Who can he trust, and how will he know if he has trusted correctly?Fatilua takes a journey through Asia, Africa, and North America, with his *eye on the bird* as he rides international waves looking for methodological answers that can nurture his soul as he lives in a post-parent world. He must carry on *the tradition*, but what tradition must he carry on? Must it be his family tradition, his community tradition, his church tradition, his Samoan tradition, his Pacific Island tradition? Or should it be the circular-migration tradition of living decades in Samoa, then decades in North America making trips to Samoa, then decades again in Samoa making trips to North America? Perhaps it is *the Samoan tradition* of sailing across the oceans and then returning to Samoa to live once more among one's own village, in one's own country, and among one's own people as a grown adult who continues to *catch the bird* while *watching the wave*. This is a tradition that intermingles, blends, interweaves, and intertwines multiple traditions to make life in the Pacific Islands not only livable but alive and flourishing.

Throughout this book, Fatilua travels far and wide, searching for these blended answers. Readers can experience the adventure of this search as Fatilua moves from chapter to chapter throughout this book. How thrilling it has been for me to experience Fatilua Fatilua's merging of his academic career with mine. Sociorhetorical interpretation was formulated out of experiences of migrating from a small mid-western farm to larger and larger metropolitan areas of the United States with major sojourns and periods of habitation in Norway and South Africa. Experiences at the fish-market in Trondheim, Norway, intermingled with fishing adventures in Minnesota, prepared me in basic ways for Fatilua's riding on the waves in this book. But little did I know when I read Christina Thompson's *Sea People: The Puzzle of Polynesia*, and then presented a review of it at an Emory Emeritus College Book Fest, that sociorhetorical interpretation had been taken to the Pacific Islands already in the late 1990s by Vaitusi Nofoaiga and would now be advanced in books like Fatilua's.

This book has A strong focus on Contextual Biblical Interpretation. After an Introduction, it presents a survey of Pacific Island biblical interpreters who have somehow brought specific oceanic experiences into interpretation of the Old Testament or the New Testament. Then he surveys African and Asian biblical hermeneutics, looking for waves he should ride to catch the bait he should use to bring his interpretation home. His goal here is to explain how contextual biblical interpretation can interweave liberation, resistance, and transformation into interpretive strategies that have an honorable presence in Western, African, and Asian biblical interpretation. The result is a rich discussion of contextual biblical hermeneutics with an eye on a distinctive way to incorporate sociorhetorical interpretation into oceanic biblical hermeneutics.Fatilua's next step is a discussion of specific aspects of politics, economy, and poverty in Samoa.

This sets the stage for a *counterintuitive* interpretation of the story of the Lukan version of the rich man who rejected Jesus' call to discipleship because he had considerable wealth. After an introduction to interpretation of the gospel of Luke, Fatilua uses sociorhetorical strategies to argue that the rich man did not simply *reject* Jesus' call to discipleship, but accepted discipleship *on his own terms*. For Fatilua, this means the rich man responded to the final commandment Jesus recited to him, that he should *honor his father and mother* (Luke 18:20). The rich man, in Fatilua's view, will honor his parents by continuing to oversee the wealth he has received from them. He will do this by making his wealth accessible to others in a generous and disciplined manner as Zacchaeus does in Luke 19:1–10, a story which comes shortly after the story of the rich man in Luke 18:18–30.

After his interpretation of the story of the rich man in Chapter five, Fatilua uses a social-scientific approach in Chapter six to explain income distribution and household economy in the Greco-Roman world in relation to their function in the Pacific Islands. Then he presents a conclusion that reads Luke 1–18 with new eyes for seeing the many people in the gospel of Luke who have wealth and argues for a *presupposition of resituated discipleship* in Jesus' responses to his disciples in Luke 18:26–30. Then at the end of the book Fatilua presents both a Samoan and a Tongan glossary for specific oceanic terminology he has used at various points in his presentation.

This is a book with fascinating information about trends in biblical hermeneutics that many readers may have little or no occasion to know about in any detail. Also, it contains a remarkable intertwining of methods and strategies to communicate challenging political-economic dimensions of life in Samoa in particular and the Pacific Islands more broadly. Enjoy the ride upon the waves!

Vernon K. Robbins, Professor Emeritus of Religion—Winship Distinguished Professor in the Humanities, Emory University

Acknowledgments

I acknowledge God's Grace, enabling and empowering in every twist and turn of this journey.

I acknowledge all whom I have crossed paths with, and while your names I have not mentioned, your advice, encouragement, and support contributed much to my personal journey. I am indebted to you all.

I acknowledge the support of the Congregational Christian Church Samoa (CCCS). Special thanks to Rev. Dr. Vaitusi Nofoaiga, Principal of Malua Theological College, Members of the Malua Faculty, Student Body and all my Malua colleagues. *Faafetai tele mo le tapuaiga.*

I acknowledge the support of the PTC Council, PTC Principal, Rev. Dr. Prof. Upolu Vaai, and members of faculty of the Pacific Theological College.I acknowledge with heartfelt gratitude my supervisor and mentor Prof. Vernon Robbins for his willingness and commitment to step in and provide advice and guidance, "re-situating" the project in its final context. I acknowledge my good friend Prof. Holger Szesnat for having trust in me and for all his support throughout this journey.

I acknowledge the support and prayers of all our aiga. *Faafetai mo la outou tatalo ma le tapuaiga.*

Finally, I acknowledge my wife Vaituutuu and our children. Thank you for your love, and for the joy that you bring to bear on this journey.

Introduction

MY ALIBI

BIBLICAL INTERPRETATION IS PERSONAL. While objectivity is intended, this book is also about my struggle to face my mother's death. I left Samoa in the late 1980s to be domiciled in Mark Twain's "most cordial and sociable city in the Union" (Taper 1963, 1), San Francisco, California. For the next decade, the culturally diverse "city by the bay" with its boundless opportunities and vibrant optimism was my home until the early 2000s when I relocated to Albany, New York, where after completing my PhD, I eventually resituated in Washington, D.C., for employment in the U.S. Capitol.

My mother was diagnosed with cancer in November 2011. This turned the tide, triggering life-changing events over the next decade. I sold my house, quit federal work, and relocated to Samoa to begin theological training at the Malua Theological College (Malua) to become a minister for the Congregational Christian Church, Samoa (CCCS). At the time, my sole motivation was the shimmering hope that God would spare my dying mother, if only for a few more years. Moreover, as if it was divinely synchronized, my mother passed away the day I began theological training. I struggled with that for a while, and eventually, I found myself drawn to the ruler in Luke 18:18–30. I identify with the ruler not out of self-pity but out of optimism that the ruler maybe represents something more. Perhaps the ruler represents my struggle as a Christian to navigate the confluence that often involves religion, politics, economics, and family life.

Re-situating myself with the ruler in Luke's narrative, I read with the ruler; I read to liberate the ruler. It is not to stand with the rich or the elites. This argument has already been advanced by those advocating for wealth and prosperity. I read with an ambition to re-situate the text to make sense of and understand life-altering events. However, it is a struggle that I feel is rich with theological and philosophical underpinnings and biblical implications.

Contextual Biblical Interpretation

Contextual biblical interpretation is as much about multiple readings as a sense of responsibility in our biblical interpretive enterprise. It recognizes that we live in a global world where everything and everyone is interconnected and interrelated. For example, the Christian Bible exists alongside other religious texts in Asia. In the Pacific Islands, it coexists with oral traditions that still resonate with people in contemporary society. In this regard, contextual biblical interpretation is cognizant that interpretation is never completed. Nor does it claim any particular reading, text, or methodological approach.

My aim in this book is to carry out a contextual biblical reading. I anticipate something akin to a deep, rich contextual interpretation of specific verses, paragraphs, and sections of the Bible. Such a contextual approach can be extended to all centuries of interpretation of the Bible from antiquity to the present, sometimes using various things "intertextually" from various writers in intervening centuries. There is much to learn from "contextual" indigenous interpretations of the Bible, especially in non-dominant cultures and societies. These previous moments of interpretation inform my contextual biblical reading as I focus "contextually" on a particular set of issues in contemporary society.

To accept the notion that there is a multiplicity of readings, contextual biblical reading warrants responsible reading. While I accept the Bible as God's word, I am equally cautious about making it the sole measure of validity. In this regard, my predispositions steer my intellect towards a pragmatic approach. At the heart of it is how to respond from a biblical basis to some of the major concerns and needs that ordinary people confront in their daily life experiences. However, instead of insisting upon a clear separation of the tangibles and intangibles, I am interested in exploring both. To bring the Bible to bear on the needs and concerns of ordinary readers, one must have the courage and innovation to break down boundaries and simple categorizations. This also suggests the need to remain critical of our reading and re-reading and be self-reflective. It is not to be critical of everything but to be able to critically engage and learn from others' particular things that are especially relevant for addressing a particular contemporary issue.

Religion, Politics, Economics, and Family Life

The subject of this contextual biblical inquiry is the confluence of religion, politics, economics, and family life. This is significant for the individual within the Pacific Island Countries and Territories (PICTs) context[1], particularly in Samoan society.[2] As a nation founded in God and with most of its population identified as Christians, Samoa is built on the three indispensable pillars of Christianity, the *faa-Samoa* (Samoan culture or way of life), and a democracy based on the Westminster model of parliamentary government. This tripartite structure governs and shapes the confluence of religion, politics, economics, and family life in Samoan society.

Since its independence in 1962, Samoa has struggled to navigate the nebulous relationship between these pillars. Tectonic movements and shifts amid the tripartite pillars have significant implications for the political-economic context of Samoan society. More significantly, they converge to shape and influence family life. To further explore this confluence on family life, I look to the Bible. I particularly look for parallels in Luke's account of the encounter between Jesus and the ruler.

The conventional understanding of Luke 18:18–30 claims discipleship as central. The ruler is interpreted as selfish, hence, his apparent discontent with Jesus' demand to sell everything and give to people experiencing poverty. This understanding, though, does much to undermine social and institutional relations in society. It underpins a seeming disconnect between a dominant construct of faith and the lived reality of the people. This view of the demand to sell everything pushes a particular

---

1. I am drawn to the term PICTs as it also recognizes those Pacific Island people that are still under territorial authority of some other foreign country. This consists of the U.S. Insular Areas including American Samoa, Commonwealth of the Northern Mariana Islands (CNMI), Guam, Palau, and the Federated States of the Marshall Islands (FSM) in the Pacific region, as well as New Caledonia and Tahiti under French rule and West Papua under the rule of the Indonesian government.

2. When I speak of Samoan society, I am referring to a broader view of Samoan ethnicity which also includes Samoans in the U.S. territory of American Samoa and in the diaspora. Be that as it may, the political and economic scope for this contextual biblical approach is the Independent State of Samoa (Samoa).

narrative that contributes much to the economic plight of people experiencing poverty.

I seek an alternative reading from my context in this contextual biblical inquiry. Could Luke be amenable to a re-situating of the ruler? Inspiration for re-situating the ruler is drawn from the Samoan concept of *aiga* (family) and the role of the *matai sa'o* (literally translated as the right one) as the head of the household. In that regard, my re-reading is a decentering of conventional understanding to emphasize instead the various institutions that shape and influence the political-economic context of family life. I am interested in the effects of institutional constraints—political and economic as well as cultural, social, and ideological factors—that shape and influence the institutional and social relations surrounding the context of Christian faith in the Pacific Island region. My hope overall is for an engagement that is transformative and liberating; that is, the text transforms me while my experience and context liberate the text.

From this contextualization of the Lukan text, inferences rendered are moored[3] in the political and economic issues facing Samoa and, to an extent, the Pacific Island Countries and Territories (PICTs). While the Lukan context and the PICTs are vastly different, the parallels transcend time and space so that a closer connection could be made, which would inform the contemporary reader. This connection also warrants meaningful dialogue with scholars from other contexts, including Asia and Africa, with comparable lived realities. I learn and borrow certain things from them that are helpful in my attempt to contextualize the Bible.

Moreover, by making this connection, I am also pursuing a secondary interest: exploring Pacific Island biblical hermeneutics. In particular, I argue the need to ground it in real-life issues confronting Pacific Island readers. A contextual biblical reading necessitates a deep exploration of the relevant issues. An issue-oriented approach goes a long way toward bridging biblical interpretation, theology and issues of justice and leadership, and the lived reality of the contemporary Pacific Island reader.

This brings me to my main argument in this contextual biblical reading. It is more meaningful and relevant that the interpretive framework

---

3. My usage of moor is inspired by the Samoan concept of *taulaga* (mooring point). The stem for *taulaga* in the Samoan language is *taula*, to anchor. Interestingly, Apia is known as the *taulaga* or capital city of Samoa. It is literally the meeting point for Samoa's rural and urban population as well as visitors to the country. Historically it was one of the anchorages for ships and fishing vessels during the colonial days. I use moor in the sense that it parallels the act of anchoring and grounding, settling and situating.

or methodological scheme of contextual biblical reading is based on the needs and concerns of contemporary society. In turn, I argue that the political-economic context of the Samoan *aiga* does much to shape the methods and tools used to explore the biblical text. As a result, the approach taken in this contextual biblical reading foregrounds the social, political, and economic relations constitutive of the Samoan *aiga*.

Guiding Questions

In re-situating the text, I ask some general questions. What institutional and social constraints could have shaped and influenced the context of Luke's "re-situating" of the rich ruler? What other possible interpretations could this reading of the rich ruler be amenable to?

My underpinning claim is that the nuances of Luke's narrative merit exploring its social and institutional relations. Subsequently, I intend to show that the ruler's response is part of a "rubber meets road" moment in Luke's narrative. The interaction indicates a critical juncture when a particular construct of faith meets social reality. To gain more clarity and make the passage more meaningful to the contemporary reader, particularly Samoa, I present a juxtaposition of the Samoan *aiga* context and that of the ruler's household. This juxtaposition is informed by exploring political-economic issues in the context of Samoan society, particularly poverty. Ultimately, I hope to produce some propositions regarding the confluence between Christian faith, politics, economics, and family life.

The *seu le manu ae taga'i ile galu* Sennit Lash

I engage Samoan traditional knowledge and wisdom to fashion a theoretical framework guided and informed by Samoan cultural philosophies and life experience. For conceptualizing a theoretical framework, I use the notion of a Samoan *faletele* (meeting house) as my frame of reference. I differentiate between the roles of the *tufuga* (carpenter) and the *fau'afa*[4] (sennit lashers) in the building of the *faletele*. While the *tufuga* is

---

4. Albert Refiti (2015, 168n517) suggests a reason for the Tui Atua bringing to Samoa the Tongan *lalava* (Tongan word for *fau'afa*) Filipe Tohi to lash and tie his house. Some of the best *fau'afa* in modern Samoa are from Fagaloa, an eastern district on the island of Upolu. The connection between Fagaloa and the Tongan royal lineage through the paramount title Ulualofaiga Talamaivao suggests that the connection could have also included sharing of knowledge on sinnet lashing.

responsible for the tectonic structures and architecture of the building, the *fau'afa* is tasked with lashing and tying the house together using the *afa* or sennit. Albert Refiti called them journeymen (2015, 168), although I prefer to think of them as gifted with wisdom and *mana* (sacred). Thus, sennit lashing gifts the house with *mana* (sacredness) and wisdom. Similarly, the theoretical framework ties the study together, providing it frame and structure. More significantly, it gives my contextual biblical reading a sense of *mana* and cultural significance.Sennit lashing is usually done in patterns and motifs. While they are usually admired for their decorative functions, the patterns and motifs symbolize values important to the fau'afa and the building. For example, one of the traditional patterns is the *sumu* (fish)[5] lash which connects horizontal and vertical joints. Describing the connection between the central post and the ridgepole of the Samoan house, Refiti interprets the *sumu* lash as a celebration of the joining together of the vertical posts as the props holding together and apart the world of men and *lagi* (heaven) and the horizontal posts signaling the spanning cosmos (Pratt 1911, 207). The *sumu* lash, in that regard, underpins the spatial connection between earth, heaven, and the cosmos.

The theoretical framework for my contextual biblical interpretation is lashed in a particular motif and pattern, underpinning specific critical values and functions. To choose a pattern or motif, I draw inspiration from another important lived reality of Samoan culture, fishing. The guiding motif is captured in the Samoan proverb *seu le manu ae taga'i ile galu*, literally translated as "catch the bird but watch the wave." These two simultaneous actions require specific skill sets. Altogether, these skill sets can be thought of as organizing or binding together the range of practices performed in this endeavor. The concept of binding together evokes the action of "sennit-lashing," a unique metaphor in the fishing culture where I was raised, permeating this contextual biblical reading of Luke.

Let me digress here and share how this helps organize my reading of Luke. From the *seu le manu ae taga'i ile galu* guiding motif, I derive three critical skillsets of steersman-ship. My contextual biblical reading is divided into three broad categories representing each skill set.

First, *seu le manu* signals the act of catching a bird. However, this catching of the bird is to make fish bait. While catching the bird is essential, the primary goal is to fish for a good catch. Thus, *seu le manu*

---

5. According to Pratt (1911, 286) *sumu* is the name of fishes of the genus Balistes. In Samoan and Tongan mythology, the *sumu* and *toloa* (duck) were both taken up to heaven and became stars. Thus, *sumu* also means a "cluster of stars," according to Pratt.

signals the attempt to acquire. To acquire in this sense suggests locating and situating a moving target. For example, the *tautai* (fisherman or steersman) must steer the canoe to locate and situate the bird in its flight. The canoe is in constant motion. Just as the bird in its flight is darting unpredictability from one point to another, the steersman must negotiate the seeming randomness of the fleeting target. A skilled steersperson must therefore locate and situate himself not only with the flight of the bird but also with the direction and velocity of the wind, as well as the depth and strength of the waves and flow of the currents. To capture the essence of this needed skill in fishing, I use the formative name *tautai seu* (the art of locating). As a *tautai seu*, I steer to locate and situate within the context of interpretation.

Second, *taga'i ile galu* signals mastery of the waves and the sea. It denotes wisdom from engaging and negotiating tidal and ocean currents, fish movement, and patterns. However, doing this in climatic conditions merits someone wise to ignore or *ama* the danger. The art of *ama* then involves navigating the shifting currents of the *Moana* (ocean) to scale the challenges ahead. It underpins the multidimensional aspect of fishing and the openness needed to receive the day's catch from the *Moana*. To capture this skill of the steersperson, I call it *tautai ama* (the art of negotiating and navigating while maintaining focus). *Tautai ama* captures the act of reading the text with a sense of navigating the possibilities by focusing on bringing home the catch of the day. It means I am partially conscious of "other things" in the context throughout the reading. As a *tautai ama*, I do not let those things distract me from the "major focus" I wish to catch.

Finally, *seu le galu ae taga'i ile galu* overall suggests responsibility and prudence. Prudence and responsibility warrant self-reflection. While the catch of the day is received, it is always in the context of what has been birthed from the belly of the *Moana*. Receiving the day's catch calls for celebrating life given and life sustained. However, it is celebrating with prudence since the catch is to be shared with others. Moreover, in doing so, others may be inspired to find spaces for further fishing. This final aspect of fishing I called *tautai a'e*. As a *tautai a'e* I call for celebration. Celebrating with prudence. In celebrating, I find a mooring point for reflection and mending. For the end is never in permanence but only a re-situating.

My contextual biblical reading is "sennit-lashed" in three parts, each representing one of the three aspects of steersmanship discussed above. They are—*tautai seu, tautai ama,* and *tautai a'e*. These are essential skills drawn from Samoan traditional wisdom and necessary at certain junctures of my reading of Luke. However, it is essential to note that just as fishing is carried out in a fluid *moana* mode, it is implausible to completely demarcate and assume boundaries between *tautai seu, tautai ama,* and *tautai a'e*. The three are sometimes intertwined and often overlap with crossing outcomes and boundaries. As the *tautai* (steersperson), I must negotiate and navigate the crossings and overlaps in the text with prudence.

Outline of the Book and Chapter Overviews

Part 1 of this contextual biblical study is called *tautai seu*. It encapsulates the idea of acquiring, locating, and situating. As a *tautai seu*, I scope the land and sea of scholarship and other steersperson to ascertain critical elements. Always keeping an open mind, I look for similarities and parallels. While similarities are essential, I embrace differences and discrepancies as well. By comparing and contrasting, I situate and locate meaning and value.

Thus, chapter 1 scopes the landscape and the sea-scape of biblical hermeneutics in the Pacific Island region. While I recognize that Australia and New Zealand are part of the Pacific family, my aim for this contextual biblical reading necessitates particularizing the concerns and issues confronting the Pacific Island Countries and Territories (PICTs). Chapter 2 seeks to locate and situate myself within other similar contexts. I steer towards other oceans with an interest to learn from other steersperson. I suspect much to learn from similar contexts like Africa and Asia. I acknowledge, though, that while regions like the Caribbean and Latin America are just as important, I am bound by the scope of the study.

The ocean is the closest representation of our interconnectedness in the global "context."[6] Thus, an "ocean" biblical reading warrants learning from other steersperson in other "oceans" or contexts. After situating and locating, chapter 3 foregrounds the political-economic context of PICTs,

---

6. As water covers more than 70 percent of the earth, and almost 100 percent of that water is found in the oceans, there is much to be said about the oceans bearing the closest analogy of global interconnectedness. I use the ocean, though, as an analogy for interconnectedness, knowing that it has limitations. In particular, several countries and communities do not have access to or are connected to the oceans. Moreover, I am also cognizant of many countries and communities that have suffered from drought and the issues relating to the lack of good drinking water. Nonetheless, the analogy underpins my own sense that there is much to learn from reviewing the works of scholars in other similar contexts.

emphasizing poverty and institutional constraints in Samoan society. Finally, chapter 4 delves into the deep *Moana* of Lukan scholarship, situating and locating placement for my contextual biblical reading of Luke 18:18–30.

Part II is guided by *tautai ama*. It represents reading and negotiating patterns and movements while focusing on the day's catch. Utilizing sociorhetorical analytics blended with insights from the New Institutional Economics (NIE), the *tautai ama* steers and navigates between the different boundaries and challenges being confronted. While the focus of the steersman is on the immediate goal, the importance of keeping a holistic view is not lost upon the interpreter. The *tautai ama* maintains a holistic view of things by focusing on the elements and their surroundings and the relationship between and among them. Part II then includes Chapter 5, which steers through the text's social, cultural, and ideological textures, navigating the relationships between and among them. Chapter 6 negotiates and navigates the boundaries of the political economy in ancient society, yet always steers prudently through and around existing relationships to other aspects of the text, including intertextural materials.

Part III represents the *tautai a'e*. The end is not the end per se, but it is space to celebrate what has been given in terms of the day's catch. In that regard, the *tautai a'e* celebrates the day's catch with prudence, recognizing that while today's catch may be plentiful, tomorrow's can only be anticipated by the shifting waves of the sea and the ebbs and flows of the current and the wind. The *tautai a'e*, therefore, is also a space that functions as the mooring point or *taulaga* to ponder and reflect on future ventures and anticipated finds. By sharing today's catch, the *tautai a'e* invites others to *talanoa* or a discussion that anticipates the challenges and possibilities of the next day's fishing. Thus, chapter 7 counts the day's catch metaphorically, summarizing the findings and restating the significance of my contextual biblical study. However, the aim also is for these findings to be moored in the political and economic context of the people in the PICTs. The chapter points out some of the study's limitations and reflections on the overall study. In the end, I hope to produce some general propositions that capture the findings and some considerations for further research.

PART ONE

Tautai Seu

1

Scoping the Land/Sea-scape of Biblical Hermeneutics in the Pacific Island Region

INTRODUCTION

THE EYES OF THE *tautai seu* locate and situate meaning, which warrants scoping both the ocean-scape and the landscape for signs and symbols. As a *tautai seu*, I steer to acquire knowledge, gaining from critical and dialogical engagement with other fishers of the deep Pacific *Moana*. It is not my purpose to formulate full-fledged Pacific Island biblical hermeneutics.[1] Instead, I am trying to re-situate within the contours of biblical scholarship in the region. I ask critical, unsettling questions, probing issues that sometimes make others uncomfortable. The motive is scoping. By scoping, I identify and locate personal predispositions and

---

1. Stanley E. Porter (2013, 31–32) gives a functional distinction between biblical hermeneutics and biblical interpretation. The discipline of hermeneutics includes elements of interpretation as well as "what it means to be an interpreter—what are the assumptions, preconditions, felicitous conditions, activities, prior commitments and human components, among other things, that enter into, and even govern, any act of human understanding, whether its object be language, culture, the physical world, even texts and much else." Interpretation however "includes the processes and techniques involved in interpretive acts, especially, but not exclusively, of texts." While I appreciate Porter's distinction between the two, I do use them interchangeably for the sake of ease.

idiosyncrasies within the broader arena of Pacific Island biblical scholarship over the last 20 years; I ask these questions. What does Pacific Island biblical hermeneutics look like, and how does it feel? What are some of the similarities and differences between and among them? What are the methodological approaches and some of the issues and challenges? How can this scope of knowledge help my intent to carry out a contextual[2] biblical reading of Luke?

I claim a partial account; the purpose is to shed light on some of the patterns and movements in Pacific Island biblical hermeneutics. Like any attempt to account for the diverse islands, people, and cultures widely dispersed across the Pacific Ocean, my attempt to circumnavigate the depth and eclectic nature of Pacific Island biblical hermeneutics scholarship has particular challenges and difficulties. One of the challenges is that many of the published works on biblical hermeneutics are Polynesian. Hardly there is any mention of Melanesian or Micronesian biblical scholars, which also signals the need for more available scholarship about Pacific Island biblical hermeneutics. While work is abundant at the level of master's theses, publication beyond this level is found wanting. As a result, I engage primarily published materials plus a couple of unpublished items selected for the sake of argument and to highlight a greater need for cultural diversity within Pacific Island biblical scholarship.

The order is chronological, based on the year it was published. I start with Jione Havea, followed by Nasili Vaka'uta, Vaitusi Nofoaiga, Mosese Ma'ilo, and Frank Smith. Peni Leota completed his thesis earlier, but publication is forthcoming. His work is exemplary, though of the breadth of Pacific Island scholarship. Under the subheading of additional interpreters, Ma'afu Palu steers a contrasting path while Iosefa Lefaoseu navigates an indigenously-driven interpretive scheme. The selection highlights salient features and perceived lacunae in Pacific Island biblical scholarship. It is not an attempt to identify the most updated or exhaustive list but to situate my reading of Luke along the contours of Pacific Island biblical scholarship. The chapter concludes with an overview and sharing of areas for possible contribution.

---

2. For the use of the term "contextual," I find the edited work of Jione Havea and Peter H. W. Lau (Havea and Lau 2020b) instructive and helpful.

JIONE HAVEA—A TRANSOCEANIC EXPERIENCE

I start with Jione Havea, who may have been the first to engage in academic publication. Havea's work exhibits a colorful flavor of the Pacific Island experience interspersed with exegetical work in biblical studies to render a framework for future Pacific Island scholars to follow. In his seminal monograph, *Elusions of Control*, Havea foregrounds his transoceanic experience showcasing the "boundary-crossing tendencies" of transoceanic readers (2003, 3). The experience of a Pacific Islander—of Tongan descent in particular, and surrounded by limited land space—colored his examination of regulations concerning women's vows in Numbers 30. The impact of regulations on divorcees and widows in ancient Israelite society is juxtaposed against the backdrop of images and metaphors from Havea's transoceanic experience. The outcome is a creative innovation, interweaving nuances of island life and Havea's exegetical prowess. Not only delivering an acute and profound sense of distinctiveness, *Elusions of Control* illuminates diligence in engaging the text.

A prominent feature of Havea's work is how he cleverly navigates between the sphere of the Pacific Island voice and his Tongan heritage. As he proceeds, Havea exposes the daunting task facing Pacific Island biblical hermeneutics scholars. For example, how does one undertake Pacific Island biblical hermeneutics in a culturally rich and diverse region? Havea's *Elusions* underpins advances and limitations in at least two arenas. First, there appear to be strengths and weaknesses as Havea tackles Pacific Island biblical hermeneutics. On the one hand, he brings his prestigious Tongan heritage into prominence; on the other hand, in specific ways, this limits his ability to emphasize Pacific Island people's culturally rich and diverse culture overall. Second, the strength and energy of his biblical exegesis, grounded in Western exegetical scholarship, at points implicitly claim a result of universal truth rather than leaving the door open to multiple individual ways of justifiably viewing specific issues.

Havea appears to be cognizant of these challenges. He skillfully mixes in symbols of his individuality, situated within a more extensive framework of Pacific Island society and culture, as he prioritizes the oceanic orientation and social location of Pacific Islanders. As Havea writes, "south pacific islanders are oriented toward the ocean." The ocean is "our island boundary, albeit a fluid boundary, and an extension of our land." The ocean is also a source of life as "Into the ocean we search for food" (4). By situating himself as a Pacific Islander, Havea highlights the text's free-flowing fluidity, enabling the exegete to cross boundaries and find otherwise difficult spaces. Islands and oceans are connected. Such interconnectedness underscores the transtextuality notion prevalent throughout Havea's reading. As Havea writes, "the boundary (ocean) that links texts (islands), the fluid expanse in between texts, in/through which readers are encouraged to cross playfully but calmly." Moreover, "the boundary is also a stepping stone, a medium, a conduit, real (textual) and/or imaginary (ideological), that enables the reader to leap from one text to another" (5).

Within this larger framework, Havea signals his individuality and Tongan heritage. By interspersing Tongan phrases and concepts throughout, Havea juxtaposes his individuality within the larger framework of a Pacific Island reader, all the while engaging with the text. For example, when Havea talks about gaps and dips in the text of Numbers 30, he draws from the Tongan *ma'ahi* (wake) and *matua* (gap) semantics concerning ocean waves. The outcome underscores a substantial degree of distinctiveness yet captures a specific Pacific Island flavor. Moreover, the Pacific Islander reader has appropriated ownership and a feeling of belonging as an otherwise imported text emerges. In this way, the coupling of historiography, narrative, legal, ideology, and transoceanic leanings (43) allows for an exciting mix, a creative and innovative way of reading the biblical text from the perspective of Pacific Island readers.

Some Consideration of Methodology

As a method for reading, Havea appears to frame everything around his transoceanic leanings and social location. One of the excellent things Havea achieved is using coherent, vivid oceanic images ("mapping the turf, watering the turf, etc.") to direct and inspire interpreters as they work with others to develop indigenous practices within Pacific Island biblical hermeneutics. Many of Havea's successors richly expand upon this excellent move in his exegetical-hermeneutical procedure. Each successor builds on this basic approach by focusing on a particular aspect of their society and culture that extends this rich, indigenous way of proceeding to interpret different elements of biblical literature. Meanwhile, the approach highlights various aspects of Pacific Island society and culture.

The undergirding element is recognizing fluidity in the text, allowing space for the reader's imagination and creativity. The primary focus appears to be the interaction between the text and the reader, giving space and value to the reader's perception, the world of the reader. It is not to say that Havea situates meaning solely with the reader. In practice, Havea recognizes that he can only start with the text (16). In this manner, he situates himself "in between, inter-esse," the texts of Num 30, and interested readers. In the following section, Havea uses textual criticism, situating Numbers 30 within its limits (18). Especially with this added move, it appears that Havea employs his transoceanic leanings to allow him space to move between multiple aspects of the context of the text and the context of his social location as a Pacific Island reader.

Havea describes how he engages the text in five segments relating to island life. The first segment, "mapping the turf," is a circumreading of the text, which highlights some of the "transoceanic leanings" and echoes of Derrida's "circumfession" (1). As Havea writes, "circumreading urges readers toward the embrace of the Other, always particular and already disclosed. It resists inflexible representations in order to account for the complexity of the around-and-across relations of texts. Circumreading is, in that regard, transgressive" (2–3).

Next, Havea uses "watering the turf" to refer to transtextuality that reflects the "cross-boundary" transoceanic perspectives of islanders (3). This watering "represents the meeting, the crossing, or intertextuality with transoceanic perspectives" to encourage what he calls "transformative and transdisciplinary reading" (page 3, fn 11). For Havea, intertextuality is concerned with both the "crossing between texts and the crossing of texts." Crossing between texts sees the text as disconnected or having space in between, while the crossing of texts sees them "intersecting, crossing, a part of, each other" (4). In this regard, it conveys a sense of looking for differences and similarities in the text. Moreover, central to transtextuality is the reader's imagination. Transtextuality "places the weight of the reading practices on the shoulders of the reader's imagination, at once reader-responsive and reader constructing" (5).

Havea also talks about dipping into the surf (6). The islander reader "rides up the wake (*ma'ahi* in Tongan) and down the gap (*matua*), while looking out for breaking waves, to face the wake behind the gap" (6). From a transoceanic view, Havea draws a parallel to transtextuality accounts for "dominant subjects (main points, wakes) and ignored and repressed subjects (the marginalized, gaps) in biblical texts" (6). Havea further states, "In the end, the transoceanic reader realizes that she can neither control nor duplicate the text. Nor can its boundaries (ocean)! Nonetheless, the reader disturbs the text (by crossing and harvesting it), and then she must let the text be" (7). Moreover, "transtextuality, therefore, also participates in the illusion and elusion of control" (7).

The fifth and final segment is overturning the surfs. He again starts with a transoceanic experience of the wave disturbances precipitated by the underside of the waves. From this transoceanic leaning, Havea draws two undercurrents of transtextuality "the affects (agency) and elusiveness of the Other" (8).

Showing astuteness and a great sense of responsibility, Havea recognizes that, as with any methodology, there are limits to his reading scheme, which he calls transtextuality. A primary concern of transtextuality is how to capture the "text and/or materialize its undersides" (8). To this question, Havea responds that it is upon the "shoulders of the reader's imagination" (8). Since what may exist in one's imagination "may be absent or insignificant" in the vision of others, "transtextual readers have a chance to resist other readings and, consequently, to free the text from readers' control" (9). In this manner, "transtextuality is a disarming practice that arms the reader while she anticipates the next departure (on/to the next text and reading)" (9).

Let me digress for a moment. It is noteworthy to revisit a suggestion I made earlier regarding where meaning is located. For Havea, his transoceanic leanings appear to express the multivalent manner in which he deals with the text. While he foregrounds his indigenous leanings and his social location, Havea shows to a certain degree a propensity to prioritize the text. His analysis begins by sifting through the text of Numbers 30 to identify the "dominant subjects" (16). The specific attention to textual evidence focusing on a translation of the Masoretic Text (BHS) and a preference for the Masoretic text is induced by "transoceanic reasons" (18) that find the "playfulness" and "variances" in the text appealing (16). These "disharmonies open the text for interpretation and hold back readers' control" (18). In this sense, Havea draws from transoceanic leanings to characterize the need to maintain the fluidity of the text, but also with a sense of responsibility, avoiding reader biases. His analysis straddles a delicate balance between the world of the text and the world of the modern-day reader. Maintaining that balance, though, I suspect, is the daunting challenge in biblical hermeneutics, no less Pacific Island biblical scholarship.

Reflecting more on transtextuality, I am reminded of Vernon Robbins's use of the intertexture of the text in a sociorhetorical inquiry (1996a, 2016). Robbins and Havea share, in my view, the notion of finding connections, or spaces for connections, between texts. Perhaps an even stronger parallel, transtextuality also resonates with the Samoan concept of *talalasi*, which Mosese Ma'ilo (2018) defines as "big telling or telling big." This, Ma'ilo cleverly employs in a re-appropriation of the biblical Prodigal Son narrative from a Pacific Island perspective. Crossing the Prodigal Son and Albert Wendts' novel-turned-into-film, *Sons for the Return Home*, Mailo highlights the challenges facing Samoans in the diaspora and their search for identity. The common denominator shared by Mailo, Robbins, and Havea is in finding narratives, stories, or texts that could be crossed with the intent of providing alternative and transformative reading. One could argue that the point at which the crossing or intersection takes place is debatable. The strength of the crossing of stories and narratives is it allows for re-appropriating the distinctiveness of the text to fit the needs of the contemporary context. Much like the Pacific Island reader, who is oriented towards the ocean, the text is fluid and, as such, is border-crossing. This is an exciting and innovative way of bridging the gap between the biblical text and the context of the Pacific Island reader.

Be that as it may, there is always a need to interject responsibility. I am reminded of what R.S. Sugitharajah writes: "To use someone else's texts and stories out of their context is to deprive them of their life and independence" (2001, 257). Much like in the Pacific Island region, which is surrounded by the vast Pacific Ocean, the difficulty is allowing fluidity of reading while also maintaining a degree of responsibility to the text, to ourselves and to the readers. This is a common thread throughout much of the biblical scholarship and will be an integral element of this writing.

Further Considerations

I am equally intrigued by the strong liberative flavor in Havea's work, for example the use of "underside,"[3] which suggests something hidden,

---

3. In my search for the meaning of underside I find that it is frequently used in liberation theology scholarship. According to Harvey Cox (1989, 386), Gustavo Gutierrez also coined the phrase "underside" although it was in connection to the phrase "underside of history." Nevertheless, I find the term has a deep connection to liberation theology which raises the question whether this could be evidence that Havea is grounded in

something below surface level but causing disturbances. This, Havea skillfully weaves into the reading with the help of the Tongan phrase "*ngalu fakaofo,*" signaling the unexpected breaking of waves caused by some disturbances triggered at the underside of the wave (7). The resulting insight is fascinating as Havea later admits that a "liberation praxis" surges as the underside current. This is an important matter given that perhaps the Pacific is arguably the last region in the world that has yet to develop some form of liberation theology.

Finally, the two dimensions that occupy the underside of Havea's transtextuality reading cannot be ignored. Transtextuality according to Havea is both transformative[4] and transdisciplinary[5] (3, footnote 11), a reference not only to the capacity to cross boundaries but also to transform the reader. In the process of reading, the text and the reader are transformed. The resulting outcome becomes the starting point for the next sphere of engagement. It is here that I venture to make the claim that Havea is perhaps suggesting the need to ground our hermeneutical reading in the contemporary context, integrating our interpretative conversation with real-life situations. Although this is not explicit I would like to think that Havea is on to something here. By insisting on a transformative element in biblical reading, the resulting outcome is an important pointer for biblical hermeneutics in the Pacific region—the need to ground our reading and interpretation in real-life issues. A great need exists to bridge the Bible with issues and challenges in the region. In this case, Havea's alternative reading of Numbers 30 and the issues confronting women causes the Pacific Island reader, at the very least in this case myself, to pause and rethink, reflecting on the role and status of women within the different Pacific cultures. Women, for example in my Samoan culture, have a special role and function. Havea's reading of Numbers 30 clearly resonates with much of the evidence that suggests women are not treated fairly, whether they be in the workplace, at home, or within society at large. Using the analogy of a canoe, in this manner, Havea's work on Numbers 30 finds anchorage or a mooring point in women-rights issues

---

liberation theology. If so, one must ponder the implications for the developing biblical hermeneutic scholarship in the Pacific region.

4. I carried out a search of the word and find that it emphasizes connections between the biblical text as the word of God and its contemporary significance (Hardin 2012).

5. This suggests the cross boundary, fluid and flowing nature of transtextuality which allows the reader to cross stories that may have not at all seem related.

in the Pacific. The treatment of women in the society is an issue that is very much part of the social fabric of society in the Pacific Islands and throughout Oceania.

A final consideration concerns a universal characterization of Pacific Island readers. While one may argue that Havea's characterization of Pacific Islanders as people oriented towards the ocean minimizes the experience of someone living on the highlands in Papua New Guinea or in the heartlands of Australia, I would add the understanding that Pacific Island people are surrounded by the vast Pacific Ocean to a degree that reflects much of life in the region. In this regard, Havea's characterization of Pacific Islanders as ocean oriented to a large extent captures the experience of most Pacific Islanders. What this reveals, again, is the difficulty in any attempt to claim any distinction for Pacific Island biblical hermeneutics within the richly diverse and broad context of the Pacific Island region.

NASILI VAKA'UTA—TU'A WISE

The second Pacific Island scholar highlighted here is also of Tongan descent. Like Havea, Nasili Vaka'uta in his monograph titled *Reading Ezra 9–10 Tu'a-Wise: Rethinking Biblical Interpretation in Oceania*, displays an array of island colors as he foregrounds his Tongan experience, worldview, context, and culture, to read through the "eyes/I" of a *tu'a*, a commoner (Vaka'uta 2011, 1). For Vaka'uta, it is important to develop a theoretical framework that is "informed by Tongan cultural perspectives and knowledge in general" with particular concentration on the experiences of the Tongan commoner. From this is borne both a methodology and a framework.

The *tu'a*-wise reading appears to be a framing borne of the need for one to show his "subjectivity and idiosyncrasies," meanwhile maintaining connection to a larger community. Vaka'uta writes as not only a *tu'a* (commoner) but also as part of the larger group of commoners. In this way, the play on words using "eyes-I" symbolizes the delicate balance between speaking as an individual and being cognizant of his relation and ties to the larger community of commoners. This play on words is not unique to Vaka'uta or the Pacific Island context. It was arguably initiated in Pacific Island biblical scholarship through Havea and continued by others like Vaitusi Nofoaiga (2017). Moreover, one can find this play on words common to other contexts.

The *tu'a*-wise reading shares the characteristics of context-based interpretation (CBI). It is culture-sensitive, context-based, liberation-focused, faith driven, and people-centered (2011, 4–5). Split into three Parts, each guided by a Tongan concept; Part 1 is guided by *tu'unga*, meaning "location," "status," or "position" (12), Part 2, *founga* designates "points of entry," or "transitory spaces" (13), and Part 3 is guided by the concept of *angafai* which suggests a "way of doing" (13). The overall impact suggests a methodology and framework that is borne of Tongan cultural and social values. It also brings into the fore Vaka'uta's goal of providing an alternative reading, one that departs from the dominant theories and methods in biblical scholarship but is grounded in a Tongan perspective.

By doing so, Vaka'uta lays out what I find to be an important element for further dialogue. His *tu'a*-wise construction is not just applying the text to the reader's context. Indeed, I think this is Vaka'uta's strength. He shows that there is a difference between "contextualizing interpretation" and contextualizing the Bible. These two separated tasks are both contextual. Yet, the former employs "indigenous categories of analysis" for interpretation whereas the latter applies the text to the reader's context. For Vaka'uta, the *tu'a*-wise reading puts more emphasis on what he calls the 'pact' of biblical interpretation (2). More significantly, I think that in here, Vaka'uta poses a nice contrast to other Pacific Island biblical scholars who would more or less appear to be analogous in nature. I will discuss this further when I turn to the works of Frank Smith and Peni Leota.

After describing his *tu'a*-wise reading, Vaka'uta begins by explicating his social location. In this the importance of social location is recognized as critical to the task of biblical interpretation. Adding a Pacific Island flavor, Vaka'uta employs Tongan concepts as categories. For example, he talks about his *tuunga* (social location, social class, commoner) (18), highlighting its importance in situating biblical text. Emphasizing his social location provides space for Vaka'uta, as someone on the inside, to explicate social class and status within the Tongan culture. His underlying motive is to highlight the "underprivileged position" (21) of the *tu'a*, commoners, and by implication share this with readers from outside. The *tu'a* as a social class in Tongan society provides Vaka'uta the space to describe the struggle confronting commoners in Tongan society. It is therefore no surprise that other themes such as resistance, liberation and transformation are also prevalent throughout the exposition (56).

This is where I find Vaka'uta instructive. Vaka'uta, through and by the construction of his social location, allows also for the biblical text to engage with an important issue confronting the contemporary reader in Tongan society. The *tua'*-wise reading appears not only as an interpretive mechanism for understanding the Bible, but also for vetting and rethinking the status quo in a class-based system such as Tonga. This for me is an important and major contribution to the notion of a Pacific Island biblical hermeneutic. It resonates with Havea's notion of a transformative interpretive that transforms the text and allows space for the reader to be transformed. In other words, the transformative essence of the interaction between reader and text bears much on both. One engages in doing critical reading of the Bible and critically assessing societal issues.

To situate the *tu'a*-wise reading, an important point for Vaka'uta's work is to highlight the nexus between contextual interpretation and postcolonialism. The intent appears to divulge a shared interest of contextual and postcolonialism readings (35). For this purpose, Vaka'uta greatly dedicates a whole chapter to establish the intimate connection between contextual and postcolonial approaches. This is an important interest of Vaka'uta as it lays the foundation for the *tu'a*-wise reading.

Vaka'uta begins by spelling out some major tenets of postcolonialism. A major aspect of the postcolonial perspective presupposes a turn to "a real flesh and blood reader who lives amongst a people situated in a particular sociocultural location in time and space" (37). The focus therefore on real-life readers is critical as from this location, "the reader approaches the Bible intending to expose oppressive mechanisms encoded in the text, and those that impede emancipation in the reading community." With this reader's mindset, he or she is "no longer trapped in history or in texts, but is located in different real–life settings" (37).

As Vaka'uta writes, this engagement with real-life situations forms the terrain between postcolonialism and contextual reading. Recognizing the Pacific Island situation bears strongly on the real-life issues confronting readers from the region. From this, Vaka'uta provides four categories that help identify or process the various strands of interpretative modes within a contextual paradigm. These modes include: cultural-ethnocentric, religious-syncretic, experiential-pragmatic, and island-oceanic mode (38). An extensive description of the four modes of reading is given, and from each mode Vaka'uta identifies an important aspect for situating the *tu'a*-wise reading. More importantly, Vaka'uta engages scholars from other contexts including Africa and Asia, on the various contextual modes of studies. By this dialogical engagement, Vaka'uta can peel off and pick up aspects of contextual framework fitting for the *tu'a*-wise reading.

More importantly, Vaka'uta also opens up other avenues for further studies. While his dialogue with a few selected scholars from other contexts is helpful, there is an emerging space for further dialogue, especially on real-life issues confronting people within each context. There appears to be a much-needed dialogue on how the Bible speaks to issues confronting people in different contexts. Grounding the discussion on an issue will also help create ways to assist people at the grassroot level.

Concerning the island-oceanic mode, Vaka'uta provides an interesting review of Havea's *Elusions*. Havea is important for giving the Pacific region voice for the first time. Moreover, he also establishes the Pacific as a site for biblical interpretation outside of the dominant modes of readings and theories. More importantly for Vaka'uta, Havea provides Pacific Island readings such as the *tu'a*-wise reading space to emerge and flourish (62).

After situating the *tu'a*-wise reading, Vaka'uta proceeds to explain his reading in-depth with its hermeneutical orientation. Subsequently, the *tu'a* wise reading uses three categories of analysis to guide its process (67). These categories "reflect the aspirations of Tongan commoners" (67). It is an alternative way to read the Bible through culturally unique and context-specific lenses, giving space for the commoners to read with the author.

The first category is *fonua* which means land in Tongan and is the equivalent of *fanua* in Samoan. The second category is *takanga* (72), which suggests a sense of community. The third category is *talanga*, which "presupposes orality, multivoicedness, and alternatives" (74). While Vaka'uta gives a detailed explanation of each category, what is more important for our purpose is that each category of analysis provides questions constructed from Tongan concepts that the reader uses to engage with the text. For example, in the category of the *fonua* lens, Vaka'uta asks: "What is the dominant perception of place? What are the drivers/bases of that perception? How is that perception constructed in biblical texts? Who owns that perception? Who is going to benefit from that perception? Who is likely to be displaced by that perception? Are there ignored perceptions? How would this ignored perception affect the current interpretations of the texts?" (72).

Moreover, through the lens of *tākanga*: "What is the dominant vision of society? What kind of society does it seek to establish? What is at stake in such a vision? What is the basis of that vision? For whom is such a society? What kind of value- and belief-systems does the vision endorse? Is there an alternative vision that is being ignored or suppressed? What implications does it have for interpretation?" (74).

Finally, through the *tālanga* lens: "How are voices represented in biblical texts? Whose voices are dominant? How is language employed to serve these dominant voices? What are the rhetorics of domination? Whose voices are repressed? How is language manipulated to maintain repression? Are there echoes of resistance? What is the rhetoric of resistance? How does the intersection of voices affect the meaning of texts and the interpretive task?" (75).

From these categories, Vaka'uta identifies key principles essential to tu'a-wise reading (76). These include a reconsideration of the "context, text, and interpretation," layered over from a Tongan standpoint (76). In describing and identifying these key principles, Vaka'uta infuses Tongan philosophies and worldview. The cultural element is undoubtedly illuminating. Indeed, the reader gets a feel of Vaka'uta's Tongan viewpoint while engaging with the text. All of these things also provide the theoretical underpinnings for the category of analysis utilized by the *tu'a*-wise reading (84).

Vaka'uta's Appeal

The appeal of Vaka'uta's work is his construction of an interpretive mode based on Tongan principles and values. What makes him stand out for me is the idea that he is not only engaging the text within his context, but he is also utilizing categories of analysis borne of his own culture to engage existing theories of interpretation. This creates a new paradigm and an important innovation for Pacific Island biblical hermeneutics, something that is evident in the work of Iosefa Lefaoseu, which I discuss later in the chapter.

Nevertheless, despite the introduction of cultural values and philosophies into exegetical paradigms, it is also important to recognize that Vaka'uta appears to be inspired and shows strong affiliation with some of the works of Elaine Wainwright and Vernon Robbins. Perhaps in this way Vaka'uta shows how indigenous concepts and principles could be intertwined with existing biblical scholarship to produce one's own reading method. It is also a strong indication that there is no singular approach, or even a pure culturally-induced way. Whether it is purely culturally induced or otherwise, the aim for biblical interpretive method is to be multivalent and interdisciplinary. Even Vaka'uta admits that

> [L]au faka-tu'a is a multidimensional methodology: the lau fe'unu method unweaves texts to reveal its structure, design and emphasis; the lau lea method directs the attention of lau faka-tu'a to the linguistic and rhetorical aspects of texts; the lau vā method focuses on the social and sacred aspects of texts; the lau tu'unga method, finally, scrutinizes texts to expose the beliefs and ideologies that shape visions and claims. (Vaka'uta 2011, 99)

Therefore, Vaka'uta in a sense broadens the gap that emerges from Havea's *Elusion*. In addition to bringing a Pacific Island flavor to engage the more dominant existing theories and methods, Vaka'uta shows just how a framework for reading can be borne of Pacific Island cultural and social values. In this way, he paves the way for others to utilize values, methods and theories from our own Pacific Island context for biblical reading. But this is in recognizing that we are never in isolation and that there is always a need for perpetual dialogical engagement with scholars of different contexts. They could be of western tradition, or others who share contextual variables similar to ours.

Finally, as an extension to the above point, there appears to be room for further dialogue on the needs of Pacific Island readers. The dynamics of the dialogue with other scholars though would serve us well if it was centered on the issues, the problems confronting readers. While the conversation on contextual approaches brings in cultural and other important values from the social location of the interpreter, to be issue-oriented would do much to assist in the practicality of biblical interpretation. Issues of varying nature, including economic, ecological, and political, raise questions that are more relevant to our circumstances and how to better connect them to the Bible. Subsequently, there emerges a need to engage a broader spectrum of disciplines and schools. In other words, there is room for a dialogical interdisciplinary engagement with scholars from different contexts and different disciplines.

VAITUSI NOFOAIGA—TAUTUAILEVA SERVICE-IN-BETWEEN

Vaitusi Nofoaiga's monograph *A Samoan Reading of Discipleship in Matthew* (2017) is similar to Vaka'uta, though it often is more explicit on the use of sociorhetorical analytical tools to bring the text to bear on his own social location. The *tautuaileva* (service-in-between) reading approach takes the position of someone, in this case *tautua*, who is at the lower strata of a hierarchical society. Like Vaka'uta's tu'a-wise, *tautuaileva* offers a critique of the reality of the contemporary reader's (Samoan) status quo, meanwhile engaging the Matthean text on a discussion of discipleship.

Nofoaiga's view of discipleship is informed by his standpoint as a Samoan living in the Diaspora. From this standpoint, Nofoaiga argues for an alternative view of discipleship, one that makes sense of his location. To assist in this, Nofoaiga fashions a formative indigenous concept that he calls *tautuaileva*. It is his own innovation based on the perspective of a *tautua* (the one who serves). *Tautuaileva* "refers to service carried out in-between spaces, as well as to a servant who stands in-between spaces. It expresses the expectation that service in a family or community is reciprocal and the needs and rights of everyone are important" (40). Nofoaiga therefore sees himself serving in between places. It is between the Samoan sense of *tautua* and the sense of service in Christian culture. In this regard, Nofoaiga occupies a "hybrid location as third space" (40). From this third space, Nofoaiga writes that

> It reveals that in times of undertaking my service role to both my family and church units, I negotiate and renegotiate the fulfillment of my needs and roles in relation to both units, depending on which unit's needs are given priority. It is the location where I stand as tautua allowing myself to accept changes and challenges in life that help me fulfill my role and responsibility to my family and church. (Nofoaiga 2017, 40).

Nofoaiga also provides a review of studies by Samoan biblical scholars, utilizing cultural hermeneutics to the Bible. The importance of this is to highlight the innovative and creative ways of Samoan biblical scholars in particular, constituting what is Pacific Island biblical hermeneutics. The focus on Samoan scholars is also important for my purpose. In trying to navigate a way forward, perhaps the question is not to pursue or define what Pacific Island biblical hermeneutics is. A more pragmatic approach and responsible way forward is to focus instead on my own social location as a Samoan. As mentioned before, there appears to be a constant struggle for Pacific Island scholars to balance their own individuality, particularly of their cultural context, and of maintaining a sense of belonging to a larger and broader oceanic categorization. In this way, Nofoaiga provides a way forward.

One of the things I find useful in my own attempt at contextual biblical reading is Nofoaiga's use of hybridity to explain his social location as a Samoan reader of the Bible in Samoa. Nofoaiga's formative concept of *tautuaileva* embodies his service to family and community which "uses any culture or material" (45). In that service, Nofoaiga writes "tautua is not monoculture" but rather "it crosses and borrows from other cultures that would serve the needs in the local society" (45). By culture Nofoaiga looks at "the cultures and traditions that have been running and controlling Samoan society" and the assumption that they "are connected to domestic and community problems such as poverty and violence." As such Nofoaiga writes that he is "more concerned with how the Christian tradition of discipleship in conjunction with the matai hierarchical social and cultural systems overlook the needs and rights of local people" (44). I find Nofoaiga stimulating in his negotiation of different cultures. While my own experience points to different cultures in the diasporic context, Nofoaiga however refers to something different. He provides space for my own pursuit of a contextual biblical reading to explore an even greater chasm that I argue is endemic to Samoan society, not only locally but also in the diaspora. As I see it, the convoluted dynamics among the three pillars in Samoan society—democracy, Christianity, and the *faa-Samoa*—provides the context for the *aiga* or the family.

The one controlling theme throughout Nofoaiga's book is discipleship. Discipleship for Nofoaiga is service, *tautua*, in between places, that symbolizes the life of a Samoan Christian, trying to balance service to the Church and the demands of living in Samoan society, Samoan cultural system. The text for analysis is Matthew 4:12–15 and 7:24—8:22, texts that deal with discipleship.

Nofoaiga is heavy in exegetical analysis, proceeding admirably along an SRI-motivated scheme, integrated with Samoan concepts and philosophies. I find welcoming the space for an extensive engagement with a mooring point. In other words, I sense that a deep and rich contextual approach to family life may add more to the conversation. Thus, in my humble attempt to do contextual biblical interpretation, it is my sense that an exploration of some of the institutional constraints that shape and influence family life in Samoan society may go a long way toward understanding the context in which the individual carries out service. In other words, a deeper contextual approach focusing on institutions creates the opportunity to challenge the oppressive situation facing the individual in Samoa, economically and politically, because of service both to the church and for cultural reasons. Be that as it may, I find *tautuaileva* to be a liberating reading that seeks to uplift the oppressive nature of *tautua*, which often leads to poverty and financial difficulties. Nofoaiga thus provides encouragement and space for seeking a mooring point in Pacific Island biblical hermeneutics.

LE VAOTOGO FRANK SMITH—ANALOGIES

Le Vaotogo Frank Smith also wrestles with the challenges of navigating biblical exegesis within one's own contemporary world. In his thesis publication titled *The Johannine Jesus from a Samoan Perspective: Toward an Intercultural Reading of the Fourth Gospel* (2017), Smith bridges two cultural worlds—that of the Fourth Gospel and his Samoan meaning system (39). Such an undertaking also captures some Pacific Island flavor similar to Havea's *Elusion*. Like Havea, Smith employs analogies. His close affiliation with Samoan culture is represented in his description of his social location, his context as a modern reader. Contextualization in this manner warrants spelling out his view of a Samoan "reality." Reality for Smith is fluid. This is attributed to the notion that no community or individual can be insulated from the influence of other cultures. In other words, Smith appears to make the claim for a reality that is mixed and hybridized. While the social construction of reality is different from culture to culture, Smith writes that the reality of a Samoan is rooted in core values that the individual holds and has internalized (25). To make his claim, Smith cites Anae, another Samoan scholar, to emphasize the notion that these values give a Samoan an identity and a sense of belonging (25). Core values including *alofa, faaaloalo,* and *tautua*, once internalized, give meaning to Samoan identity. Moreover, they inform the Samoan of an understanding of his or her reality.

The appeal in Smith's approach is the bridging of the world of the modern reader with his or her counterpart in the first century. To enable such bridging or connection, the text as the medium of communication is accentuated. This is an important consideration and a common denominator shared also by Havea, Vaka'uta and Nofoaiga. A view that has long been touted by Vernon Robbins, the text as the medium of communication is embedded with social, cultural, and ideological textures, which for me have the appearance of data for analysis. It is interesting for me also that this perception is quite common among Pacific Island scholars (Mailo also exhibits this). It is probably no coincidence that one finds this view prevalent among Pacific Island cultures, mostly among scholars of Tongan and Samoan ancestry. This is probably attributed to a certain degree of affinity for oratory and rhetorical construction in many Pacific cultures.

Smith's approach exhibits a similar affinity. He would use the text or narrative to create for the real reader, or in other words the contemporary reader, an "analogical situation" (2017, 57, figure 5). That is, the real reader understands the text in terms of analogies evoked and shaped by his or her own reality. Nevertheless, Smith clearly recognizes the potential of introducing bias into his reading approach (57). Using analogies increases the chances of introducing bias into the analysis. The dangers in ethnocentrism and anachronism are real and have been a critical consideration in biblical scholarship. And while there does not appear to be an elaborate solution, Smith though thinks the benefits outweigh the dangers. The appeal in using the analogical situation is to give rise to questions. These questions enable the contemporary reader to re-construct various possibilities in how the text could have been made meaningful for the first-century reader. In other words, the contemporary reader engages with the text to re-create the analogical context of the first-century reader.

After describing this analogical method, Smith focuses on three texts from John: 5:1–47; 13:1–20; and 15:1–17. At this point, the practice to re-orient the text within a Samoan context is prominent. Smith in this case exhibits a similar trait with his other Pacific Island colleagues. His discussion of the narratives is interwoven with analogies evoked from his own Samoan sociocultural location. For example, in his reading of John 5:1–3, Smith writes that the "spatial and the temporal dimensions of vv. 1–3 and the way these verses are arranged evoke for me a spatio-temporal category codified as *taeao*" (64). Smith notes, from his social location as a Samoan reader, that *taeao* has several nuances of meaning. They may refer to events in the past "which are significant in the history of the community and recalled in the present" (64). In a way it is also accepting an "interpretation of an historical moment that has been accepted as the truth" (64). The overall sense from its use is the understanding that "the temporal location and the geographical location cannot be separated because the experiences of such events are located in time and space" (64). For Smith then, through his reading of the text, the image of *taeao* is evoked due to the temporal dimension of the text—it signals a festival and an important geographical location in John. From here, Smith makes the claim that the healing is not the central point in the narrative. Rather, it has become the central point by which "Jesus makes a particular claim about himself" (64). Thus, the healing has become the *taeao*. It has become a "symbolic event and recalled for a particular purpose here" (64). By using the analogy of *taeao* as well as other intertextures, Smith then asks questions of the text. In particular, Smith asks questions that would help re-construct plausible scenarios for which the reader in the first century may have given meaning to the text.

Let me digress here. The use of analogies conjured from one's social location as a contemporary reader both has weaknesses and strengths. With the recent trend in Pacific Island biblical scholarship, I am interested to further explore the value that the use of cultural elements brings to the analysis of the text. For example, I find Smith's use of historical and literary critical tools sufficient to provide an adequate description of the social and political dimensions of the biblical context. Describing Jerusalem as where "the elite owners of the land make their home" and "land is the primary source of wealth" makes this an important economic aspect in the discussion. In other words, I ask if the social political and economic aspects of the textures could have been unraveled without Smith's use of the analogical situation of *taeao*?

In that regard, Smith exhibits both weaknesses and strengths in the use of cultural elements. On one hand, historians emphasize the great differences between antiquity and the present because everything virtually present to the contemporary reader is new. On the other hand, cultural elements and values help to bridge biblical texts and the lived reality of the contemporary reader. Anthropological studies of humans show amazing similarities among all humans everywhere, even when they are engaged doing very different things.

That for me is an important aspect of Smith's work and probably something to consider with respect to Pacific Island biblical hermeneutical studies. In my humble opinion, there is a need to steer a balanced approach. The utilizing of cultural elements and the values that they bring to the discussion needs to be critically analyzed with respect to the exegetical value that such undertaking would add. The potential benefits from such engagement would be to strengthen and firm our own analysis against potential bias including ethnocentrism and anachronism. These are some of the important issues confronting Pacific Biblical Hermeneutics. The aim therefore is to be cognizant of this challenge. Moreover, to be self-critical in our biblical interpretation is to maintain a balance between the desire to add cultural value and a responsibility to biblical exegesis.

Therefore, the contextualization of the Christian Bible has great value to readers of the Pacific Island region. Re-orienting and re-reading the Bible from a Pacific Island context has great value hermeneutically. At the same time, there is a need for restraint and responsibility. The challenge remains to not only color and frame the Christian Bible in Pacific Island musings and renderings, but also to broaden the meaning and depth of the text for our own understanding. Discussing this struggle with steersperson or scholars from other oceans or contexts is in order and something I will turn to in the next chapter.

MOSESE MA'ILO—TRANSLATION MATTERS

I also bring in Mosese Ma'ilo's work to illustrate another important aspect. In particular, Ma'ilo in his book *Bible-ing My Samoan* critically vets the Samoan translation of the Bible (2016). Using his expertise in the Samoan language, Ma'ilo challenges the colonial mindset and undergirding philosophy that appears embedded within. Ma'ilo uses several texts to illustrate his claim. For example, one text in particular is Romans 13:1–7. The use of the word *usiusita'i* instead of *va-tapuia* reinforces the ideology of a parent-child relationship rather than a leader and the people. Mai'lo writes, "In the Samoan protocol of social interaction, the term *usiusita'i* is more related to the parent-child relationship, while the *vatapuia, va fealoai* (both literally referring to the va or 'space' of 'reciprocal respect' between people) appropriates the relationship between a leader and a people in his/her leadership" (191). By highlighting this, Ma'ilo notes that the "use of *usiusita'i* is ideologically motivated to perpetuate the sense of complete silence, surrender, and emptiness of the ruled as a 'melted' presence that fades into a weaker substance in the presence of the ruler" (191). In other words, the choice of semantics reflects a certain western ideology, perhaps of the Western-missionaries, continuing a colonial mindset for reading.

Within this context, Ma'ilo appears to echo an important aspect of postcolonial readings. One of the important aspects of postcolonial readings is to recognize that the Bible received by the indigenes is heavily-laden with western-induced configurations and framings. Thus, for the reader or interpreter in the Third World context, critical questions are to be asked from their perspective (Sugirtharajah 2001). In this manner, while Bible Translation is not a direct focus of this paper, Ma'ilo nevertheless offers some intriguing questions concerning the final form or primary unit of analysis, which is the biblical text. If the biblical text, as Ma'ilo alludes to it, is an instrument perpetuating a colonial mindset and a certain mission-oriented paradigm, what does this do to our interpretation and reading? This is an issue that Havea also talks about, explicating the need to account for the different Scriptures existing in Oceania (2017, 11). Similarly, Sugirtharajah also discusses this from the perspective of Third World readings, or voices from the margins (2013).

Ma'ilo in this regard, challenges Pacific Island Biblical scholars to liberate the biblical text from its strong-colonial ancestry. This is more than just bringing the Bible closer to the Oceania context as others like Havea ruminate. To some extent, Ma'ilo challenges Pacific Island scholars not only to question the final form of the Bible, but also the authoritative manner to which we as Pacific Islanders have accorded the Bible. In this manner, I find Ma'ilo and R.S. Sugirtharajah share similar sentiments regarding biblical interpretation. Biblical interpretation underpins the important task of scrutinizing the Bible for its "colonial entanglements" (Sugirtharajah 2001, 251). As such, the exegete scrutinizes biblical narratives "not as a series of divinely guided incidents or reports about divine-human encounters, but as emanating from colonial contacts" (251).

In addition, the notion of logic is implicit in Ma'ilo's work. In particular, Bible translation also calls into question principles and theories concerning Samoan logic. By delving into issues concerning translation and textual construction, Ma'ilo appears to impel the Samoan interpreter to re-examine the Bible within the scope of Samoan logic. This includes the notion of ambiguity. In Samoan culture and society, ambiguity is critical to navigating, nurturing and maintaining relationships. The logic within indicates a culture that is less inclined to definitiveness and frankness. On the contrary, the Samoan language and rhetoric underscores a culture that places great value on building and nurturing relationships and connections. This adds tremendous pressure on the need to find resolution, to solve problems. Yet, there is a sense that even a solution is only good for the problem at hand, and not to offer it as formulaic and generalized to other contexts. It is this nature of Samoan language and logic that in my humble opinion is implicit in Ma'ilo's work. Vernacular and rhetoric play a critical role in Samoan logic and by extension Pacific Island biblical interpretation.

PENI LEOTA—MORE ANALOGIES

While his published thesis is forthcoming, I find that Peni Leota, in addition to his teachings during his tenure as a Lecturer in Malua, adds an important contribution to the dialogue on Pacific Island Biblical hermeneutics. This is also evident in how frequent he is cited (Havea 2014; Nofoaiga 2017; Alama 2018). In his work "*Ethnic Tensions in Persian-Period Yehud: A Samoan Postcolonial Hermeneutic*" (2005) Leota offers more perspective on the notion of Pacific Island biblical hermeneutics. While Havea can be considered eclectic in style Leota on the other hand is more guarded. In many ways, Leota and Smith share a lot of commonalities, one in particular is the use of analogies. In his exploration of the ethnic tensions behind the Ezra-Nehemiah and Chronicle texts, Leota is guided by Mark Brett's "dialogical style of engagement with the text" (1). Key to this dialogical style is accepting the diversity of interpretive interests and frameworks that shape the exegete's view of the text.

For Leota though, the consideration of ethnocentrism weighs heavily. The interpretative turn, Leota writes, is

> [A] continuum between a strong form of epistemological holism that regards ethnocentrism as unavoidable (a position often identified as 'postmodernism'), and weak holism that seeks to present another life form in a way that does justice to both the interpreter's culture and the one under examination. (2)

Leota, much like Smith, uses his Samoan context to draw analogies with the context of the text and to inform his situatedness. The manner in which Leota does this reflects a certain degree of respect for the context of the biblical text. Much caution is taken to draw analogies from the

Bible to inform issues of identity in the Samoan context. In this case, the "ethnic tensions in Persian period Yehud provide analogies for viewing the development of Samoan ethnic identity" (185).

Let me digress here. I find that Leota's approach is a timely reminder of the need for a sense of responsibility in our contextual biblical reading. Do I presuppose autonomy in the text? As a *tautai seu*, I situate and locate the text within my context. I do accept that once penned, the text becomes disassociated from the source. As such the text is open for multiple interpretations and may also be applied to the contexts of other readers (McLean 2012, 237). In that regard, there is space for multiple interpretations and meanings. Nonetheless, as a *tautai seu*, I am also cognizant of the need to steer and situate in other oceans. This warrants an equally important need for restraint and responsibility in biblical readings. What amounts to responsible reading? I am cognizant nonetheless of the needs of my contextual biblical reading that merits a deep rich contextual approach to the biblical text. I intend to explore the social, cultural, ideological and political-economic dimensions of the Luan story of the ruler. My hope then is to integrate this with an attempt to construct a contextual biblical reading that is moored in a particular issue critical in the lived reality of the contemporary society.

One can make the claim that some tension exists between Havea and Leota as the latter appears to fall short of the transdisciplinary essence of the former's transtextuality reading. The threat of ethnocentrism weighs heavily on Leota, and rightly so. The notion that the text is bent to weave in the interpreter's story has significant implications on the objectivity and universality of interpretation. Be that as it may, it is unreasonable to expect any notions of autonomy in the text (Thiselton 2009, 29). The moment the interpreter engages, explores or reads the text, is the moment that there is a reasonable crossing of boundaries between the text and interpreter. The text shapes the interpreter as well as vice versa.[6] Ethnocentrism is unavoidable.

---

6. I am aware that there is a huge debate within reader-response scholarship regarding the nature of this interaction between the reader and text. Stanley Fish for example, argues that there is nothing in the text to interpret. It is the interpreter that brings meaning to the text. In other words, it is the response of the reader that gives text meaning (see discussion in Thiselton 2009, 29–34).

Another important aspect is Leota's attitude towards one's social location. Like many of his Pacific Island colleagues, Leota is very much cognizant of his social location and of his own Samoan culture. Much like Vaka'uta, Leota also recognizes that there is no avoidance of the fact that culture changes. As he writes, this is "no way a nativist attempt to recover Samoan traditional culture for its own sake, but self-consciously written from the perspective of a Samoan reader whose interest in culture affirms the views of Jürgen Habermas and Norman Gottwald that treat culture in relation to economics and politics" (3). Leota therefore recognizes the vanity in attempting to recover a pure Samoan culture. The understanding of the Samoan culture or any culture is very much a function of the person's situatedness. To try and recapture a pristine culture is to indulge in naivety and ignorance. Culture changes as society develops.

Personally, this is critical for my contextual biblical study. The emphasis on cultural elements in biblical interpretation can easily detract from the exegetical value that such undertaking may add. An even more beneficial undertaking is to integrate contextual and cultural elements within historical and literary paradigms. By this I mean that I am constantly negotiating between my need to gain further clarity through historical as well as literary data. Meanwhile, I do see the text also as a tool with historical, literary, social, cultural, ideological, and theological values.

Others

In recent years, there has been a great influx of Pacific Island scholarship including some of the recent doctorates like Charles Edward Kolohai (2013), Seumaninoa Puaina (2016), Arthur John Wulf (2016), andSamasoni Moleli (2018). Much can be learned from their contribution, but I will highlight two works in particular to better frame my argument for a contextual biblical reading of the Lukan story of the ruler. I find the two contrasting views beneficial in my own attempt as a *tautai seu* to negotiate the context of the biblical text and the needs of my own contemporary context.

Ma'afu Palu—A Counter-Argument

Choosing to include the works of Ma'afu Palu in this review is for the purpose of contrast. The point is to present a Pacific Island region that is diverse in cultures as well as philosophical tendencies. Not everyone shares in the excitement of utilizing indigenous epistemologies to read the Christian Bible. Although the essence of his disputation is theological, Ma'afu Palu (2003) has something to add to biblical interpretation. How does context shape biblical hermeneutics? Palu starts with the process of exegesis by which the text is studied to render meaning. Hermeneutics is the "effort to interpret the text to us here and now" (Palu 2005, 25), and homiletics is the application which for Palu is the "specific application to the contemporary congregation" (25). From there, Palu explicates the hermeneutical gap, the notion that the biblical text is anachronistic to our contemporary issues and challenges. God's word does not fit today's modern world. To redress this hermeneutical gap, Palu argues for a single "biblical worldview" (39). He uses the apostle Paul as an example. Palu argues that Paul himself "did not seek to re-dress the Biblical truths in cultural outfits more pertinent to those respective audiences. The Biblical truth that everyone is in need of repentance, for instance, remained true just as much for Athenians. . . as it does for those of us in the Pacific in the 21st century" (39).

Therefore, while the current trend favors employing the reader's context in biblical hermeneutics, Palu contends that there is one way to understand the biblical narrative, that is, the Christian Bible is to be recognized within its Jewish context, the history of Israel, its culture and social elements in which it was written. For Palu, the point of departure for the Pacific reader is as an outsider. He writes, "rather than constantly seeking ways in which the biblical message can be transported to the local soil of the Pacific, I suggest that we attempt the reverse. Beginning as Gentiles with a vantage point 'outside' the biblical narrative 'world' we therefore seek primarily to understand our 'context' aright and then 'enter' the biblical narrative world by faith as the proper response to the invitation offered by the cross" (Palu 2006, 21–22).

Overall Palu demonstrates a deep connection to classical evangelical hermeneutics. Bringing up Palu also at this juncture showcases that the current trend in Pacific biblical hermeneutics is not without its detractors. Like the Pacific Island region is diverse and vast, so are the extant challenges and issues in the discipline of biblical studies.

Iosefa Lefaoseu—Indigenousness in Reading

Iosefa Lefaoseu is also relevant just for the fact that he continues the journey towards constructing a Pacific indigenous hermeneutic (see Vaka'uta above). In his *tosi-lasi* reading of the Book of Job (2018), Lefaoseu utilizes all the various dimensions of mat-weaving including the activity of gathering the materials, processing the materials and weaving of the fine mat as a hermeneutical framework to read and interpret the Book of Job. Borne of the idea that Mikhail Bakhtin's polyphonic concept "cannot completely capture the aspects of relationality from a Samoan context" (12), Lefaoseu constructs a reading approach that utilizes the Samoan art form of *lalagaga* or "weaving for a purpose." In this construction, one can make the claim that *tosi* (strand) is analogous to the "text." As Lefaoseu writes:

> *Tosi—lasi* reading is a dialogical approach, appropriating the idea of *faafaletui* in a way this work refers to as *lalagaga o le ola*. This is firstly expressed in the interactions of the living *tosi* of the reader, the living *tosi* of/within the text, and the living *tosi* behind the text. It is essentially dialogical in the sense that it emphasizes the *faafaletui* of three worlds: the world behind the text, the world of the text, and the world before the text. (Lefaoseu 2018, 30)

The above parallel between *tosi* and "text" reminds me of Vernon Robbins's use of the weaving metaphor. The Latin word *texere* means "to weave," and Robbins builds on the weaving metaphor to the concept of a text as a thick tapestry. With this in mind, instead of the text being a series of windows and mirrors, the text is like a tapestry that is "not simply a 'thing unto itself' but is also a 'message which is read'. As a message, it is a communication" (Robbins 1996b, 19).

In saying this, my point is to showcase how the construction of an indigenous reading paradigm is often in dialogue with existing scholarship. It thrives and emerges from engaging in constant dialogue with scholars in other contexts with other value systems. In this regard, while contextual biblical interpretations emphasize one's own context, I am conscious of the fact that there is much to be gained from exploring the historical and literary context of the biblical text. It does not necessarily mean, though, that every vernacular parallel and cultural construct contributes to the exegetical purpose.

Lefaoseu's appeal is that he represents an indigenously-induced reading approach. First, he adds to the contributions of other Pacific

Island scholars by bringing to the fore additional voices from the Pacific Island region. His goal is not in any way to replace or to neglect the underpinning values and principles of existing biblical scholarship, but to engage and extend the dialogue to include voices that are usually without a forum. Second, the responsibility to make sense of the Christian Bible within our own context warrants taking ownership of our own methods of reading and hermeneutical lenses to produce our own interpretation. The goal is to include the original context of the author and reader, but it is also to recognize that the imposition of imported value belief systems upon Pacific Island life and experiences fractures and uproots the integrity of indigenousness. Therefore, connecting the Bible to new contexts requires significant re-thinking and re-orienting to maintain the transformative element of this connection.

Whatever one may think about the discussion above, at present there appears to be a strong tendency to emphasize the cultural value that indigenously-induced methods of reading and hermeneutical lens could bring to the dialogue. In this, I think that Lefaoseu also points to a gap that could be filled by further studies and would bring additional exegetical value to the PICT region of biblical interpretation. There is space not only for metaphorical musings, but also for engaging with the text through historical and literary critical means. In saying that, I recognize that I find myself in a position where I have to constantly steer on the edges of the waves of historical-literary criticism and social-cultural-ideological, textual criticism. Just as the *tautai seu* seeks the bird in its flight, I find myself facing the daunting task of situating and locating my moving canoe in the fluidity of the deep *moana* of biblical interpretations. Nonetheless, in my contextual biblical reading, it is my hope to navigate and negotiate these challenges through a more pragmatic approach.

OVERVIEW AND CONTRIBUTION

As the *tautai seu*, the aim in this chapter has been to understand the layout of the existing scholarship on biblical studies in the region for the purpose of situating and to locating my own interpretation of the biblical text. From my perspective, the review holds the potential to enhance my own approach, methodology and framework for reading and engaging with the text of Luke 18:18–30. Beginning with a survey of Pacific Island biblical interpretation and hermeneutics makes it possible for me to better situate the scope and purpose of my study. To bring my discussion of the survey to a conclusion, I will repeat some key aspects of the scholarship here.

It is my observation, based on my review of the scholarship, that the Bible is not deemed in contemporary interpretation as just an object of interest but is intertwined with Pacific Island experience. Experience, feeling, emotion, and imagination are constituent parts of the re-thinking, re-orienting, and re-reading process as island readers engage with the text. Contextualization of the Bible is prevalent in current scholarship.

The majority of the scholarship so far has shown an affinity for utilizing indigenous concepts, theories, and methods for the purpose of drawing parallels or making analogies with the biblical text. Two strands of contextualization—these I have called interpretive and methodological—are distinct. The interpretive strand utilizes indigenous concepts and images as analogies and metaphors—borne of one's social location, including diasporic context—as reading lenses. The use of "island" and "Pacific indigenous" vernacular is often employed to bridge the gap between the contemporary Pacific Island reader and the biblical text.

The methodological focus, on the other hand, aims for the contextualization of interpretive instruments. To this end, the approach is to utilize indigenous concepts and theories to construct a Pacific-oriented methodology or framework while also using elements of historical critical as well as literary critical tools. So where does this leave me?

For my own contextual appropriation of the biblical text, I hope to explore the social, cultural and ideological textures of the text as well as its political-economic context. My approach to this will be to engage a deep and rich contextual exploration of the biblical text utilizing sociorhetorical critical tools and elements of the New Institutional Economics (NIE) to explore the social, cultural, and ideological dimensions of the text as well as its political-economic context.

The review also raises an important issue for consideration, in particular, how to incorporate Pacific Island logic in our biblical readings. The challenge here is that talk about Pacific Island logic can easily distract from the rich diversity in cultural, social, linguistic, and political aspects of the Pacific Island region. As indicated before, the challenge is how to reconcile the universality of the region with the distinctiveness of the different cultures it encompasses. This is an ongoing battle in the universe of biblical scholarship and appears to be the case also with Pacific Island biblical hermeneutics. In this study I argue for a pragmatic approach that is grounded in the lived reality of the contemporary reader. To help in that contextualized approach I also engage fishers in other oceans to pick out things that can help. The goal is not to impose or to transform, but to learn and to be transformed from a dialogical engagement with others.

Overall, my review of biblical scholarship in the Pacific Island region has led me to believe that the current trend is to foreground biblical interpretation in one's social location. From there, questions emerge that inform the exegete about methodology or interpretive framework. While the emphasis on cultural elements has helped bridge the Christian Bible with the world of the contemporary Pacific Island reader, my view is that consideration of the socioeconomic nature of Pacific Island life and institutional constraints in this context have been found wanting. For this reason, I intend to foreground institutional constraints and political-economic context in my attempt to carry out a contextual biblical reading of the biblical text.

It is also my view that a word of caution is warranted about the trendy use of indigenous concepts and methods in creating reading constructs and the attraction of doing something indigenously "Pacific." This justifiable and important approach to biblical interpretation has led at times to lamentable neglect of the historical and literary context of the text. As a result, the lines between ethnocentrism and indigenousness are often not clear. A greater need for responsibility in contextual biblical reading is in order. This is a major way I hope this study makes a contribution. As much as the cultural and the indigenously-induced interpretive construct adds Pacific flavor to biblical interpretation, much can be learned from exploring the institutional constraints and political-economic systems embedded in the social, cultural, and ideological textures of the text. This warrants a multi-method approach that asks historical and literary questions in the context of the other questions being asked.

It is my hope in this contextual biblical study to foreground the institutional relations that shape and constrain the lived reality of the contemporary reader. These involve the political-economic structures including distribution of resources and goods as well as the cultural and social elements that shape and influence one's circumstances. From this, questions will be asked of Luke's story of the rich ruler. Using historical as well as literary critical tools, I will then ask particular questions of the text to ascertain some of the institutional constraints on the ruler in Luke 18. This is interesting from the perspective of exploring the correlation between the lived reality of the ruler and the expectations and social context of discipleship. It is also an interesting phenomenon in the context of some of the political-economic issues confronting the church and its members in Samoa as well as in the larger Pacific Island region.

2

Engaging *Tautai* (Steersperson) in Other Context

INTRODUCTION

AFTER STEERING IN THE deep *moana* of biblical interpretation in the Pacific Island region, the *tautai seu* (a locating steersman) is now ready to cross borders and engage with our counterparts in other regions. I draw upon the wisdom of other fishers in similar contexts. In this regard, contextualizing or re-situating the Bible in contemporary contexts has long been a staple of both African and Asian biblical hermeneutic scholarship. My purpose for this chapter is for the discernment of the methodologies and theoretical underpinnings in their undertakings. These are informative and instructive in my attempt to engage the Lukan narrative with the political-economic context of the Pacific Island Countries and Territories (PICTs). The underlying aim is to situate and locate my own re-appropriation of the Lukan narrative within the larger scheme of contextual biblical scholarship.

I begin with a review of African Biblical hermeneutics focusing on the works of Itumeleng J. Mosala, Justine Ukpong, Musa W. Dube, Jonathan Draper, and Gerald O. West. One may argue that these scholars are mainly shaped by the South African context. This in turn reflects the potential risk in any attempt to generalize, often to the outcome of ignoring the rich and diverse cultures throughout the African continent. Nevertheless, the above list is not exhaustive and is only intended to highlight some aspects of African contextual biblical interpretation. Moreover, it is for the purpose of demonstrating variance by comparing and contrasting with the works of scholars in other contexts. Thus, in the subsequent sections, I also look at Asian Biblical hermeneutical scholarship. In particular, I include the works of R.S. Sugirtharajah, John Ahn, Hisako Kunukawa, Kwok Pui-lan, and Lily Fetalsana-Apura. Concluding the chapter, I provide an overall summary with some general observations on contextual biblical interpretations. More significantly I compare and contrast these findings with my review of Pacific Island biblical hermeneutics from the previous chapter.

AFRICAN BIBLICAL HERMENEUTICS

As a *tautai seu* (a locating steersman) I am always cautious not to offend or impose as I locate and situate myself with other interpreters. To speak of an African Biblical Hermeneutic in a continent consisting of more than fifty contiguous countries does not do justice to the richness, depth, and breadth of biblical scholarship in this vast region. Moreover, in order to situate and locate, the *tautai seu* is cognizant of the need to respect borders and boundaries when traversing different contexts—*seu le manu ae taga'i ile galu*, catch the bird but be careful of the wave. As a Pacific Islander, to speak of other contexts calls for caution and prudence especially as it is presumptuous or even intrusive to attempt a single categorization to qualify the richness and eclectic history and culture of the African countries. This means that the following discussion is an attempt to respect the context of the interpreters whose work is reviewed. At the same time there is an attempt to find connection and overlaps across the many cultures and rich history across the African continent. I am emboldened by Andrew M. Mbuvi's claim that "cultural trends may reflect enough overlaps that we can very cautiously retain a concept of a unified ABS [African Biblical Studies] identity" (Mbuvi 2017, 151). While diversity and multiplicity of readings is to be recognized, there is much to be gained from finding space for connection and room for bridging and establishing trans-contextual dialogue.

African biblical studies is an emerging field that "have sought to articulate, engage and critique the Bible in juxtaposition with African religious, political, economic, cultural and social realities" (Mbuvi 2017, 151). At the heart of it is an attempt to bring the Bible to bear on the concerns and needs of the people. Hence re-interpreting the Bible contextually is quite prevalent (Dada 2010, 161). It underscores the perpetual significance of the Bible in the African context. Despite the Bible being utilized as "an ideological tool of suppression and oppression" two factors are crucial to its perpetual relevance: first, for most African Christians, the Bible continues to serve as the reference point in "issues of faith and practice"; second, the Bible has become for the ordinary African reader a resource in their struggle for "survival and liberation" (Dada 2010, 161).

African biblical hermeneutics can be broadly characterized as consisting of three poles, or tri-polar. The first two poles consist of the biblical context and the African context. The third pole is viewed as playing a mediating role, establishing relational dialogue between the first two poles. Gerald O. West observes that the third pole can take different forms and often results in "at least six intersecting yet different emphases in African biblical interpretation: inculturation, liberation, feminist, psychological, postcolonial, and queer biblical hermeneutics" (West 2016, 44). Of the works discussed below, I find Justin Upkong, Musa Dube, and Gerald O. West to be some of the closest examples.

Jonathan Draper adds his own characterization of the African biblical hermeneutical process which includes: distantiation, contextualization, and appropriation (2015, 9). Distantiation is an attempt to identify the biblical context and the context of the exegete. By establishing the historical context of the biblical text, there is a conscious effort to avoid a personal bias as a result of too much emphasis on the context of the interpreter or the reader. Contextualization establishes the connection between the two. The third pole is the appropriation which can be characterized as the dialogical relation between the biblical context and the context of the reader. Combined, the three poles suggest a process in motion and any one of the three poles can serve as the starting point.

In my opinion, a key principle in African contextual biblical hermeneutics is the transformation of the African context, something that is vital to the well-being of society (Adamo 2015, 32–33). The Bible or the biblical text is re-read against African world-view and culture. The aim is to integrate and adapt "African religious and sociocultural concepts as well as the economic, political and missionary heritage of diverse African concepts" (West 2007, 16). I am listing some of the prominent works below.

Black Biblical Hermeneutics

Itumeleng J. Mosala, describing "black biblical hermeneutics," argues that the history and culture of the interpreting community are essential (Mosala 1989, 3). In this regard, one can assume that the Bible is read through the eyes of the African community so the interpretive enterprise is a function of African history and culture. But it is not enough for Mosala just to consider African history and culture. Rather it is also important to clarify and differentiate one's ideology and theoretical framings from those of the dominant practices and discourses. This is a significant point of Mosala's claim.

Mosala gives a convincing critique of sociological approaches. Despite claims of locating themselves "midway between the metaphysical idealism of philosophy and the positivist empiricism of natural science" (Mosala 1989, 56), sociological approaches reintroduce "ideological hunches inherent in the historical-critical methods, but it hides them under the cloak of a more systemic approach" (Mosala 1989, 58). While sociology-based analysis has drawn attention to the social dimension of the biblical text, Mosala warns that

> It has taken us two steps back by adopting some of the subtle ideological maneuvers of modern society, lending an academic aura to what is essentially an ideological political method. More significantly, it conceals its ideological and political agenda by using recognized and respected academic methods within bourgeois society, such as the Weberian interpretive sociology and the Durkheimian structural-functionalist sociology. (Mosala 1989, 65)

Implicit in Mosala then is a sentiment to be freed of ideological and political influence which employs the Bible for class-based interests. His objection therefore is not so much to the use of sociological approaches per se but rather for the purpose of openly acknowledging class-struggles inherent within them. Black biblical hermeneutics needs to provide an "ideological break with biblical criticism" (Mosala 1989, 66).

A key assertion is that black biblical hermeneutics, or any other form of modern criticism, supports some form of struggle. Mosala's sentiment for such struggle echoes that of Terry Eagleton who notes struggle is an integral part of criticism. While there may be contemporary dispositions of critics in fields like semiotics, cultural theory, and psychoanalysis, etc., the common concern for Eagleton has always been "with the symbolic processes of social life, and the social production of forms of subjectivity" (Eagleton 1984, 124). In this regard, "the role of the contemporary critic is *traditional*" (123), to critique forms of subjectivity. Like Eagleton, Mosala (1989), therefore, sees value in grounding black biblical hermeneutics in the struggle against the apartheid system in South Africa. While Mosala welcomes the sociological concerns shown by the proponents of the new sociological approaches to the Bible, he laments that they continue to sustain ideological tendencies inherent within historical-critical approaches. What is needed rather is an approach that considers the text for what it is: products of definite historical and social material conditions (Mosala 1989, 7). Hence, an essential element of black biblical hermeneutics is to challenge and critique the dominant narrative that continues to perpetuate subjectivity.

Let me digress for a moment. I find Mosala useful, at the very least, to situate an approach to examine political-economic constraints contributing to what one can call a form of subjectivity—the impoverishment of people in the Pacific Island Region. While class struggle in the Pacific may not be as blatant and conspicuous as it was during the era of apartheid in South Africa, I share in the sentiment that liberation is not just about the relationships among specific groups of people, but also between people and their productive forces—means of production including land, water, machinery, tools, etc., plus labor forces (Mosala 1989, 67). This is not to say that there are no class-struggles in the Pacific region (see Tongan noble system or the Samoan *matai* system). Class-struggle is often a function of history and culture, and exists in different forms in every society. Moreover, liberation is not just spiritual but also material. As Mosala writes, "it is the liberation of these elements of social and material life" that makes for both spiritual and material freedom (65). While class-struggle is critical, discernment of the institutions that shape and influence the way of life in society adds to a deeper appreciation of the root cause. Mosala's notion of liberation theology though is not to be confused with liberation theology that is usually associated with certain Latin American activist-scholars like Segundo, Gutierrez, Assman, Bonino, etc. As Mosala asserts, "liberation of theology" is a generic movement of Third World people in a struggle against imperialistic regimes that perpetuate the political and economic exploitation of the people (Mosala 2006, 134). As such, the focus is to challenge the factors that contribute to the political and exploitation of the people.

While I concur with Mosala about the value of challenging institutional sources of material imbalance in society, I am cognizant of the discrepancies in contextual framings between the contemporary Pacific and South Africa in the 1980's. I would err therefore on the side of pragmatism. This is not in any way condoning the killings of many innocent people and the oppressive regime of the apartheid system. However, I hold a strong conviction that the passion to resist against injustice in any society and ruling institutions should not overwhelm a conscientious attempt to bring the Bible to bear on issues of social and political-economic nature whether locally or globally. History is filled with revolutions[1] that did not end well. What is much needed, and a currency in the Pacific region, is the desire to talk and dialogue. Consensus, to be sure, is like a leviathan[2] that cannot be captured nor domesticated or like a *talanoa* (story, telling, conversation) (Havea 2010) that is influenced and shaped by a hierarchical, cultural structure. Yet, the goal is for the interpenetration of empathy and compassion that may lay the foundation for moderation and level-headedness in peace-building and conflict resolution in the region. Simply put, I value the goal of challenging existing institutional elements of society that subjugate people. Yet, I urge caution so it does not grow into unbridled passions that spark fires of violence and bloodshed. In that regard, I find resonance with Chief Albert John Mvumbi Luthuli (1962) who fought for non-violent resistance against the apartheid regime of South Africa. His leadership during the 1950's, a tumultuous period in the history of the country, is a model. Luthuli's non-violent leadership conjures up similar images of Samoa's own *Mau* Movement[3] (struggle for independence) leader, Tupua Tamasese Lealofi III. Even at the point of giving up his life, Lealofi appealed for peace, underpinning his leadership with the Samoan notion of *tautua toto* (service through

---

1. What I mean by revolution here is of a "violent" nature. The point here is to emphasize dialogue and diplomacy which in the Samoan context is captured in the notion of *soalaupule* (sharing authority). Filemoni Tuigamala (2012) in his B.D. thesis uses the *soalaupule* concept to propose Christian leadership for peace and justice in Samoa. The concept underpins a sense of giving space to shape and influence relationships reconciled to dialogue and diplomacy, seeking justice, peace for the community.

2. Job 41:1 provides the basis for the thought, a metaphor to signal a task that is difficult to achieve or something that is hard to situate or control.

3. For a description of the Mau movement and Samoa's struggle for independence against the colonial administration of the New Zealand government, see Michael Field (1991).

spilt blood) (Tominiko 2020, 115). Put simply, service rendered even to the point of sacrificing one's life has the potential to avoid violence.

From a *tautai seu* perspective, Mosala in South Africa steers an approach that is helpful in shaping my own contextual biblical reading. Three modes of productions—namely communal, tributary and capitalist—foreground his analysis of the causes and consequences of injustice in the South African society. This foregrounding is the starting point from which Mosala derives and weaves together strands of black biblical hermeneutics. In doing so, Mosala presents a challenge. In particular, whether a black biblical hermeneutic can help in my re-appropriation of the Bible within the Samoan context, which is starkly different from the African context. For example, as suggested above, class struggle is nonexistent in Samoa, or at least not as blatant as in the days of apartheid in South Africa. As such, the challenge is to develop a methodological apparatus that allows for trans-contextual analysis. This is where I find Mosala useful. While he is strictly focused on the African context, Mosala steers an approach that can reasonably engage both the context of the contemporary reader and the historical context of the biblical text. Discerning hermeneutics as consisting of four phases—context of the text, the text, context of the reading community and the reading community itself—Mosala moves programmatically toward the priority of the reading community itself. In his words, the "social-ideological location and commitment of the reader must be accorded methodological priority" (1989, 123). Prioritizing the context of the contemporary reader frames the scope for the historical research in addition to fleshing out questions to be asked of the text. Foregrounding the socio-economic and political context, or whatever is the context of the exegete, is critical. This is an important aspect of my study as I hope to foreground the political-economic context of Samoan society. The aim is to gain clarity on some of the institutional constraints that contribute to the political-economic struggles confronting families in the Samoan context.

Methodologically, Mosala brings together sociological and historical-materialist tools to bear on "the grid of black history and culture in order for them to enable the development of a specifically black biblical hermeneutics of liberation" (1989, 5). To do this he draws upon various perspectives from the sociology of literature, discourse analysis, empirical sociology, and political literary criticism. Even more significant, Mosala does not see this as a methodological shift from that of the "humanities" to "sociological" methods. Rather, fundamental questions of "ideology, culture, gender, race, and politics" (1989, 8) are made integral in the pursuit of liberative biblical hermeneutics.

Known as "materialist," Mosala's method is based on the assumption that "how a society produces and reproduces its life is fundamentally conditioned by its mode of production" (1989, 103). The corollary of that assumption is the assertion that the "legal, religious, political, and philosophical spheres of society develop on the basis of the production mode and refer back to it." Mosala's materialist method, therefore, endeavors to account for the following aspects of society: 1) the nature of the mode of production; 2) the constellation of classes necessitated by that mode; and 3) the nature of the ideological manifestations arising out of and referring back to that mode of production. Looking at each aspect, I share the sentiment of some of Mosala's critics that a strong sense of socialism tints his endeavor. Since the breakup of the Soviet Union in the mid-twentieth century, though, the "place of explicitly Marxist analysis has become largely muted in South African biblical exegesis" (McKay 2015, 372). This is not to be misconstrued as celebrating market-based economy or capitalism. Indeed, far from it. I am only highlighting a stronger need to be diversified in our analysis. A variegated approach is needed to capture those institutional constraints that contribute to the impoverishment of society.

As will be discussed in the next chapter, I intend to incorporate some aspects of a materialist approach by utilizing elements of the New Institutional Economics (NIE). Combined with sociorhetorical interpretive (SRI) analytics, I intend to explore the political-economic context of the Lukan text. Questions will be asked of the text especially with respect to institutional constraints confronting the household in first-century society. Nonetheless, in my own humble opinion, methodology should emerge functionally out of the studied phenomenon. In this regard, a multi-method approach is called for by the variegated and often complex nature of the institutional constraints shaping the political-economic context. To move successfully toward this goal, more thorough review of the political-economic context of society in first-century Mediterranean is necessary.

Inculturation Hermeneutics

Another critical aspect evident in African Biblical Hermeneutics is the notion that the methodology and hermeneutical framework of an investigation is borne out of the world and culture of the people who are being investigated. Justin S. Ukpong talks about inculturation hermeneutics—a form of "contextual hermeneutic methodology" that utilizes the "conceptual frame of reference" of the people under scrutiny to interpret the Bible through their own social-cultural context (Ukpong 2002, 12). For Ukpong then, it is not enough to read the biblical text in its original context and apply it to the context of the interpreter. Nor is it appropriate to read the context into the biblical text. Rather, the central tenet of inculturation hermeneutics presupposes that the conceptual framework, the methodology, and the interpreter, are all functions of "the world-view and life experience" of the culture that is the subject of interpretation (Ukpong 1995, 5). In this there are close resemblances between Ukpong and Nasili Vaka'uta's (2011) *tu'a*-wise reading. They both exhibit what I called "the contextualization of interpretive instruments" (see chapter on Pacific Island Biblical hermeneutics, page 35), which comprises not only contextualizing the text but also utilizing indigenous concepts and theories in that contextualization.

Ukpong shares in the sentiment that western academic biblical pedagogy tends to be intellectualist, seeking objective truth as an interpretive interest and insisting upon universal principles. For Ukpong, western biblical pedagogy underscores rigidity and singularity with outcomes that are usually applied universally. African biblical hermeneutics on the other hand is both existential and pragmatic (Ukpong 2002, 19–20). It is contextual as it does not claim universality, nor does it claim to capture the totality of meaning of a text. Rather, it is done in a context that is mediated through a framework borne of the world-view or social-cultural context of a particular community (Ukpong 2002, 21). While inculturation hermeneutics may be particular, it also allows enough space for dialogue and conversation with other readings.

Based on the presupposition that the Christian Bible is both the word of God containing norms for Christian life and a literary ancient document, Ukpong places the locus of interpretation on the connection between these two categories and on the theological meaning of the text in contemporary society (Ukpong 1995, 9). The goal of exegesis therefore is "to actualize the theological meaning of the text in a contemporary context" (9). Given that the Bible is an ancient literary document, the use of historical-critical tools is inevitable, although with caution. Sharing Peter Stuhlmacher's (1977) sentiment, Ukpong warns that the historical tools are to be used "precisely as servant not as master" (Ukpong 1995,

9). This implicitly means there is a need to diversify one's tool box (Temin 2012, 69), if we may be permitted to use this analogy, since the interpretive enterprise warrants a variegated approach.[4]

The need for a variegated approach is reinforced by the presumption that the text is plurivalent—capable of having multiple meanings depending on one's point of departure. But while the text may have multiple meanings, not all readings are correct according to Ukpong. As a result, there is a need for standards against which to measure and critically engage multiplicity of readings. Accordingly, all readings "must be judged in the light of the meaning of the entire Bible" (1995, 10). Moreover, the theology of the text "must be judged against the basic biblical affirmations and principles like existence of God as creator and sustainer of the universe, love of God and neighbor (sic) etc." (1995, 10).

This point is important, one that resonates with my own desire to exercise critical discernment within my contextual biblical reading. In particular, while I consent to the notion of multiplicity of readings, there is an even more critical need for some framework of reference. Without a clear framework of reference, there is no standard or point of reference from which to critically engage and discern our interpretive enterprise. Nonetheless, the obvious challenge is the discernment of a standard and who is to be accorded the burden of judging. Thus, while there is an argument for a point of reference, I am not as bold as Ukpong. In particular, I have reservation about judging readings against some creedal or universal standards. My reservation is based on a conviction borne of the principle of *seu le manu ae taga'i ile galu* (catch the bird but watch the wave). Metaphorically, my approach is undergirded and encompassed by pragmatism. Borne of the experience of fishing out in the open sea, one must exercise courage and accept unlimited challenges. There may be an unlimited catch to be made, but there is perhaps a greater potential for rogue waves and unanticipated climatic changes. Similarly, while there is virtually no limit to the multiplicity of meaning of a text, in my humble opinion, a sense of responsibility is critical. While the Bible as the locus for biblical interpretation has validity, I argue that the greater responsibility

---

4. I find that the idea of a multi-method approach in biblical readings resonates also with other disciplines in public management and the tools approach which underpins the sense that the choice of tools involves values. In both disciplines, the choice of tools reflects values endorsed by the researcher as well as shaped by the nature of the problem. For further reading on the tools approach see Lester M. Salamon (2002) for its use in public management and Robert T. Nakamura and Thomas W. Church (2003) in public policy.

lies with the exegete, the interpreter. As history has informed us, the Bible has been utilized for all sorts of purposes, good and bad. To militate against this, self-reflection is necessary with openness to critical examination and questions. The point is that while space is warranted for multiple readings and meanings, self-reflection is required to harness a sense of responsibility and prudence. This has important implications. Primarily, that the process of interpreting should not be considered "completed" or absolute. Rather, it is a perpetual process riding on the ebbs and flow of social changes and the fluid context of the interpreter.

That the text is plurivalent also implies a more sophisticated and nuanced methodological reading endeavor. While Ukpong, in his context, may have preferred historical-critical tools, the fact that the text is plurivalent suggests the need for a more variegated arsenal of methodological tools. This is one of the reasons why for my study, I am pursuing a sociorhetorical exploration—"an approach that evaluates and reorients its strategies as it engages in multi-faceted dialogue with the texts and other phenomena that come within its purview" (Robbins 2010, 192). SRI enables the goal of bringing the Bible in contact with the many needs and concerns of the people in a particular society.

As a matter of fact, Ukpong's description of the procedures for doing inculturation hermeneutics resonates well with SRI. In particular, according to Ukpong, the first step is to identify "the interpreter's specific context that dynamically corresponds or approximates to the historical context of the text" and then to clarify the interpreter's perspective in relation to the text (1995, 10). This suggests finding a connection between the historical context of the text and the contemporary context. But while Ukpong does not explicitly mention it, he just might have been referring to the social location of the author of the text or that of the reader. One of the appeals of SRI is mediating connections between the context of the reader and of the text. It is very much connected to West's description of the third pole, or pole of appropriation (West 2016, 43). Draper is also in support adding that "it is precisely the particular reader's "ideo-theological orientation" (the goals and choices she makes) which brings the text and context into dialogue and enables the production of meaning and hence transformative praxis" (2015, 13). In other words, to make the connection between the context of the text and the reader significantly meaningful, much depends on the ideological dialogue between the reader and the text. It is precisely for this very reason that I find SRI fitting. In particular, the ideological texture of the text gives space for the ideology of the reader to interface with that of the text (Robbins 1996b, 194). The ideological dialogue between the reader and the text is critical to SRI.

Reading with Ordinary People

Endeavoring to bring the Bible to bear on the African context, Gerald O. West, inter alia, advances the idea of contextual biblical reading. His work on "reading with the ordinary people" lays the foundation for how to do Bible studies in different contexts, and especially eliciting community perspectives. By "readers," West echoes the "well-charted shift in hermeneutics towards the reader" (West 1999, 10). His use of the term reader is both literal and metaphoric as it encompasses also those who are "illiterate, but who listen to, retell and remake the Bible" (10). The term "ordinary" designates those who read the Bible "pre-critically" and those who are poor and marginalized. By readers also, West is inclusive of the "socially engaged biblical scholar" (10).

West's "reading with the ordinary people" is an exercise to bridge the seemingly inevitable schism between critical and pre-critical readings of the Bible. This he demonstrates by advancing a step-by-step contextual bible study process with the purpose of taking seriously the readings of the ordinary people guided by the trained scholar. As West describes, "contextual Bible study begins with the needs and concerns of poor and marginalized communities" (1999, 131). The Bible reading is driven by questions that emerge from the communities rather than having been dictated by academic biblical scholars. They are elicited from the "life interests" of the participating group. Their experiences shape the question or questions to ask of the text. This creates a "framework of accountability" for Bible reading. Such framework allows both biblical scholars and ordinary readers space to participate fully and to be held accountable. As West writes,

> By deliberately choosing to work in those contexts in which it is possible for subject positions and power relations to be vigilantly foregrounded, the reading interface in which socially engaged biblical scholars and ordinary 'readers' participate is subject to subject—is 'reading with'. (West 1999, 132)

Implicit in the above quote is a desire to create a platform for equity between intellectuals and the grassroots. It is in a sense recognizing the vast discrepancies in the world of academia and those moored in real-life issues away from the limelight.

Another important aspect of a contextual Bible study is the possibility of (also) reading the "unknown, neglected and abandoned texts—texts from the margins of the Bible" (132). As West argues, "the danger with well-known texts is that they already have strong reception histories and marked effects, and it is not always easy to read against the damage they have done" (132). In saying this, one can make the claim that Luke 18:18–30 is a well-known text. Notwithstanding any marked effects and strong reception history, I argue though that the text remains vital to an understanding of the relationship between material and spiritual life, especially in a place like the Pacific Island region. Much can be learned from exploring the social dynamics surrounding the rich ruler, theological meanings that are valid lessons for Christians in the Pacific region.

Another key feature of contextual Bible study is the emphasis on resources. By resources, West appears to refer to different critical reading methods claiming that "in order to read the Bible critically we would need to draw on the resources of biblical scholarship" (2013, 44). For West, "the 'critical' resources of biblical resources offered sets of questions that probed the structural and ideological relationships within and behind the biblical text" (44). Choosing which resources to use depends on the needs and concerns raised by the participating community or readers. They create the generative theme that actually activates the reading resources. By generative theme, West seemingly resonates with Paulo Freire's assertion that "the generative theme cannot be found in people, divorced from reality; nor yet in reality, divorced from people" (Freire 1970, 106). As such, according to Freire, "to investigate the generative theme is to investigate people's thinking about reality and people's action upon reality, which is their praxis" (106).

As a *tautai seu*, the idea of a generative theme resonates with my own preference to ground my contextual biblical reading in the lived reality of the people. It is for this reason that I foreground the political-economic context of the Pacific Island Countries and Territories (PICTs) and in particular the Samoan context in my contextual biblical reading of Luke. That is as a *tautai seu*, the lived reality of my Samoan context is just as significant as the context of the text in my contextual biblical reading of Luke.

Because of this connection between people and their reality, the context of the participants is important to West. As he writes, "because critical modes of reading tend to create some distance between readers and text they come second and serve whatever resources and readings are already present" (West 1999, 135). But by starting with the context of the participants, "the often urgent demands of the context usually hold forms of engagement and forms of critical distance together in a creative dialectic; the tentative testing and articulating of 'working' readings (and theologies) seems to require the use of both local community resources for reading and critical modes of reading" (135). West's bible study process therefore is neither "a naïve and romantic listening to" nor "a paternalistic and marginalizing reading." Rather it is a process in which "we vigilantly foreground our respective subject positions and where we become explicit concerning the power relations implicit in the reading process" (West 1999, 135–36).

Also implicit in West's idea of the process of contextual Bible study is a sense that the locus of interpretation needs to bear on the needs of the ordinary people. From this perspective, the Bible is viewed as often utilized as a tool and instrument for the oppressors as well as the oppressed (Adamo 2015, 34). It has been used "to legitimate imperial conquest, to suppress resistance to tyrannical regimes, to bolster male patriarchy and sometimes violent domination of women" (Draper 2015, 11). More significantly, biblical interpretation itself is colonized in many ways as it is often an exercise in the hands of the privileged, the academicians. Andrew M. Mbuvi sees this as a failure in African biblical interpretation where the majority of African scholarship written in western institutions failed to bring the African context to bear on the readings (Mbuvi 2017, 153). Regardless of the mode of reading, the interpreting community is more often exclusive and privileged, dominated especially by academia. Contextual Bible study, therefore to some extent, seeks to reverse this and more, including breaking the hermeneutical hegemony and ideological stranglehold that Eurocentric biblical scholars enjoyed (Adamo 2015, 34). Engaging ordinary people presumes a shift in the locus of interpretation where meaning is no longer a prerogative of just a privileged few, but requires engaging also common, unsophisticated people. Meaning resides even with those whose needs and voices are often neglected in biblical interpretation.

A word of caution is offered here. While the promises of a contextual Bible study are certainly a worthy cause, how to concretize this transformation to liberate remains a critical challenge. There is no clear evidence that the transformation taking place from reading with the ordinary people translates into action. The relationship between the reading and transformation is at best, "complex and much less direct than is often claimed" (Wit and Dyk 2015, 2). Even if the locus of interpretation resides with the disenfranchised community or those whose voices are often neglected, the fact of the matter is there are institutional constraints that continue to undermine the connection between any contextual reading and meaningful actions. This is not to say that the liberation aspect of contextual Bible study is to be taken lightly. But without successfully challenging and altering the institutional landscape that governs and designs our interpretive enterprise, it would be difficult to ascertain any real benefits to ordinary people. This could mean that a deeper appreciation of the institutional constraints contributing to the current status of the people is in order. Addressing those constraints will go a long way towards mediating some of the political and economic obstacles impeding the attempt for social justice.

Postcolonial readings and beyond

More recent attempts to feature African issues and concerns in biblical reading seem to have taken a postcolonial turn. Sharing many of the sentiments among several scholars on the African context, Mbuvi offers that

> (T)he recognition of the impact of colonialism on all major aspects of African life—politics, religion, language, economics, culture, etc.—and its continuing impact on society today has led to postcolonial studies whose premise is to expose the colonial project in all its forms and then to decolonize the colonized or formerly colonized. (Mbuvi 2017, 164)

I will focus on the work of Musa W. Dube in particular for its feminist aspects as well as how Dube explicitly connects liberation theology and work. The imperialistic nature in which the Bible was weaponized for the purpose of colonization underscores the challenge facing biblical interpretation in the African context. Exacerbating the challenge is the fact that the same Bible was employed to subject the people of Africa to imperial rule and colonial subjects. To demonstrate this loss of sense, Dube tells of an anonymous oral short story, the version of which noted here is repeated from Takatso Mofokeng (1988). Dube explains

> During the decades of the armed struggle for liberation in sub-Saharan Africa, an anonymous short story, orally narrated and

> passed on by word of mouth, became popular. The story held that "when the white man came to our country he had the Bible and we had the land. The white man said to us, 'let us pray.' After the prayer, the white man had the land and we had the Bible." (Dube 2000, 3)

For Dube therefore, it is her quest to provide a response. But this in itself gives the sense that postcolonial issues are something in the past. Dube though offers a view of postcolonial issues that are continuous. She notes in particular that through "multinational corporations, universal media, and international monetary bodies, military and ideological muscle imperialism has proven its capacity to mutate and persist in ever new and remarkable forms—what is now termed globalization or neocolonization" (Dube 2000, 48).

Moreover, Dube adds that globalization, especially in this age of information superhighway, has had the effect of enhancing the flow of information from "former colonial metropolitan centers" to the rest of world. This latest form of imperialism has created an overall impact on global relations "affecting men and women, privileging some and oppressing others, and finding ways to repeatedly justify and maintain itself across the globe" (48). For Dube therefore, postcolonial studies and method endeavor to challenge elements of "powers of oppression" in academic institutions and establish "an oppositional body of literature that seeks to understand and expose the making of global expansion and exploitation as well as to search for better ways of imagining and building just international relations" (48).

While postcoloniality[5] "affects all the social institutions of the concerned nations and races," Dube's particular focus is on the literary materials available and how they continue to perpetuate colonial aspects of African history (2000, 48). In that regard, Dube uses the term postcolonial to refer "to literary theories developed from studying literature and its participation in the institution of imperialism" (48). Adding further, "*postcolonial* [Dube's emphasis] does not denote that colonialism is over, since the latter did not simply consist of geographical and political domination but also included cultural and economic structures that persist to this day" (48). For Dube, therefore, postcolonial "refers to an overall analysis of the methods and effects of imperialism as a continuing reality in global relations" (48). One can detect a certain degree of suspicion in

---

5. For further readings on postcoloniality see Anna Runesson (2011).

Dube towards certain methods for reading the Bible. This is a prominent feature of Dube's postcolonial approach.

Dube starts by outlining postcolonial theories of literature. In sum, postcolonial theories of literature "examine the making and the subversion of imperialism, which in the past tended to lead to geographical colonialism" (Dube 2000, 52). Literature is viewed as "an essential instrument in imperialism's power struggles" and as such analyses of both literature of the colonizer and the colonized are essential. The focus of such analysis is on how literature "constructs or responds to the traveling, the entering, and the taking control of foreign lands by imperialistic nations" (Dube 2000, 52). To shed further clarity, Dube shares from several anthologies of postcolonial aspects for analysis. Several aspects are listed including:

> The West as an imperialist center, nationalism, nativism, diaspora, hybridity, identity, language, education, history, media, intertextuality, place and displacement, production and consumption, universality and difference, representation and resistance, intellectuals and institutions, subalterns and resistance, and gender representation in imperial domination or Subversion. (Dube 2000, 52)

The importance of the above is to discern the various features of postcolonial reading. As Dube offers, postcoloniality "is a very complex phenomenon that involves texts from different times, places, and cultures and whose boundaries often blur" (Dube 2000, 52). This multiple-textual nature of postcoloniality presupposes "a myriad of methods and theories, all of which examine literature and its participation in the building, collaboration, or subversion of global imperial relationships" (Dube 2000, 52–53). Moreover, one can detect aspects of intertextuality in Dube's postcoloniality.

After a brief overview of postcolonial theories on literature, Dube then proceeds to provide an extensive illustration of postcolonial reading, focusing in particular on "the literary methods of imperialism's power struggles" by analyzing certain texts. The aim is to show "how the desires and revolts of the institution of imperialism are concretized in the production and reproduction of recognizable literary-rhetorical patterns" (53). The first step in Dube's illustration is to look at the "imperializing text" or the text of the colonizer which tends to claim power over foreign and populated lands (53). By doing so, emphasis is on the impact of the colonizer, giving voice and shape to the imperialistic text. The literary-rhetorical methods that were used to justify taking control of distant and foreign lands become the focal point of interest for Dube's postcolonial approach (53).

From a *tautai seu* perspective, what I find especially intriguing is the use of extra-canonical literature to read alongside the Bible. Part of Dube's approach looks at other imperializing extra-canonical ancient texts. This warrants the use of intertextuality and interdisciplinary tools in the analysis, a prominent feature of Dube's postcolonial approach. As Dube argues, the reading of the Bible together with ancient secular texts is merited for several reasons. Sharing Susanna Heschel's (1996) sentiment that Christian feminist writings tend to negatively portray Judaism, Dube writes that the "interdisciplinary, intertextual, boundary-transgressing postcolonial feminist approach" protects against anti-Semitism. For Dube, reading of the Bible side by side with secular texts does much to "demystify the isolation of Christian texts from other cultural texts, an approach that tends to shield them from various critical investigations as well as to perpetuate some of the oppressive ideologies of the Bible" (Dube 2000, 54). Also, Dube argues that "biblical feminists' isolated focus on Jewish literature seems to hide the fact that patriarchy is prevalent in many other non-Jewish classical narratives" (54). More significantly Dube sees the reading of secular and sacred texts together as paying closer attention to one's "own postcolonial experience" (54). Learning the English language and the Christian mission were both instrumental in the colonization of Africa. As Dube observes in particular, "imperialism was instituted through both the church and the English departments of schools" (54).

Vetting Dube's postcolonial reading of Matthew 15:21–28 also sheds light on some of the methodological tools she employed. The nature of the exegetical work carried out suggests that it is mainly literary in nature. In this regard, it is a reading which according to Dube is "on and through the text that does not equate Matthew with historical facts" (Dube 2000, 127). Rather the focus is on "the rhetorical text engineered within and by a particular historical setting." Dube's admission here is an important one for me as it bears greater affinity to the notion of a "social and cultural texture" of the text. The focus though for Dube's exegetical work is on power relations. It is re-construction of the text presupposing what the implied author perceives as the reality "associated with the power struggles that pertain to the Roman imperial occupation" (127).

As a *tautai seu*, what is intriguing is that while Dube's approach is presumably literary in nature, there is also an integral element of historical critical tools involved. In my humble opinion, this is evidence in support of a more integrated methodological approach. In Dube's exploration of empire in Matthew, the focus shifts towards two important elements of the text—historical and ideological features. The establishment of historicity based on the text helps to bring clarity on its underlying ideology. As Dube states:

> The historical perspective seeks to establish whether the Matthean text is rejecting the imperialism of its time or seeking its favor. The ideological view, on the other hand, seeks to establish whether the Matthean intertextual perspective is geared toward rejecting or accommodating imperialism. The latter presupposes that Matthew stands within the Hebrew Bible foundation myth of the promised land, which was shown... to embody imperialistic values. Although the approach seeks to separate these two aspects, they are quite interconnected. (Dube 2000, 128)

The connection between ideology and historicity is vital for Dube as it presages bringing into bearing one's own social location. In doing so, Dube undertakes the task of bringing the text to bear on the African context. From Dube's social location, history is recounted noting that "the historical experience of sub-Saharan African people finds an intimate relationship between empire and mission" (129). Moreover, "popular African folklore and critical writers such as Ngugi wa Thiongo, Ali Mazrui, Canaan Banana, and Kwesi Dickson... emphasize an ideological interconnection between biblical mission passages and imperialism" (129). By bringing in her social location, Dube formulates questions to challenge the Matthean text. In this regard, one can presume that Dube's social location and question formulations also appear to transform the interpretive process. In the process, the text is transformed as much as the reader.

ASIAN BIBLICAL HERMENEUTICS

Connecting the Bible to the Asian context presents a different set of challenges. But while there is a stark contrast between the history and culture of Asia and Africa, there are also intersecting areas especially in how they negotiate religious, cultural, and colonial elements of the Bible.

One of the vexing problems in bringing the Bible to bear on the Asian context lies in trying to identify the locus of Asia. To attempt to trace the contours of Asian biblical hermeneutics, one has to begin by appreciating the onerous task of defining Asia as a concept and of finding a single term in the Asian languages that can represent the whole region like the term European does for that continent (Sugirtharajah 2013, 1). Adding to the conundrum is the inability and refusal of the multiple religious, linguistic, and ethnic groups that inhabited the continent to see themselves as a collective unit (Sugirtharajah 2013, 1). Part of it also is the fluidity and complexity the word Asia represents. For example, the term Asia in Chinese characters can be deduced to having the meaning of "inferiority." The result places China in the center while everyone else is termed the "others" (Sugirtharajah 2013, 1). Given the fact that historically China has long been an empire, this is very telling. In this regard, it is reasonable to assume that to call someone from China "Asian" is ambivalent.

Another challenge is based on the fact that Asia's geographical and identity boundaries are fluid. In fact, in terms of geographical location and cultural identity, Asia is appropriately identified as consisting of four groups—West Asia, Central Asia, East Asia, and South Asia (Havea and Lau 2015, 2).

Further complications for clear definition and explanation of Asian biblical hermeneutics come from the introduction of Christianity to Asia since the region was already rich with outstanding living traditions including Hinduism, Buddhism, Confucianism, Taoism, Shamanism, and Islam when Christianity began to arrive (Bae 2004, 392). Scriptures from these living traditions had already been deeply influential on society, the culture and history of many Asian countries. As a result, Asian biblical hermeneutics is cognizant that it exists alongside other scriptures with equally influential impact. Hyunju Bae sums it up nicely:

> The scriptures of many of these constitute a significant part of Asian indigenous culture, and Asian people breathe the cosmological and anthropological instructions and views of life of those traditions, wittingly or unwittingly, because they are the

classics of Asian culture. The contemporary interdisciplinary approach to the Bible in the West often derives from its status as the Western classic, not merely as the scripture of Christian religion. In contrast, the Asian biblical scholars and theologians live in the culture in which the notable classics are the *Analects* of Confucius, Buddhist scriptures, *Tao Te Ching*, *Chuang Tzu*, the *Vedas* and the *Koran*. (Bae 2004, 393)

Against this background, one can see the many challenges Asian biblical hermeneutics has to navigate as a discipline. Moreover, presumably the Asian context implies traditional literacy, whereas the African context does not. On the other hand, the interesting question is who was able to read in the Asian context and whether that was strictly an elite consideration. It is noteworthy that in Asia oral transmission of the major authoritative bodies of words is the dominant mode in many religious traditions. In many Asian cultures, "the scriptures have been chanted, recited, memorized and performed for millennia because the spoken words are considered more sacred than the written texts" (Pui-lan 2000, 53). Christianity's introduction of "written scripture" into Asia, and perhaps particularly into India, introduced a significantly different understanding of authoritative religious word. It was not until printing and popular education became affordable that the written text became important.

As a *tautai seu*, I situate some of the selected readings from the Asian context with some of the wisdom already gathered from the African context. A notable characteristic is the diversity of the methodological approaches and theoretical orientations that scholars employed (Segovia 1994, 371). The presence of a wide range of methods including comparative analysis, literary criticism, cultural criticism and cultural studies manifests great affinity to methodological approaches and theoretical frameworks that have emerged from Western biblical scholarship. While one may argue that this is an indication of the breadth of religious and cultural aspects in Asia, R.S. Sugirtharajah laments that there is no distinctive Asian mode of reading (1994, 251). While African contextual biblical interpretations have seized on terms such as black biblical hermeneutics or inculturation hermeneutics, Asians according to Sugirtharajah have no such distinctive mode of reading. This is not a bad thing. Rather it is a function of the history and culture of the region. Understandably, there is a greater need and available space in Asia for "alternative indigenous reading theories"

(Sugirtharajah 1994, 251). Notwithstanding the lack of an Asian mode of reading, for the sake of discussion Sugirtharajah describes two broadly grouped headings—metropolitan and vernacular strands of reading (1994, 252). These groupings are not clearly demarcated nor are they particular to Asia. While they are grouped under different umbrellas, they do share many common factors with other contexts. Exploring these discrepancies and similarities is instructive and informative.

Metropolitan Reading

Metropolitan reading reflects the social reality of today's world in which globalization has managed to connect the world together through the information highway, multinational corporations and migration. From the perspective of metropolitan reading, to understand contemporary social life one must extend the unit of analysis beyond the local into the global context. This has introduced a global trend that has deeply influenced biblical interpretation (Sugirtharajah 1994, 252). One of the major results of this global trend is that contextual biblical hermeneutics is often dominated by methodologies and approaches influenced by western values and principles. Even some of the recent approaches including *minjung*, *dalit*, and *burakumin*, according to Sugirtharajah, are "based on and re-work western models." In a context of spreading western influence, methodologies and approaches with origins in western academies have been creatively adapted by a "metropolitan family" of Asian scholars who understand themselves as "a collective hermeneutical family" (252).

A major import of metropolitan reading is that the local context is very much a function of the global context and vice versa. The implications of this are significant. For one, even when the focus is on a particular context, the analysis is likely to use collective tools and methods that are predominantly western in origin. As a result, there are no strict boundaries demarcating the utilization of methods and tools. Indeed, metropolitan readings regularly acknowledge and recognize the presence of methodologies and theoretical approaches that have originated in western academies but are then being creatively utilized and put into use to fit Asian contexts (Sugirtharajah 1994, 252).

This is an important point as it reflects something critical about contextual biblical interpretation whether in Asia, Africa or even in the Pacific. Because we are all connected, the intersection between mainline methods of biblical criticism—mainly historical and literary criticism—and contextual biblical interpretation is inevitable. The fact is, many scholars in Africa and Asia do use some version of western or mainline methods (Havea and Lau 2020a, 7). Proof of Sugirtharajah's metropolitan categorization lies in a statement by Jione Havea and Peter H. W. Lau, where they express similar approval for this inevitable intersection.

> In our experience, we find contextual biblical critics using mainline methods (to look *behind* and *into* the text) whereas mainline biblical critics do not wander into the fields of contextual interpretation (to look *in front of* the text). The problem therefore is not with contextual biblical critics but with the strictly mainline biblical critics... There are two facets we wish to stress here with respect to methodology: the first facet is that pitting historical and literary criticisms over against contextual biblical interpretation is unfair because these are not blockaded from each other. One does not defile the discipline by adding contextual interpretation to one's literary and/or historical reading. And one's contextual interpretation is shallow without literary and historical readings as well. The second facet is that methodology has been used to erect a political arena so that, in other words, what happens in the reading room overflows into the board room. (Havea and Lau 2020a, 7–8)

The above quotation therefore underscores the inevitability of integration between mainline and contextual biblical interpretation methods. Moreover, it suggests the need to disrupt and dismantle the "inferiority" barrier confronting contextual readings. While metropolitan readings imply the need for some degree of integration, contextual readings have some hurdles to overcome. In particular, social and political stigmatization exert pressure on contextual readings to meet or adhere to certain standards established and institutionalized through western academics, societies and associations. This is the dilemma facing contextual readings.

Vernacular Hermeneutics

According to R.S. Sugirtharajah, while liberation-focused biblical hermeneutics privileges liberation, vernacular hermeneutics "mobilizes indigenous cultural nuances for theological enterprises" (1999, 11). It is context-sensitive and "privileges indigenous culture as an authentic site for doing theology" and moreover, vernacular hermeneutics "focuses on native characteristics and ideas" (12). It is not just focusing or employing indigenous language, concepts or ideas. Much more than this is the focus on the people, their needs and concerns. As Sugirtharajah assesses the situation, vernacular hermeneutics is "postmodern in its eagerness to celebrate the local, and postcolonial in its ability to disturb and dislodge the reigning imported theories" (12).

According to Sugirtharajah, instead of borrowing from western exegetical practices, vernacular reading is an attempt to rediscover Asia's past (Sugirtharajah 1994, 253). It reclaims ancient reading theories and methods of storytelling. Borrowing mainly from Indian scholars, Sugirtharajah offers several examples of ancient readings that have been reclaimed for the purpose of reading the Bible. One in particular is the use of an ancient Indian method of reading *dhuani* which stresses "the suggestive possibility of the text, its evocative nature and its emotional grip on the reader/ hearer/ spectator" (253). Another example is the use of ancient Indian storytelling, a method used by "religious teachers to instruct their followers" (253). It is not so much the re-reading of an old text but the retelling of old stories for a new context.

Sugirtharajah's description of vernacular hermeneutics suggests a turn for indigenous-sensitive readings. The aim appears to be an independent and inclusively indigenous approach to biblical interpretation that prioritizes non-mainline tools and methods. Yet, one gets the sense from Sugirtharajah that something is lacking if our biblical enterprise simply focuses on an indigenous-sensitive reading. While the aim is to establish indigenous readings, Sugirtharajah appears to argue for something more, a method that "can conform to the ground rules set by the western academics" (1994, 254). Overall, his approach offers encouragement to pursue more indigenous oriented methods, pushing beyond mainline biblical interpretation toward non-mainline tools based on indigenous values and beliefs. This is an honorable task and something to be taken with much seriousness.

But as discussed above, Sugirtharajah further expounds on an even deeper concern and perhaps a flaw in our current biblical interpretation scholarship. He regularly points to political barriers often faced by scholars from contexts in the margin. Barriers often exist as remnants of a colonial academia that continues to function as a gatekeeper that controls the flow of the global biblical enterprise. As a result, indigenous interpretation regularly disrupts remnants of colonialism institutionalized in the biblical enterprise at the same time it is using the Bible to establish and perpetuate subjective issues within indigenous society. This is a sentiment shared by several scholars especially those from the margins including women and children (Boer and Segovia 2012; Sugirtharajah 2017). Of importance to the purpose of contrasting and comparing across the Asian, African and Pacific Island context, I mentioned in particular Nasili Vaka'uta (2011) and Iosefa Lefaoseu (2018) from the Pacific context, and Justin Ukpong from the African context. The aim of contextualization is not just on the text and meaning, but also the interpretive tools and methods that have been set up as standards for doing biblical interpretations.

A word of caution is in order. The rich exegetical value in indigenous methods and approaches have not been fully realized. While there is much to be learned and gained by doing indigenous methods exclusively, a much more fruitful enterprise warrants starting with the needs and concerns of the people. To make the Bible more relevant is to moor biblical interpretation in social reality. That could be the first goal. It is also on that basis that our methodologies and tools of reading will emerge. The question of method or interpretive framework is a function of the issue studied. In other words, contextual biblical interpretation gains much by being issue-driven. That is my hope in the attempt to make the connection between the Lukan narrative and the political-economic context of the PICT's. It is also for that reason that I find the SRI framework most fitting.

Asians in Diaspora

To gain breadth in perspective, I also want to highlight some of the other readings I find intriguing and relevant. John Ahn (2019) in an edited work compiles essays from local Korean scholars as well as those in the diaspora. These essays offer an overall view of some of the discussions on what constitutes Korean biblical hermeneutics.

One of the interesting aspects of the Ahn volume is how there is a conscious effort to capture both Korean and Korean American scholarship in an attempt to distinguish what is Korean biblical hermeneutics. This conscious effort underscores the value of the interpreter's social location. From Ahn's perspective, the social location of the interpreter provides the center from which any attempt to distinguish Korean and Korean American biblical hermeneutics departs (2019, 3). The challenge though is finding consensus on what constitutes the core. Further confounding matters is the challenge of someone living in the diapsora[6]. Ahn summarizes this as follows:

> What constitutes, demarcates, fosters, and makes Korean and Korean American biblical interpretation distinctive from Asian American or other cultural interpretations? If social location is seminal, what additional noticeable similarities or differences are found in interpretation framed by a South Korean point of view over against a North Korean, or for that matter, a Korean American one? (Ahn 2019, 4)

Key to Ahn then is the need to construct a center and periphery or centers and peripheries. Despite challenges, including ethical issues concerning the notion of center (Holter 2010, 93), Ahn asserts that "the diachronic task of historical and textual criticism and the synchronic task of locating the *Mitte* [Ahn's emphasis] are necessary for a better understanding of the text" (4). As a result, Ahn shares the sentiment for a more synthesized approach.

> There is a consensus that, in Korean and Korean American biblical interpretation, our task is not to replace existing modes of interpretations, but rather, as biblical scholars, work within biblical studies and with social sciences, ethnic studies, and global issues to create and foster something distinctive. If the outcome is a carefully constructed new creation, a new transnational mode of interpretation, which encompasses past and present methods, factoring in social constructions of realities, solving critical problems, bringing awareness to important modern and ancient issues, and offering new insights, a synthesized model has been achieved. If not, much work remains ahead of us. (Ahn 2019, 4)

In the above quote, Ahn sums up the challenge and goal for Korean and Korean American biblical scholars. But the overall volume also offers sound advice for other contexts and for my study. It underscores the need for a more integrated and interconnected approach to biblical interpretation, one that also warrants an interdisciplinary approach. For Ahn though, distinctiveness is to be found between existing western

---

6. For the sake of time and word limit, the center of my attention is on Asian biblical scholars based mainly in Asia. Nonetheless, I am aware of the richness and depth that would have been gained through the works of those in the Diaspora in particular Asian American including Sze-kar Wan (2000), Gale A. Yee (2009), and Khiok-Khng Yeo (2011).

and non-western tools within this integration of methodologies and approaches. While I agree that integration is necessary for both our purpose and could be the way to pursue distinctiveness, I do diverge somewhat. Perhaps there is not much differentiation to be made, especially given the effect of globalization. But more significantly, I would argue instead that the emphasis should not be methodological but rather issue-centered and people-focused. Because we are surrounded by different social constraints, ecological, political, economic, the issues that we face can be the distinguishing factor for biblical interpretation. The next section can be considered evidence.

Asian Feminist Biblical Hermeneutics

Hisako Kunukawa (2014) in an edited work compiles papers presented at the third meeting of the Society of Asian Biblical Studies in 2012. The theme of the meeting was on migration and diaspora. The contributors—all feminists/scholars from Japan, China, and Korea—undertake readings of the biblical texts within their social and cultural contexts. A distinguishing aspect of Kunukawa's edited work is the fact that while the writers are all writing from different social locations, they do share one thing in common—a commitment to find justice for women.

> Though our social locations are diverse, all of us are committed to finding justice for women in our countries and in our contemporary living through our dialogue with biblical texts. Our struggles for survival in society and our fight for a voice and a space within a patriarchal academy are hard and painfully severe. Despite the resistance, we Asian women/feminist scholars have made efforts to transform the current situation by striving against the discrimination we encounter in our lives as women and as scholars. (Kunukawa 2014, 2)

Thus, justice for women becomes the focusing-issue for Kunukawa and other Asian feminist scholars.

Kwok Pui-lan (2000) in her monograph provides further clarity on the nuances of Asian feminist theology. It started as a grassroots movement borne of the context and real-life experience of Asian women. Because of their sensitivity to the word feminism, many of the Asian women prefer to call their theology something far less radical (2000, 9). Many preferred Asian women's theology over feminist theology, "to avoid the negative connotations of a militant, separatist and man-hating stance" (9). Pui-lan though prefers women's rights movement to convey her own discernment of "Asian feminist theology not only as a form of theological reflection but also as a political movement to transform the church and society so that women's freedom and dignity will be fully recognized" (10). Hence, we see in Pui-lan how the Bible is viewed as having the dual responsibilities of both being transformative and liberating. Women's rights provide the focusing locality.

Pui-lan provides a helpful description of the various models of feminist hermeneutical approaches to the Bible (51). One of the approaches attempts to recover the memory of women in the Bible. In a church culture that is dominated by males, biblical female figures, especially those in the life and ministry of Jesus, are noted for their significance. By emphasizing their engagement in God's ministry and contributions to history, this approach shows that biblical women can be role models for contemporary Asian women (Pui-lan 2000, 53). The difficulty for this approach from Pui-lan's perspective is the continuing curtailing of women. For example, women are always depicted in secondary roles especially in a male-dominated society. Moreover, this approach fails to refute the constant portrayal of women as property, as whores, or as victims of society (53).

Scholars of Asian feminist theology also prefer oral presentation and transmission of the Bible. By oral presentation, the text is a "re-tell" not so much for its historical context, but rather for how it is received by the listening audience. A couple of key points are accentuated. First it is democratic and participatory similar to how Gerald O. West's "ordinary people" are solicited. Second, this approach curtails the dominant narrative that the written and literary cultures are more sophisticated and advanced. Third, this approach also undergirds the view that the written and oral text exist in a continuum (Pui-lan 2000, 54).

Strategies for this approach include giving voice to women in the Bible and re-creating their dialogues. Another strategy is by re-telling the biblical stories from the perspective of the woman, placing the woman as the narrator. This re-casting can also be carried out in the form of a poem, drama, skits or dance (Pui-lan 2000, 54). The effect is to reclaim the voices of the women as subjects giving the reader a chance for a sense of self-identifying with those feelings, thoughts and voices. In other words, the approach seeks to bridge divergences between the Asian and biblical contexts.

The socio-political approach according to Pui-lan attempts to read the Bible within the frame of contemporary socio-political events in Asia (56). Questions borne of today's contemporary situation are then employed to engage the Bible. These questions shape one's interaction with the Bible as well as determining the methods for reading the biblical text (56). The implications are significant in particular, according to Pui-lan, since there are many parallels between ancient biblical times and contemporary Asian politics (56). Moreover, contemporary questions concerning social relations in a multi-ethnic society including issues of religion, politics, economic justice, harmony and conflict are as relevant today as in biblical times (56).

To illustrate some of the above approaches to feminist theology Pui-lan cites works of Hisako Kunukawa that pay particular attention to the sociological as well as the anthropological aspects of society. Particular mention is given to the social aspects of honor and shame. Not only that, Kunukawa puts emphasis on the use of rhetorical critical methods to explore the rhetorical function and persuasiveness of the text.

Pui-lan then describes her work on postcolonial reading as another approach to Asian feminist theology. Using the story of the Syrophoenician woman as an example, Pui-lan illustrates the underlying power dynamics in the text. Literary evidence illustrates the way the unequal position of the woman is portrayed "set in a dense web of oppositions: Jewish homeland/foreign lands, inside/outside the house, Jews/Gentiles, cleanliness/uncleanliness, children/dogs, disciples/woman, and people with faith/people without faith" (61). Another key feature of postcolonial reading according to Pui-lan is the insistence that the woman is not curtailed only by her gender but rather that her identity is also a function of "class, language, ethnicity and so on" (62). Hence, such a reading "makes room for a consideration of the differences among women, because it does not focus solely on the sex/gender system at work in the story" (62).

More recently, some scholars have attempted to employ drama and theater as the medium for reading the biblical text. One in particular is the use of *noh* drama which originated in Japanese farming communities "as popular performance ritual depicting stories about the gods and the ancestors" (62). What is significant is the notion that it provides "an occasion for meditation on issues of life and for collective catharsis" (62). For Pui-lan though, "further investigation into the social and political aspects of biblical *noh* drama will be needed if the medium is put into feminist use" (64). Moreover, "a hermeneutics of performative arts will need to be developed, taking into consideration the use of masks, symbolic gestures, dance and movements, which would be quite different from the hermeneutics of words, both oral and written" (64).

The significance of Pui-lan's work is to highlight some of the variations in the search to bring the Bible to bear on contemporary issues of concern and need in society. In particular, Asian feminist theology brings the Bible to bear not only on gender issues but also social, political and economic aspects of society. More significantly, it foregrounds what people experience in real-life. The biblical text is moored in the life-realities of the people. In doing so, it offers "a critical assessment of what the Bible did and does in the complex political reality of both church and society on the one hand, and a sympathetic retrieval of the meanings one can construct from the creative interpretation of the Bible on the other hand" (Bae 2004, 391).

Moreover, Pui-lan is important as evidence of the creativity that emerges out of focusing on issues of justice for women. This clearly suggests the direct correlation between issue/need and methodology. That is, preference of methodological approach and interpretive framework is shaped and defined by a deeper appreciation and awareness of the nuances of challenges and obstacles facing women in society. Therefore, foregrounding life experience does much to lay the platform for our biblical interpretive enterprise.

A word of caution I must add. While I value foregrounding real-life experience in biblical interpretation, it is not in any way suggesting that the Bible is nothing less than God's word. It is however recognizing how the Bible has been utilized to serve the interests of those in authority to create an unjust political-economic context for others. Hence, the foregrounding of experience is to give voice to those without, and those suppressed and constrained. By accentuating social reality, questions are raised of the biblical text.

For example in a recent monograph, Lily Fetalsana-Apura (2019) uses her experience and social situation as a Filipino woman to look at the Bible. Her analysis of Joshua 1:1–9 further highlights what she terms resistance reading—resisting the colonial influence that also shaped how the Bible is read and interpreted in the Philippines. Underscoring resistant reading is the assertion that while "the Bible can be interpreted to perpetuate oppressive human structures, resistance hermeneutics can be a powerful tool to recover and rediscover the contextual meanings of biblical texts (Fetalsana-Apura 2019, 4). Moreover, by "employing contextual and social scientific approaches, resistance hermeneutics has the capacity to examine the ideologies reflective of dominant contexts" (4).

DEEPENING OUR UNDERSTANDING OF CONTEXTUAL BIBLICAL INTERPRETATION

The purpose of this next section is to summarize and discern some of the key aspects of contextual biblical interpretation. Comparing the African context and Asian context with each other and with the Pacific Island context can help to bring clarity to my own work. In particular, I come away with some general observations regarding the different methods and approaches employed. As a *tautai seu* (locating steersman) my purpose is not to impose but rather to locate and situate my contextual biblical reading of the Lukan narrative.

As I proceed, I am aware that Nasili Vakauta's (2011, 35–61) categorization of contextual modes of reading hovers over my work. While Vakauta's categorization is based on an assessment including Latin America and other contexts, my own effort is to deepen some of the nuances and complexities in particular with knowledge about contextual biblical interpretation in Africa and Asia. While this particular focus still may be limited, it adds further depth and richness in detail. My own discernment of biblical contextual interpretation belies my belief that contextual biblical interpretation is adaptable and fluid. Because it is a function of the social, cultural and political environment, contextual biblical interpretation is subject to change necessitating reflection and adjustment. Finally, my motivation in all of this is to gain clarity on how contextual biblical interpretation is utilized to shed light on social, political and economic issues in society. Subsequently, I locate a framework and methodological scheme to bring the Lukan narrative to bear on the political-economic context in the Pacific Island Countries and Territories (PICTs) and in particular, Samoa.

Contextual Biblical Interpretation Grounded in Lived Reality

A common feature of the works discussed above is to bring the Bible to bear on issues that matter to people in contemporary society. Itumeleng J. Mosala for example sees the class-based system in the African context as the site for struggle. A class-based system is at the core of many injustices in society and undergirds the attempt to revitalize a black biblical hermeneutic. Similarly, the emergence of feminist theology in Asia parallels the search for justice on issues of gender, and since then has taken on the struggle for social and economic justice. The works of scholars like Kwok Pui-lan and Hisako Kunukawa are exemplary.

Approaches to connect the Bible to contemporary contexts have made use of methods and frameworks from social science, cultural studies and sociology. While these approaches are variegated, a common aspect has been an emphasis on the social location of the reader. This appears to be a central element of doing contextual biblical interpretation. The implications are significant. Social location for me parallels the social realities surrounding the reader. Much like reader response[7], the cultural, social, economic and political context of the reader contributes to the interpretive scheme. The distinguishing factor for me though is the supplementary integration of historical and literary critical methods. Contextual biblical interpretation hence warrants continuing dialogue between the biblical context and the context of the reader. This warrants a careful review of a combination of tools to ascertain the variables.

The challenge therefore appears to be in choosing where the emphasis should be. Whether it is on the biblical text or whether it is on the experience of the reader, the determining factor to locate emphasis depends on readership. For the purpose of my study, my interest is to see how the biblical context could inform or otherwise help us confront the political-economic struggle facing Christians in Samoa. In that regard, my study is issue-oriented. By this I mean that the issues and their specifics are foregrounded. While this may be similar to the tri-polar approach, my intent is to add a fourth dimension.

It is my hope that by the end of the study, I will arrive at a discussion of its implications for my current social location, social realities. This is my mooring point. Using the fishing analogy, after the task of fishing there is a period of mending, re-evaluating and re-appropriating. It is in this phase of *tautai a'e* (steersman celebrating and reflecting together) that the dialogical relation between the contexts is brought to bear on the issue of the concerns and needs of the people. It also allows for reflection on the process, leaving the conversation open for alternatives and further movement. In this regard, the process is always fluid and is not absolutized.

7. For further reading on reader response see Stanley Fish (1980) and Robert M. Fowler (1996).

Liberation, Resistance, and Transformation

Because contextual biblical interpretation emerges as a result of a struggle for justice, there is a closer parallel to liberation theology. Part of the struggle for justice therefore from a contextual biblical interpretation perspective is to remove the Bible from the monopoly of the imperial and intellectual powers. In other words, the aim is to liberate the Bible as well as the Bible serving as a liberating tool for the colonized, marginalized and the ordinary.

Because contextual biblical interpretation is mostly associated with grassroots level, and especially those in the margins, it encapsulates a form of resistance. Lily Fetalsana-Apura evidences how the Bible is employed as a tool to resist against oppressive government and injustice in society. In this regard, it can be a tool for adherents of democracy and advocates of human rights. Contextual biblical interpretation is an attempt to resist based on dialogue and utilizing as much diplomacy as possible.

Given the liberating and resistant nature of contextual biblical interpretation, the overall effect is that of transformation. The reader as well as the biblical text are transformed. More significantly, contextual biblical interpretation seeks to transform society. Because it attempts to place the Bible within the social, cultural, political and economic reality of society, transformation is inevitable. Subsequently, contextual biblical interpretation includes some form of advocacy. In other words, a major component of contextual biblical interpretation encapsulates advocacy for justice, for change, for the improvement of the current status of people at the grassroots level.

Revival, Creation, and Integration of Indigenous Modes of Reading and Interpretive Frameworks

Contextual biblical interpretation underscores the desire to revive indigenousness. In the struggle to rediscover cultural identities and reclaim a sense of history, contextual biblical interpretation signals a prevalent sentiment among scholars of Third World countries to resist against western influence. Inculturation, postcolonial, cultural, and vernacular hermeneutics are some of the different terms employed although they all share similar goals, that is to revive indigenous modes of readings and to rid the Bible of its colonial aspects.

While many prefer the indigenization of methods and approaches, more recent scholars have come to realize and accept that perhaps instead of attempting to replace all mainline tools such as historical and literary criticisms, a more pragmatic undertaking is warranted. Blending of both mainline and contextual biblical interpretation tools is in order. This is an important point in light of my attempt to connect the Lukan narrative and the political context of the PICTs. I refuse to adhere entirely to what some recent scholars have identified as the need to utilize an indigenous concept or framework. Instead, I am of the belief that the interpretive framework or methodological scheme should be a function of or foundation based on the needs and concerns of contemporary society. Buoyed by this belief, the political-economic context of the Samoan *aiga* does much to shape the methods and tools to be used in this study. In this regard, my approach foregrounds the social, political and economic relations constitutive of the Samoan *aiga*.

Connecting Ordinary and Learned Readers; Lateral Readings

One of the strongest claims of contextual biblical hermeneutics is it can help diffuse the dominance and control of academics and people with resources. West's reading with ordinary readers is exemplary. So long as the distribution of resources favors those with more, there is a need for contextual biblical reading to remain critical and challenge material disparity and intellectual domination in society.

More significantly, contextual biblical interpretation challenges the notion of the inerrancy of the Bible. While it does not diminish the significance of the Bible as the word of God, it does compel the reader to reconsider and reevaluate one's presuppositions and beliefs about the Bible and the validity of certain interpretations or interpretive schema.

Moreover, it seeks to incorporate ideological perspectives from ordinary readers. In effect, the outcome is to change the locality of biblical interpretation. Instead of focusing on one locality, contextual biblical interpretation emphasizes the relationship or connection between biblical context and the social realities of contemporary society. This connection is vital and an essential component of the advocacy element of contextual biblical interpretation. For transformation to be initiated, biblical interpretation is to be moored in the social realities of the people, their needs and concerns. I hope to provide at the end of this study a re-reading of the Lukan narrative that can address the struggles facing the Samoan *aiga* especially within the political-economic context.

3

Political-Economic Context, Poverty, and Institutional Constraints in Samoa

INTRODUCTION

DRAWING UPON THE WISDOM of my Pacific Island fishers and counterparts in the Asian and African context, I then situate and locate parts of the deep sea to fish as a *tautai seu* for the day's catch. In this way, I situate myself with the lived reality of contemporary society. In order to carry out a deep contextual reading of the Lukan passage on the rich ruler, I first situate myself with the lived reality of today's society. In particular, I foreground the issue of the challenging state of the political economy[1] in the PICTs with an emphasis on poverty in Samoa as a case study. A rich and deep contextual understanding of the political-economic context of the PICTs and poverty in contemporary Samoan society can help my contextual biblical reading of the biblical text. In this regard, one can make the argument that the issue also represents the hermeneutical lens to read the Lukan narrative. Notably, this is neither a comprehensive study on poverty nor an extensive analysis of the political-economic context in the PICTs. Rather the objective is to gain a deeper understanding

---

1. I am using the term political economy to refer to the nexus between politics and economics. This reflects my bias towards political institutions as I see the economy shaped and influenced by political institutions. It highlights the critical juncture that exists between politics and economy.

of some of the dimensions of poverty in the political-economic context of contemporary society in Samoa. In saying this, I am not making any specific claim about poverty and the Lukan narrative on the rich ruler. Rather the approach taken in this study underscores an innate desire to ground biblical hermeneutics in real-life issues. As a *tautai seu*, the hope is to situate my contextual reading within the lived reality of society. Much can be gained from real-life concerns and challenges confronting people in the Pacific[2] region or anywhere else, to help me contextualize the Lukan narrative.

In this chapter, I attempt to foreground the political-economic context of contemporary Pacific Island society in my contextual reading, which necessitates drawing upon the wisdom of fishers from other disciplines. As a *tautai seu*, I locate and situate myself within the wide range of scholarly materials on other subject matters, including political economy, institutional analysis, and government affairs in the Pacific Island region. Always with prudence, I humbly seek to engage a deep contextual reading of the political-economic issue or issues that are shaping and influencing family life in the Pacific. In particular, I situate and locate myself with the institutional constraints on the *aiga* in the Samoan context. Meanwhile, I situate and locate with a keen awareness that the ultimate focus of this fishing process is to engage the Lukan passage on the rich ruler later.

The chapter outline is as follows. I begin with a brief description of my approach and design, namely an institutional analytical approach. The institutional approach involves moving through three different levels of analysis—macro, meso, and micro level. At the macro level, I sketch the general contours of the political economy context of the PICTs. At the meso level, the focus is on Samoan society, while the institution of *aiga* (family) is the emphasis at the micro level.

From there, I move to my point of departure. I find the Island of Hope (IOH) report enabling in my attempt to sketch some of the perceived issues and challenges facing the people of the region. The IOH document provides an overview of the region's political-economic context from the churches' perspective. While the data may have changed

2. I recognize that there is an ongoing debate regarding the name Pacific and whether it should be Pasifika or as some prefer, Oceania. I claim the name Pacific as my way of telling my story. It is also for the purpose of making the task of reading simple for readers external to the Pacific region. That I am using the name Pacific in this study is not in any way trying to stake a claim in the ongoing debate on what to call the body of waters surrounding my place of birth.

since the report was published 20 years ago, there is great value in ascertaining some aspects that have become institutionalized over time. After perusing some of the details in the IOH report, I revert to my social location[3] from which the life justification proofs or *lagisoifua*[4] of my perceptions are drawn on the political-economic issues of the region. This is an important shift as it helps shape the context of the study. This is followed by an overview of the discussion on the political-economic context of the PICTs, which is framed and constrained by my social location and the *lagisoifua* embedded within.

Following the overview of the political economy of the PICTs, I then look at Samoan society as a case study. The section on Samoan society highlights the institution of the *aiga*, a vital element of the discussion on poverty. The discussion is interwoven with some scholarly views making for some interesting observations and further assumptions. The final section discusses the prospects of linking my world with that of the Lukan narrative. The discussion focuses on how the linking or connection is enabled by utilizing some aspects of sociorhetorical interpretation, particularly social, cultural, and ideological textures (Robbins 1996a). After this, I discuss the design for exploring parallels between the political-economic context in the text and that of my contemporary world. The chapter ends with a summary.

INSTITUTIONAL CONSTRAINTS

As a *tautai seu*, I locate connections between my world and that of the Lukan narrative by exploring parallels between the institutional constraints on the *aiga* and the response of the rich ruler in the Lukan narrative. I claim that the rich ruler is not just an individual but also part of "an institution," his *aiga*. Much can be gained from exploring the possibility that institutional constraints play an important role in the Lukan narrative

---

3. For further readings on social location and its implications see Kathy Ehrensperger (2019, 65) and Vernon K. Robbins (1996b, 194).

4. See Aiono's (1996) description of *lagisoifua* from which I borrowed the term. It is simply used in this study as referring to life justification. These are life justifications as a result of one's life experience, and other key factors including education, upbringing including church, family and society. It is inclusive but also particular to my social location, from my particular point of view, shaped by where I am situated, as a Samoan transcending the Samoan Diaspora but with ties to families and land in Samoa. As much as I don't want this to be a narrative about myself, it is very much about who and what I am.

of the rich ruler. While institutional analysis has been a major part of analysis in the social sciences, including subjects like political science, economics, and law, I attempt here a similar approach by highlighting the cultural, social, ideological, and political-economic context of the Lukan narrative.

Concerning the locating and situating of myself, my time studying at the Rockefeller College of Public Affairs SUNY Albany in methods and approaches in Public Administration and Policy is a major influence in the decision to use aspects of institutional analysis in my reading of Luke. I am drawn to the importance of institutions, especially in shaping decision-making and individual responses. Individual decisions and choices are shaped and influenced by institutional constraints[5]. In this regard, I see the rich ruler in the Lukan narrative as someone surrounded by social, cultural, political and economic constraints. As such, his response to Jesus's imperative to sell everything shows someone strategic and cognizant of his surroundings.

Institutions are not the same as organizations. Using Douglass C. North's analogy of sports, institutions are the rules of the games shaping how players perform and play on the field. They provide the framework for human interactions (1990, 3). In addition, institutions shape and influence relations or interactions between people, between organizations and between countries. These can be relations or interactions in the social, political, economic, or even cultural context.

Institutions can include any form of constraint that human beings devise to shape human interaction. They can be formal or informal. Formal institutions include rules or orders which human beings devise while informal institutions include conventions and codes of behavior. The constitution of a country for example is an institution consisting of rules and statutes created by a body of representatives to govern and lead a country. On the other hand, institutions can also be simply something that evolve over time like common law. For this study, I am referring to both the informal and formal meaning of the word institution. Institutional constraints include "both what individuals are prohibited from

---

5. My doctoral dissertation at SUNY Albany explores multiple influences constraining decision-making ability of rulemaking agencies. Part of the study reviews the decisions of the individual commissioners sitting on the Federal Communications Commission during the biennial review of telecommunications from 1996 to 2000. Similarly, I am interested in exploring such institutional constraints on the ruler in the Lukan narrative.

doing and, sometimes, under what conditions some individuals are permitted to undertake certain activities" (North 1990, 4).

An institutional approach usually involves three levels of analysis—macro, meso, and micro (Holland 2007, 31). For this chapter, the focus at the macro level is on the PICTs, with particular emphasis on the Independent State of Samoa. The meso-level highlights the overall Samoan society while at the micro-level I specifically explore certain aspects of the *aiga*.

MY POINT OF DEPARTURE—THE ISLAND OF HOPE REPORT

As a *tautai seu*, I locate my point of departure for this chapter in the Pacific Council of Churches' (PCC) Island of Hope (IOH) document. In 2001, PCC published an important yet frequently overlooked document, with the title, Island of Hope (119). Funded by the World Council of Churches (WCC), the document is the outcome of a consultation of Pacific church leaders which offers a view of economic globalization from the perspective of the Pacific Island people. It encapsulates a collective response of the regional churches on alternatives to economic globalization presenting, perhaps for the first time, a clear concept that was to serve as a platform for future action and movement.

The usefulness and relevancy of the report resides in its broad overview. It provides a macro-level perspective of the political-economic context in which PICTs are situated. I submit that after 20 years, much of the data in the report may be outdated. Nevertheless, the institutional constraints (Moraski and Shipan 1999) and basic foundations of many of the problems within the region remain unchanged. Discernment of these institutional constraints lends much to the nature and extent of the current social and political-economic issues in the region.

Overall, the Island of Hope (IOH) document is a strong critique of the adverse impacts of economic globalization on the Pacific Island countries and offers an ecumenical alternative to address the impact of globalization and economic development in the region. Central to the report is its critical assessment that the promises of the globalized free market system have not been realized among the people of the Pacific Islands, indeed quite the contrary. Among many of the adverse impacts are an increasing number of families living under the poverty line. This situation has become the impetus for an emphasis on poverty as the "real-life" issue to read the biblical text about the rich ruler.

While recent numbers show a decline in world poverty, the COVID-19 pandemic may have destabilized any progress made. Moreover, as the IOH report indicates, the continued reliance on liberal economic policies which encourage investments and competition, have also led to the neglect of social issues like education, health care, and social welfare (for example, the measles outbreak in Samoa in 2019). As a result, low wages and poor working conditions are prevalent. For example, a garment worker in Fiji (mostly women) gets paid $1/hour compared to the same person in Australia making $10/hour (World Council of Churches 2001, 119).

Exacerbating the challenge is the fact that the church is implicated in the report. Cultural forces as well as social expectations compel people to give much to the operations and development of the church communities[6] (119). While the IOH report does not elaborate on the influence of the church on individual families, I find this space inviting. Aside from the role of the church I attempt to bring to the forefront some of the causes and the extent of the political-economic context in the PICTs. For example, while the number of poor people may have changed over the last 20 years, indicating some progress, there are institutional constraints that have remained over time. By institutional constraints I am thinking about more than just simply structure, or organizations. Rather, I am envisioning also institutions in terms of processes, rules, traditions, ways of doing things. These can be cultural, social and even ideological. Moreover, these institutions underscore key philosophies and ideologies about how certain communities or societies do things.

While I concur that the church plays a role in the political economy of Samoan society, I am not in any way suggesting that the church is the single or most prominent cause, since there are other contributing agencies. There is much to be gained from also ascertaining other social, cultural factors as well as institutionalized ideological and philosophical underpinnings that merit attention and exploration. In particular, the tendency to idealize Samoan indigenous living while also maintaining a modern consumer lifestyle raises some interesting questions. On one side, the outflow of Samoan immigrants to countries like New Zealand,

---

6. For a sense of the amount people contribute to the church in Samoa, see for example the newspaper article from the Samoa Observer (Feagaimaali'i 2019) regarding the increase in offering to the Congregational Christian Church, Samoa (CCCS).

Australia, and the United States underscores a deep-seated desire for an improved quality of living. On the contrary, the tendency to idealize a return to some state of indigenousness has morphed into a dominant narrative which seeks to reclaim what is native and indigenous to the Pacific Island countries. Thus, the strong rhetoric to rediscover indigenous lifestyles belies the heavily modern consumerism in the region. One only needs to visit Apia, Suva, or Port Moresby to encounter this.

Samoa like many other PICTs is at a disadvantage given their limited resources and economies of scale. With a population of just less than 200,000[7] (South Pacific Commission 2020) Samoa for example faces a tremendous uphill battle in trading with overseas partners. Exports made up 5.8 percent of its total GDP in 2019, but an export/import imbalance of 46 percent created an overall trade deficit of—40.2 percent (Samoa Bureau of Statistics, 2019). To make up for this deficit the government often has relied on external grants, foreign investments, and overseas partners for economic development in the country. Subsequently it begs the question whether it is possible to sustain a modern consumer lifestyle in a geographical geopolitical place like Samoa.

The other side of this picture is the global context of Samoa's political-economic context, which has significant implications for the overall situation. The same interconnectedness that is important to Samoan society at the local level can be a hindrance at the global level. In other words, the standard of living and measure of poverty in Samoa is very much a function of its relationship to the global context. As the basic unit of Samoa society, the *aiga*, a network of familial relations, is surrounded by internal as well as external institutional constraints which underscore some of the challenges in Samoa's political-economic context. To understand some of these constraints I share my life story, reconciling existing views on poverty with my social location and where I stand in light of the political economy of the PICTs.

THE *LAGISOIFUA* OF MY SOCIAL LOCATION

While the approach in this study emphasizes the influence of institutional constraints, the views and assessment expressed throughout this paper are largely a function of my social location. I owe much of how

---

7. According to recent estimates, without migration, Samoa's 2019 population would have been 354,000 (Howes, Orton, and Surandiran 2020). Samoans in the diasporas constitute about 60 percent of the domestic population.

I situate my social location to Vaitusi Nofoaiga's (2017) description of his *tautuaileva* (service-in-between) in which he identifies himself as a Samoan shaped by his sense of place. Place is a space identified by various situations emergent from interactions among people with their values. In this regard, place is a location lived and controlled by people. It is where I learn how to live and relate to other people. It is also the environment where I experience (un)familiar situations based on the human values accepted by people who inhabit that place. In this way, understanding the particular place to which I belong in a society determines how I see and experience other places. More importantly, it shapes how I see other people in other places. Thus, a sense of place is important in defining who I am as a Samoan (Nofoaiga 2017, 34).

As a *tautai seu*, I situate myself as someone "in-between" the diaspora and my country of birth. In this regard, one can say that my journey in life is my "location." The viewpoints and ideology expressed throughout these pages are borne of the life-justification proofs, or *lagisoifua*, embedded throughout my location as an individual who exists "in-between." *Lagisoifua* in this regard are the evidence, the "life-proofs" as experienced. They are attestations that form the justification of my views and presuppositions, borne of my social location. Such a view resonates with Fanaafi Le Tagaloa Aiono's. Explaining the connection between the role of the *fatuaiupu* as a keeper of language and tradition in Samoan society and *lagisoifua*, Aiono writes:

> The study of Samoan Language and Culture has revealed in the institution of the *Fatua'iupu* that Samoan Culture recognized the existence and power of change and has provided formulae and procedure for its recording and study ... The *Fatua'iupu* of yore seemed such enlightened and tolerant beings, ever ready to hear different views and versions, but always insisting in the "life-justification proof ["] the life-sources or *lagisoifua* of the particular statement and opinion. It does not matter how outlandish my view or claim the *Fatua'iupu* would merely request that I play the life-giving poem of my views or the *lagisoifua*. (Aiono 1996, 2)[8]

While Aiono's statement above is directed towards the role of the *fatuaiupu* in Samoan language, it illuminates the extent to which "life-justifications" or the *lagisoifua* merits grounding claims and viewpoints

---

8. The italics are added in the quote for consistency.

in our reality. The concept of *lagisoifua* forces one to find justifications in one's own vantage of reality subject to one's social location.

While I integrate some of the ideas and views drawn from the scholarship on poverty, the perception and ideology expressed favor a particular vantage point shaped by my location as a Samoan living "in-between." As such, my ideas and views are weighted in self-reflection and my own ideological and philosophical predispositions. It is who I am, which as I intend to show later in the study also shapes how I interact with the biblical text. This is not to say that I lack respect for the biblical text and the history therein. Far from it. In my view, responsible reading[9] merits reflection and action on the context of the biblical text. Therefore, I am inevitably constituted towards who I am and my purpose. From the perspective of *tautai seu*, I seek to re-situate myself both with the Lukan story and with the political-economic context in contemporary Pacific region.

A Dream Born in the Village

"We exist because these stories exist" (Larry Smith 2017).

As a Pacific Islander, as a Samoan living "in-between," it is important to tell our stories, tell my stories. Telling my story is critical. Instead of being looked at, examined, and dissected, I am telling my story from my perspective. This is not to ignore the fact that science plays an important role in our lived reality and the fact is we are living in a world of numbers, statistics, and data. Statistics matter. Thus, I weave my personal story around this reality, my own attempt at doing scientific research, of weaving a good story.

Growing up in the villages, life for me included a combination of subsistent living and a little bit of entrepreneurship. My parents ran the only store at the time in the whole district and people from across the bay would come in canoes to purchase the essentials including sugar, flour, and salt. In those days, the difference between education in the rural areas and Apia, the capital of Samoa, was night and day[10]. The dream for

---

9. I find Jan Botha's (1994) explanation of responsible reading persuasive. In particular, the onus is on the interpreter to uphold a sense of responsibility when engaging with the biblical text.

10. Recently, the Samoan government has been more proactive in improving the level of education in rural areas through more funding and grants.

many families was to relocate to Apia in pursuit of a better education and the opportunity to find employment in government or in the growing business community. This was not lost on my parents. It was also in the pursuit of the same dream that I moved to California in the late eighties.

Life in the diaspora was not always that special. That awareness took on deeper meaning in my work with the Samoan Community Development Center (SCDC). As a community-based organization which partnered with the city of San Francisco to offer assistance to its low-income neighborhoods, the SCDC exposed me to the nuances of struggling families. The need to have access to a good education, health care, shelter, steady income, and stable environment, were often complicated by rampant drug and substance abuse, shootings and violence, staples of the San Francisco Bay Area low-income neighborhoods in the early nineties. For a Samoan "fresh off the boat"[11] navigating the line between the pursuit of a good quality life and the struggles of living in the low-income neighborhoods at times can be quite overwhelming.

For many Samoan families living in low-income neighborhoods, the high-risk environment was a small price to pay in the pursuit of the "American dream" which often translates to a good education and a good job. Nonetheless, the need to give to the church and send remittance[12] back home was never lost on many Samoan families. Despite the difficult challenges confronted in their new lived reality, sending money for the *aiga* in Samoa was worth the sacrifice for many Samoan families and also a matter of pride for some.

---

11. I find Larry Smith's (2017) description of the phrase appealing in the sense that it speaks to the stories of immigrants. I exist because my story exists. My story is that of a Samoan living in the U.S., returning to Samoa, and then moving to Suva, Fiji, for further studies. Shortly after completing my Ph.D. in Biblical Studies, our church, the Congregational Christian Church, Samoa (CCCS), called me back to Samoa to teach at the Malua Theological College.

12. Based on data provided by the South Pacific Commission (2020), remittance remains an essential source of family income within the PICTs, contributing not only to daily consumption and basic needs but also to education and health-related expenditure as well as to traditional and cultural events and obligations. Remittance, also at the macro level, is an essential source of foreign exchange to pay for imports. For example 2018, remittances to Samoa made up almost 17 percent of the total GDP. This number changed drastically, especially during the COVID-19 pandemic with flight and border restrictions. According to some projections, Tonga and Samoa are most vulnerable to declines in remittances, followed by Marshall Islands, Tuvalu, Kiribati, and Fiji.

POLITICS, ECONOMICS, AND THE PICTS

Later in 2017, I was fortunate to re-situate my experience of struggling families within the broader context of U.S. politics. Working for the Office of Congressman Eni Faleomavaega Hunkin in the U.S. Congressional House of Representatives, I was assigned to oversee and monitor legislation pertaining to the U.S. Insular Areas and the Pacific region. That afforded exposure to some of the issues confronting PICTs in the context of U.S. relations and presence in the Pacific region. While the scope of my work was mainly to focus on issues pertaining to the people of American Samoa, I found myself also drawn to the larger Pacific region. In particular, it allowed me the opportunity to triangulate my own *lagisoifua* and a viewpoint of poverty on the level of the individual with the macro level overview of the political-economic environment of the PICTs.

The PICTs remains a strategic arena in global geopolitics. The Pacific Ocean covers one-third of the earth's surface. Spanning the Pacific Ocean are the 7,500 islands which comprise the 22 PICTs (Hunkin 1998). For the 12 million people (South Pacific Commission 2020) that consider the PICTs home, the Pacific Ocean represents a kind of oxymoronic challenge. While rich in natural resources and other blessings with its large territorial waters and seabed rights,[13] the Pacific Ocean is also a boundary isolating and insulating people of the region from the outside world. Depending on one's emphasis, opinions on the quality of life in the islands vary. PICTs to a large extent represent a strategically significant constituency in the global political economy. Home to some 12 million people, the Pacific Ocean is untapped for its natural resources, yet easily exploited for its strategic location in geopolitics. One can only go back in history to discern the struggles facing the Pacific Island region.

Historically, the Pacific Island region was a strategic location for the allied forces to win against Japan in World War II (Hunkin 1998). Critical battles waged in Guadalcanal, Midway, Wake Island, Guam, and Saipan saw the Pacific Island people fighting and working alongside the Americans. Even during the Cold War, the Pacific Island people continued to side with the Americans and the West. More recently, the increasing

---

13. Deep-sea mining (DSM) remains a highly disputed issue in the Pacific region. On one hand, are a growing number of scientists and Pacific civil society networks calling for a precautionary pause on the fledgling sector. On the other hand, are a number of smaller island nations like Nauru that are pushing through legislation in the International Seabed Authority (ISA) to commence exploration of deep-sea mining in the region ("Deep Sea Mining by 2023 Gets Green Light in Pacific" 2021).

presence of China has made the strategic location of the Pacific Island region even more critical.

Yet, while the PICTs are strategically critical to geopolitics, the fact that the region is isolated and surrounded by the wide Pacific Ocean made it susceptible to exploitation by the developed countries. A case in point was how the U.S. after World War II determined that it was obviously dangerous to explode atomic bombs anywhere in the continental United States. A place far and away was needed. As a result, the U.S. military command chose the Marshall Islands as the place to conduct its nuclear testing program. Overall, the U.S. exploded some 67 nuclear bombs in the Marshall Islands including the explosion of the first hydrogen bomb ever in the history of the world. The hydrogen bomb that the U.S. military command exploded in the Marshall Islands in 1954 was known as the Bravo Shot, and it was measured as a 15-megaton nuclear device, a thousand times more powerful than the atom bombs that the U.S. dropped on Hiroshima and Nagasaki (Hunkin 2007). To this day, the people of the Marshall Island have made tremendous sacrifice at the hands of the more powerful United States.

The recent emergence of China as a major power of influence has served also to reignite interest in the region. In a recent Congressional Research Service (CRS) report to the U.S. Congress, it was noted that Chinese domination of the South China Seas (SCS) and East China Seas (ECS) could substantially affect U.S. strategic, political and economic interests in the Indo-Pacific region and elsewhere (O'Rourke 2021). Moreover, given the current difficulties and challenges facing the economies in the PICTs, it is reasonable to assume that China has the resources to gain influence and presence in the region.

Based on recent numbers from the World Bank, many of the economies in the Pacific region have been hit hard by COVID-19 (2020). As mentioned above, the tourism industries in countries like Tonga and Samoa are feeling severe effects. Even in before the pandemic, some of the Pacific Island countries were still recovering from the adverse effects of natural disasters like the Tropical Cyclone Harold that hit Tonga, Vanuatu and Fiji in April 2020 (Parc and Spieth 2020). Even Samoa in late 2019 was also hit hard by the measles plague (Forrester 2019).

These calamities have adversely affected the economies of many of the PICTs. For example, Samoa's economy contracted by 3.5 percent in FY2020, while Fiji and Papua New Guinea contracted by 1.3 and 3.3 percent respectively (World Bank 2020). While some of the island nations like the Federated States of Micronesia showed a steady increase over the past five years (1.4 percent increase through September 2019), the reality is the economies of the PICTs are most vulnerable given the large scale of dependency on the tourism industries and other service-related industries. Many of the economies depend on a single industry. For example, American Samoa largely depends on its tuna canning industry (Gootnick and Richard 2020), Solomon Islands on its logging industry (Katovai, Laurance, and Edwards 2015), and Kiribati and Tuvalu on fishing licenses (Gillett 2016). The outlook on many of these small island economies depend significantly on their post-COVID responses and the "resituated-ness" that is taking place. This is added on to the already constant pressure to diversify and attain sustainable economies.

The uncertainties in the current political economy context of the PICTs are not new. The challenges of COVID-19 only highlighted the unstable political economy in the region. Existing institutional constraints based on location, geopolitics, population size, susceptibility to natural disasters and so forth, continue to threaten the livelihoods of the people in the region. That Pacific Island people have managed to exist for centuries throughout these ordeals is testimony to their resourcefulness and resilience. Traditional institutions have also helped. That many have migrated to their more developed neighbors in New Zealand, Australia, and Hawaii seeking a chance for a better life is also part of the lived experience of the Pacific Island people. Perhaps it is also a reflection of Pacific Island identity as navigators of oceans and boundaries.

Let me digress here. Pacific Island people are oriented toward re-situatedness. To talk about Pacific Island life in the region warrants also talking about Pacific Island people in the diaspora, those navigating the "in-between" diaspora and homeland. When I first moved from Samoa to California in the 1980's, I found myself going through a process of "re-situating." Relocating from Samoa to the U.S. involved a process of re-situating, of re-appropriating who I am. In other words, re-situating merits re-appropriating of the "I am." It is not only just moving from one physical location to another, but there is also a sense of navigating the institutional constraints embedded within the extant social environment. The notion of re-situating is an important element in my contextual biblical reading of the Lukan narrative to be discussed in a later chapter. That is, I want to highlight this notion of "re-situatedness" taking place in the Lukan narrative.

CASE STUDY—THE INDEPENDENT STATE OF SAMOA

Samoa is a country that is heavily dependent on development aid and family remittances from overseas. What little the country can produce internally and export only amounted to about 5.1 percent of its GDP in 2018. As indicated above, the largest main source of revenue comes from its tourism industry at 30.3 percent, and remittances at 16.4 percent (South Pacific Commission 2020). To understand the gravitational pull that shape and influence Samoa's political economy, I start with the basic unit of Samoan society, the *aiga*. Samoa, even way before contact with the Europeans was made, has always had a decentralized political structure (Meleisea 1987b, 4). Indeed, in the history of Samoa, it is rare to find a "King of Samoa" and it was one of the banes frustrating the colonial powers, first the Germans and then the New Zealanders. Controlling a people who are accustomed both traditionally and culturally to a decentralized political structure proves a critical aspect of Samoan history. Malama Meleisea dedicated a whole chapter of his monograph to the "struggle for monarchy." The rivalry between the two Malietoa factions in the 19th century led to a long bitter conflict among the locals compounded by the quarrels of the local Europeans and their respective nations (Meleisea 1987a, 89). Without a centralized government, relations and kinships created through the reach of the *aiga* were and remain critical institutions in Samoan society.

Aiga—The Basic Unit of Samoan Society

The basic unit of Samoan society is the *aiga* (family) (Tofaeono 2000, 30–34; Meleisea 1987b, 6–9). In ancient Samoa, the *aiga* is self-sufficient, a consumer and producer in one. The need to produce more than what is necessary for its livelihood hardly exists. *Aiga* can comprise of not just kinship relations (extended family) but also non-relatives. The immediate *aiga* consists of the parents and their children. Extending beyond that basic level we have other members of the household connected not only through kinship but also through marriage and other means. As the household extends, the degree of kinship becomes less pronounced to the point that even someone alien to the household can be a member, all bounded within the *aiga*.

Nuu (village), *itu-malo* (district) and the *faa-Samoa* (Samoan culture)

From an institutional perspective, one looks for structures and avenues of relations within society. In this regard, the next level beyond *aiga* is the *nu'u* (translated as village) which may comprise of groups of *aiga* with shared heritage. The relations between the *aiga* can even extend beyond the *nu'u*. In that regard, a group of *nu'u* made up an *itu-malo* (district). The word *itu-malo* can be literally translated as the "winning side" but may also connote "alliance" according to Malama (1987b, 6). I can understand Malama's point. The *itu-malo* and its honorifics often come as a result of a political alliance during battle or other historical circumstance. But instead of focusing on the larger political entity of *nu'u* or *itu-malo*, I find the *aiga* a more fitting start. All actions at the outer layers are shaped and influenced by the inner core just as much as the *aiga* is shaped by the outer layers of the *nu'u* and *itu-malo*. Discernment of some of the institutional challenges facing the *aiga* warrants exploring the Samoan way of life, or the Samoan culture.

The *faa-matai* (chief system) and the *faa-Samoa* (Samoan culture)

The *faa-Samoa* (Samoan culture) is simply the Samoan way of life (Samoa Law Reform Commission 2017, 9). One of its central institutions is the *faa-matai* (chief system). It provides the institutional framework that permeates Samoan society. The word *matai* is translated by George Pratt as "the head of a family" (Pratt 1911, 212). Malama explains that it comes from the phrase "*mulu-i-ui*" which has the connotation of someone who is set apart. Thus, the *matai* is someone who is set apart or someone who is "consecrated" (1987b, 7). I agree with Malama's definition except that I find the notion of the *matai* as someone who is consecrated problematic. This has effectuated the common misinterpretation among many chiefs and politicians that a *matai* is one of the *sui vaaia ole Atua* (representative of God). This is a cause for concern, for it has often been utilized for political motives. Further confounding the problem is the fact that constitutionally only a *matai* can run for parliament in Samoa. That further exacerbates the misinterpretation that *matais* are representation of the divine.

There are two types of matai. The *matai tulafale* is an orator who is assigned to speechmaking and the *matai ali'i* is a paramount chief for ceremonial purposes. This division of roles and functions demonstrates one of the guiding principles in the Samoan way of life that everyone has a role to play in Samoan society. The Samoan proverb *"o Samoa o le atunuu ua uma ona tofi"* can suggest that "Samoa is already hierarchically divided within families, villages, and the larger community" (Samoa Law Reform Commission 2017, 9). More significantly, the saying also underpins the notion that roles and responsibilities within Samoan society are already set and defined. Thus, the way of life in Samoa is set in protocols, traditions, and rituals. There are protocols for the relationship between parents and children, between siblings, between the church minister and the village council and so forth. The *faa-matai* (chief system) and the *faa-Samoa* (Samoan culture or Samoan way of life) are manifested in protocols and rules that govern relations between families, villages, districts and the larger community. These are critical formal and informal institutions in the Samoan context.

Matai *sa'o* (high chief) in Samoan society

Presiding over the affairs of the *aiga* is the *matai sa'o*. While there could be more than one *matai* (chief) in the *aiga*, the *matai sa'o* is the primary title holder, the steward of family lands and *matai* titles, and the *fatua'iupu* (keeper of myths and oral tradition) of family lineages, wisdom and knowledge concerning family affairs. Within the village setting, the *matai sa'o* is the primary representative of the *aiga*, sitting in the village *fono* (council), which deliberates and adjudicates matters concerning the village. When there are special occasions like a wedding or bestowal of title, and even funerals and other matters, the *matai sa'o* presides over how members of the aiga could contribute or assist. In this manner, the *matai sa'o* plays a role similar to that of a manager or chief administrator, juggling different responsibilities and navigating complexities for the well-being of the *aiga*. One can argue that to a certain extent, the *matai sa'o* resembles a similar role to that of the ruler in the Lukan narrative. This resemblance will be highlighted later.

The *matai sa'o* plays a crucial role in the political economy of Samoan society. Together with other high chiefs in the village community, they would see to it that there is enough food supply for the village. In ancient times, village communities, under the direction of the chiefs, would store, for example, fermented breadfruit in pits especially in times of famine (Meleisea 1987b, 9). From there, the food supply is rationed and distributed to all households. Thus, the chiefs, as the primary political-economic institution in the village communities, are able to preserve whatever scarce resources are available. The *matai sa'o* also has the authority to declare and impose an interdict (*sa*) on certain crops or a piece of land (Meleisea 1987b, 9). This authority could be extended to ban the fishing of certain species of fish at particular times, or even the use of non-traditional methods of fishing damaging to the environment. Through these restrictions, the *matai sa'o* has significant influence on the sustainability of food supply and enforcing environmentally and ecologically friendly measures.

The Samoan Law Reform Commission (SLRC) Report

The authority and role of the *matai sa'o* has come under scrutiny recently. Increasing complaints against the abuse of power became a cause of concern, and in 2015 the Samoa Law Reform Commission (SLRC) was given a directive by the Prime Minister at the time to explore these public complaints. Public consultations commenced in 2016 and in 2017, the SLRC published its final report with recommendations for reforms. Concerning complaints brought before the Lands and Titles Court of Samoa (Court), the report reveals that about 10 percent of cases filed against a *matai sa'o* were successful in removing the *matai sa'o* while 90 percent were unsuccessful (7, fn #2). Allegations of abuse had to do with decisions that affected the welfare of the family, the lack of prior consultation between the *matai sa'o* and members of the family regarding matters pertaining to the use, settlement or leasing of land, or family funds under the control of the *matai sa'o*. Some of the examples discussed during consultations include:

> The *Matai Sa'o* depositing family money into his daughter's account without prior consultation with other family members; proceeded with a *umusaga o le fale o le aiga* [dedication of a new house] without consulting all sides of the extended family; misusing family funds under the control of the *Matai Sa'o*; being unable to resolve family disputes; failing to carry out duties in acting as a trustee (*osiaiga*) for the *aigapotopoto* [extended family] in maintaining family assets; performing actions which

brought shame upon the family. (Samoa Law Reform Commission 2017, 7, fn #3)

The issue of authority was also raised during public consultations. A majority of submissions noted the need to limit the authority and the power of the *matai saʻo* in accordance with the *faa-samoa* (Samoan way of life, Samoan culture). That is, the *matai saʻo* is to be a custodian or trustee of the family, whose authority derives from and depends on the consensus of family members (8). Moreover, the overall purpose of duties and responsibilities of the *matai saʻo* is to promote the social and economic welfare of the family as well as to maintain peace and stability (Samoa Law Reform Commission 2017, 12). The underpinning concern is to provide a system of check and balances against the abuse of power and to minimize its effects on the welfare of families. In the end, the report makes several recommendations, legislative and non-legislative measures pertaining to various aspects including eligibility for appointment, duties and responsibilities, removal, the issue of having multiple *matai saʻo*, and the process for dispute resolution.

One of the critical issues raised in the report underpins the growing influence of state government on the Samoan way of life. The concern orbits around the question of whether the recommended actions in the report are to be legislated. That is, the question is whether the state government should legislate and therefore restrict the ability of families and villages to make decisions pertaining to their way of life. While the report is cognizant of this sensitive intersection between the power of the state government and the right of the *aiga*, the general consensus among many of the submissions received by the Commission reflect the need for some legislation.

I find it interesting therefore that the call for reforms and changes has given the government of Samoa legal capacity to shape and influence the way of life in society. This means government legislation to shape and influence the *aiga* and its institutions, traditions, and social environment. The effect is to limit and put several institutional constraints on the capacity of the *matai saʻo* (high chief) and the *aiga* (household, family) to effectively shape their lived reality and adapt to social changes.

For example, the government amendment in 2008 of its Lands and Titles Act, effectively altered the traditional perception of the role of the *matai saʻo* with regards to customary land. The amendment establishes a Torrens land system which mandated registration of ownership of customary land in Samoa (Government of Samoa 2008, Part 3). The aim is to attract foreign investors and entrepreneurs in the interest of economic development and growth. Meanwhile, the amendment effectively undermines existing cultural understanding of lands and titles. One in particular is the very essence of what the *matai sa'o* (high chief) stands for. The *matai sa'o* as a concept undergirds fluidity. Registration of customary land only guarantees the certainty of ownership threatening the very fluidity that is essential to Samoan culture. The outcome is a weakened family structure and the depravity of the rights of all members. On the contrary, the *matai sa'o* is only to be a title holder, representative of the different relations that constitute the very essence of the aiga. In this regard, the *matai sa'o* is to be dyadic, self-less, and representing the needs and interests of all members of the household including not only those with lineal claims to the family title, but also non-relatives.

A point of digression is in order. I must submit that often times the *matai sa'o* is not always what he ought to be. As cited above in the 2017 report, vested with authority and power, there is always the possibility for the *matai sa'o* to seek to maximize self-interest. Instead of deflecting the *viiga* (praises) the *matai sa'o* is all too caught up in the pursuit of power and glory. In this regard, I am reminded of a speech given at the Malua Graduation Ceremony in 2001 by the late Governor of American Samoa, Tauese Sunia (Goodnews 2001), in which he discussed the notion of deflecting praise in Samoan culture. Praise is heaped on an individual as a token of respect. To gain respect is also gauged by the number of praises one gets. Sunia uses the term *"eu ese le viiga"*—deflecting the praise/glory," to suggest the need to be vigilant and remain humble in the face of praise.

I do agree with Sunia that one of the fundamental values of the *faa-Samoa* (Samoan way of life) is in deflecting praises. It is in the utmost interest of the Samoan culture that *viiga* is deflected. If one person in a relationship takes a lower position, it is in the interest of the other to take an even lower position. This is one of the greatest values in the Samoan culture. Thus, when a *matai sa'o* fails to deflect praise then that person has lost focus on what is good leadership and justice in the *faa-Samoa*. In such a system, it is easy to see why there are many challenges and difficulties facing the Samoan culture, especially in light of the dominant capitalist economic model.

POVERTY AND SAMOA

From the perspective of a *tautai seu*, this next section situates and locates some of the scholarship and general observations on poverty in Samoa. These are important in order to further explore the political-economic context of contemporary Samoan society and in particular the issue of poverty.

A full picture of poverty in Samoa is often masked by several factors. While Samoa has seen several economic developments over the last 20 years, there is still ample evidence to suggest poverty exists in the country. In a report on hardship and poverty, the Samoa Bureau of Statistics (2016) offers that changes are needed to better address the issue of poverty in Samoa. While "extreme poverty and hunger do not exist in the form envisaged in the MDG/SDG [Millennium Development Goals / Sustainable Development Goals]," these indicators do not reflect the reality in Samoa. As in every other society, there are those who are less well-off than average. Attributing factors include "poor education, poor health, location, the impact of natural disasters and many other reasons." Therefore, even though Samoa does not exhibit statistically a high incidence of people living in extreme hardship, "there are some who are unable to enjoy a standard of living comparable to others in Samoa" (Samoa Bureau of Statistics 2016, 13).

The Samoa Observer, the primary daily newspaper in the country, is more telling. Pictures and stories in its weekly section on "Village Voices" paint a vastly disconcerting narrative of families, even some living in the Apia town area, without safe drinking water, shelter or electricity (Fruean 2020). They are to be a constant reminder of the struggling conditions in many parts of the country. One gets the sense therefore that all is not well in Samoa. Despite the many developments in the country for the past 20 some years, there is evidence to suggest that a significant number of people in Samoan society lacks basic needs. This murky picture of poverty can be attributed also to challenges in defining poverty.

Poverty Is More Than Just Numbers

While poverty is widely accepted as part of the human experience, there is no consensus on how to best define and ascertain its various dimensions. Measuring and determining the nature and extent of poverty continues to be a matter of contention and discussion. These discussions shape policies and political responses to address poverty. There are two broad trends with underlying ideologies.

On one hand, the tendency among economists is to associate poverty with individual wages and incomes. Poverty is measured by how much an individual takes home in terms of income and wages. At the national level, the country's Gross Domestic Product (GDP) serves as basis for whether the country is classified as having developing or developed status. Together, these money-centric framings have been the basis for many of the policies endorsed and practiced by global institutions like the World Bank and the International Monetary Fund and other major financial multi-national corporations. Even among many members of the United Nations (U.N.), there is a general acceptance of a money-centric framing of poverty. In a resolution adopted by its General Assembly on 25 September 2015, the U.N. declares as one of its goals the eradication of extreme poverty specified as $1.25/day (United Nations 2015). The outcome is for policies aimed at increasing the level of income and level of production.

On the other hand, there is an increasing awareness that this money-centric basis does not fully capture all critical and integral dimensions of poverty. More than a statistical numeration, poverty should be viewed as a social phenomenon that encompasses "deprivations in multiple dimensions, including health, standard of living, education and political participation" (Odekon 2006, vii). Discernment of poverty based on income alone fails to capture other important dimensions in life. In other words, there are other critical considerations for quality life.

Mehmet Odekon attests to this, adding that "unless it is coupled with social, political, and economic freedoms, it does not suffice to enhance individual capabilities." In this regard, having a regular paying job is only part of what adds "to healthy life, to education, and to participation in the surrounding political, cultural, and economic life." The individual also needs access to good health insurance, access to education, and to be able to participate in democracy just like any other citizen. Moreover, liberating poverty from the single context of income-based measurement makes it more meaningful even in affluent and industrial countries or "otherwise, poverty would be an issue only in developing countries" (Odekon 2006, viii).

Let me digress here. The difficulties in defining poverty in the Pacific Island region is due in part to strong family ties which often result in the perception that there is no, and should not be any poverty (Abbott and Pollard 2004, 1). That parallels what I would call "shared-poverty." Drawn from the Samoan notion of *mativa-fesagai* (poverty face-to-face), shared-poverty implies that the effects of poverty or situation of lack are shared by other members of the aiga, even those living in the diaspora. The expectation for the individual in the diaspora is to help with family matters and events in the homeland. For example, even at about 6000 miles from Samoa, it is expected by members of the *aiga* that Samoans in the U.S. are to send money to care for the needs of their families in Samoa. In FY 2018, remittance made up about 17 percent of Samoa's GDP (South Pacific Commission 2020). This is money sent home contributing to daily consumption and basic needs as well as paying for school fees, cultural and family affairs. For Samoans, sending money to the *aiga* in the homeland underscores the importance of maintaining relations and kinship, one of the pillars of the Samoan way of life and part of Samoan identity. Thus, shared-poverty underpins relationships and connections with others.

The importance of maintaining relationships and connections to the *aiga* is manifested also in the "service-in-between" by Samoans in the diaspora. In recognition of their contributions or service to the domestic *aiga*, *matai* titles are bestowed on those living in the diaspora. These transnational *matai* titles are a gesture of approval and acknowledgement of the relationships and connections between the domestic and the diasporic *aiga*. The notion of a "transnational" *matai* is becoming more significant, given that Samoans in the diaspora already outstrip the population in Samoa (Anae et al. 2017, 38). I remember when I started working in the U.S. Congress, I was given a chief title by my maternal family in Samoa. I could have just asked some of the chiefs to come to Virginia where I was staying at the time to do the necessary traditional ceremony. However, I did not want to look like I was using the occasion to gain *viiga* (praise). I decided to take leave from work and fly to Samoa for the traditional ceremony. It was important for my mother especially that I came home and paid my respect to the *aiga* and the village. Moreover, it was also part of my *tautua* or service as it also meant offering money, fine mats, and food to the chiefs. These were all part of the Samoan way of life in order to maintain good relations not only within the *aiga*, but especially navigating the intricacies of village life. For me, making my mother happy was all that mattered.

A similar sentiment underscores the need to give to the church. Many of the first Samoan churches in the San Francisco Bay Area maintained religious affiliations with the churches in Samoa. By virtue of those connections, giving and offering to the church was sustained even when it meant the monetary benefits from giving often stay in Samoa. Moreover, many of the congregations in the U.S. have pastors and ministers who have graduated from the local theological colleges in Samoa and, thus, still maintain close ties to the native homeland.

Giving, therefore, is all part of maintaining the cultural and philosophical circles of the *aiga* and an obligation for members of the *aiga* living in the diaspora. While these may vary over time, there is enough cultural as well as institutionalized ideology and philosophies remaining that often shape and influence decision making of the *aiga*. Thus, to understand poverty and the political-economic context of Samoa, one has to take into account other contributing factors beyond solely individual income. These are institutional constraints that often shape individual choices and performances in society. Cultural wealth in Samoan society is more than just about having material wealth. Wealth in the *faasamoa* (Samoan way of life) also emphasizes relationships inherent within (Glass 2012, 24). From a relational perspective, poverty can also be seen as absence of relationships, being isolated and being alone.

The wisdom of the *tautai seu* is not just in situating and locating. Rather there is always a sense of caution. Thus, a word of caution is offered here. While relations are important, they can impede on the individual. Relations based on respect for example can easily be exploited to manipulate the individual to act in accordance with the interest of one single dominating narrative. In this regard, one is always mindful that relations can be exploitative and manipulative. Nevertheless, I argue that incorporating a relational dimension of poverty is useful for the purpose of this study. It underscores the claim that the individual is embedded within a social, cultural, and political-economic environment. Ascertaining the institutional constraints within this environment does much to explain and exhibit the social and political-economic context of the individual.

Beck et al agree that there is more to poverty than just gauging it based on a money-centric framework. Poverty is "a socially relational problem involving deprivations in multiple dimensions, including health, standard of living, education and political participation" (Beck, Hahn, and Lepenies 2020, 1). I am aware of the importance of statistics. The essence of statistics is to provide the basis for ascertaining the extent and magnitude of the issue. One gets an acute sense of what people are facing if numbers are available. For example, about 1.2 billion of the world population lives on less than a $1/day, the parameter for extreme poverty. Of that number about 42 percent live in South Asia, 27 percent in Sub-Saharan Africa, and 24 percent in Asia and the Pacific (Odekon 2006, viii). The remaining proportion is shared among regions including Latin America. Using statistical data also shows that there is a glaring contrast in incidence of poverty among different countries. In that regard, Ethiopia and Uganda both show 82 percent.

But while statistics and monetary-based framings are helpful, the concern is the lack of attention given to other possible dimensions because of a money-centric emphasis. In his essay, Daniel Putnam (2020) argues along similar lines. Contending that there is benefit from perceiving poverty as a social relation, Putnam claims poverty is a kind of social phenomenon "defined by the character of the interpersonal relationships a person is susceptible to losing or falling into in virtue of occupying that position" (Putnam 2020, 41). The main argument therefore is "we should include a conception of poverty as a social relation in our repertoire if we think that one purpose of the concept of poverty is identifying individuals who are disadvantaged in a morally relevant sense due to lack of resources" (47). In other words, poverty is a function of displacement in which the individual is disadvantaged due to the lack of resources.

The idea that the individual is constrained by the social environment is also supported by Odekon (2006). Reasons for poverty can either be temporary or permanent. There are temporary reasons, for example a recession, which can be alleviated with an improving economy. However, it is different when there are institutional constraints that cause permanent poverty. This can be the result of "historical, cultural, or social factors, such as colonialism, international economic relations, or apartheid. In these cases, different policies to combat poverty are called for. Inequality in the distribution of income and wealth tops the list of long-term causes of poverty" (Odekon 2006, ix).

Poverty Warrants a Multi-disciplinary Approach

The recent trend in scholarship on poverty embraces a multi-disciplinary approach. Gottfried Schweiger calls it the "ecological approach" (Schweiger 2020, 14). The ecological approach appears to be more interested in the different environments in which "the individual and her social life is embedded, and in which her condition of poverty is structured, caused and reproduced." Writing on the relationship between recognition theory and poverty, Schweiger argues that

> This is not meant to supersede the individual or to neglect the plasticity of poverty and the possibilities of poor people being able to shape and alter their own condition. Rather, it is intended to acknowledge—as it is also a core understanding of recognition theory—that poverty and human life in general are embedded in cultural, social, economic and political structures and orders that not only influence our lives but also shape our own self-understanding and autonomy. (Schweiger 2020, 14)

This is an important point for the purpose of this study. The "ecological environment" underscores the notion that poverty is a function of the overall environment that surrounds the individual including social, cultural, and the political-economic context. It follows then that while some aspects of poverty may correlate with economic performance, there is much to be gained by looking into the institutional constraints embedded within the "ecological" environment of the individual. This is the perspective I take in this study. Ascertaining the institutional constraints embedded within the ecological environment warrants a comprehensive approach that merits a multidisciplinary approach.

Not only this, but I take the position that poverty is also about social relations. This is something I take from recent trends in the literature on poverty. In the introduction to their volume of essays on poverty Beck et al write that:

> The unifying theme connecting this volume's contributions is that poverty needs to be understood not only as a multidimensional, but also as a socially relational phenomenon, and that this dual understanding can improve existing efforts toward measuring and alleviating poverty. In order to advance the debate on poverty, we provide a forum for much needed dialogue between philosophers and more empirically oriented researchers, because philosophically sound analysis of and truly global research on poverty's social embeddedness must go hand in hand. (Beck, Hahn, and Lepenies 2020, 3)

Because poverty is a social phenomenon, it merits a multi-discipline approach. As a *tautai seu* locating and situating my reading of the Lukan narrative, I do anticipate pursuing a multi-discipline perspective. With this in mind, later in this study I will pursue the possibilities that the actions of the ruler in Luke may have been the result of institutional constraints within his "ecological" environment.

Poverty and the Question of Ideology

There are also certain ideologies that underpin the debate on poverty. The consensus among even the most critical scholars, especially those in the capitalist arena, is global poverty has fallen over several decades before COVID-19. Yet questions persist on the nature of data and statistics to measure poverty. These are important questions as they affect institutional schemes to provide for growth and development in the global context. Responses to those questions are often based on particular ideologies. Especially in the advent of global setting exercises in the new millennium these data and statistics "have been marshaled to legitimize the reigning international economic order" (Fischer 2018, 17). Concerns and doubts start to creep in on the authority of World Bank production of global poverty statistics. More importantly, it brings up the question of what and whose ideology spearheads the discussion on poverty in the global context. Is it an ideology that sees the continuation of exploitation, increased subordination and oppression, or one that highlights progress or in the views of others, liberation (Fischer 2018, 18)? As Fischer frames it, the basic question is whether the world has become any better since the end of the Cold War and the fall of communism. Confounding matters and at the core of this question is the "fanfare" of ideologies that surrounds it (18). Ideology in a sense encompasses "the stories and ideas that we live out as members of particular communities in order to establish ways of understanding about how best to live together" (Fischer 2018, 21). The pejorative sense of ideology manifests itself when those in power "can and do manipulate and enforce these stories in order to support their own interests" (21). Poverty statistics are employed in very much the same manner often to push a particular narrative. As Fischer aptly describes:

> [P]overty statistics are often even marshalled to legitimise oppression, as is common in occasional publications that seek to defend colonial legacies on the basis of health and education improvements in many colonies in the later nineteenth and first half of the twentieth century... Poverty statistics are also often used to justify occupation and forced incorporation... Similarly, global poverty statistics have been marshalled in various

ways to legitimise the reigning international economic order. The global-setting exercises of the new millennium have been more specifically oriented towards legitimizing the recent and particularly virulent phase of capitalism variously coined as 'neoliberalism' or more euphemistically as globalisation. (Fischer 2018, 22)

The above quotation highlights how statistics on poverty can be utilized to further certain ideologies. Statistical data and money-centric framework such as GDP and personal income dictate the narrative on growth and development. They reinforce the critical impact of institutional constraints that are exogenous to the PICTs. Monetary value is often emphasized over social well-being and welfare. More importantly, the dominant narrative is how to improve GDP and personal income. This has caused much disparity in income and distribution of resources.

This dominant narrative of growth and development have further deepened the dependency mindset among PICTs. Perhaps it was one of the many lessons learned from the recent COVID-19. As noted above, the economies of the PICTs suffered losses as a result of the shutdowns in overseas countries like the U.S., New Zealand and Australia, countries with large Pacific Island populations. The impact was especially felt in the tourism industry. Travel restrictions and border closures caused great strain on the economies of countries like Cook Island, Fiji, Guam, Palau, French Polynesia, Samoa, Tonga and Vanuatu with tourism making up more than 20 percent of their GDP. Other tourists' destinations like Papua New Guinea, Solomon Islands, New Caledonia, American Samoa, Federated State of Micronesia, Kiribati, Marshall Islands, and Tuvalu, all faced huge losses to other tourism-related industries such as transportation, service, and food.

With this said, the point is to engage the interconnectedness between PICTs and the global context. Because of the heavy reliance on international donors, PICTs are highly susceptible to exploitation. Interconnectedness is an advantage as well as a risk. For the PICTs, connectedness to the outside world has effectuated economic dependence and inadequacy as they face the difficult task of providing a government that is sufficiently funded and effectively providing for the needs of its population (Hezel SJ 2012, 25). The deepening crisis of economic dependence and inadequacy in the Pacific region has accelerated a narrative that idealizes indigenous living. PICTs are adopting a narrative that pushes for a rediscovery of traditional knowledge and wisdom as well as reconnecting with the land and the ocean.

However, the indigeneity narrative should not and cannot mask internal institutional constraints that continue to bare adverse effects on the people. In particular, PICTs have to revisit some of the internally generated elements including beliefs, norms and cultural values that have been institutionalized. Explaining some of the difficulties impeding the effectiveness of foreign aid, Mary M. Shirley (2008) observes three characteristics about institutions that are relevant. They are as follows:

1. A society's fundamental beliefs, norms, and rules tend to be durable, often lasting for centuries. Changes occur on the margin in less fundamental laws or organizations, but these are seldom sustained if the broader institutional framework remains unchanged.

2. Institutional frameworks endure because they are congruent with underlying power structures. Powerful groups who benefit from the institutional status quo will actively oppose changes that threaten their power and wealth. Even without active opposition, humans' habits and beliefs tend to resist revolutionary change. Without drastic changes in power structures and shared beliefs, institutional reforms in most poor countries will lead to large disparities between laws on the books and laws in practice, and between how laws are applied to the powerful and to the powerless.

3. Sometimes changes in beliefs, power structures, and institutional frameworks do occur and move countries incrementally toward more open access to economic and political power. Sustainable progress results from heterodox experiments that evolve gradually in response to competition and through adaptation to local conditions. (Shirley 2008, 59)

The important point is to acknowledge that certain social,cultural and ideological aspects of the Pacific way[14] are standing against our own pursuit of a quality life. This underscores the value in exploring some of the externally imposed and internally generated institutional constraints to fully ascertain the social environment in which one is situated. In

14. My use of Pacific way here is just an attempt to capture the holistic Pacific mentality, which is pretty ambitious of a goal, in order to illustrate the need for the people of the Pacific region to be self-reflective rather than unquestioningly following a certain narrative which in my opinion tends to divert from the collective goal of shared responsibility.

particular, the ability of the individual to make decisions is often hamstrung and constrained by one's relations with others in the community.

CONNECTING MY WORLD WITH THE LUKAN NARRATIVE

After surveying the discussion up to this point, the *tautai seu* is ready to situate and locate the biblical text within the lived reality of today's society. Taking a page, or line, from Jione Havea and Peter H. W. Lau (2020a, 1) I pose the question "is there gain in reading?" By reading, I present a particular kind of interpretation of the story of the rich ruler in Luke. Like Havea and Lau, I put this question at the forefront of my reading of the Lukan text. Everyone has something to gain from reading the biblical text. Some "gain joy, pleasure, enlightenment, pain, frustration, confusion, and even despair—but gain we certainly achieve" (Havea and Lau 2020a, 1).

As a *tautai seu*, I read to situate the biblical text not only within meaning but also within my context, my re-situatedness. This reading warrants exploring the political-economic context of the PICTs, in particular Samoan society. It is a deep contextual reading of the biblical text based on a contextual understanding of my contemporary world with regard to a particular issue. Such an undertaking has been the subject of debate among scholars resulting in a slew of works on how to best acquire meaning across contextual and cultural framings (Ahn 2019, 3; Fetalsana-Apura 2019, 167; Havea and Lau 2020a, 4; Mbuvi 2017, 151). Like the *tautai seu*, I situate meaning in the nuances of the issue confronting the reader in contemporary society. In particular, I am attempting to find meaning for the Pacific Island Christian who has to navigate the ebbs and flow of contemporary political-economic challenges. The purpose is not to dominate nor impose, rather, to explore alternatives. In a region where resources are limited, geographically isolated, and heavily dependent on foreign investors and development aid, there is a need for spiritual guidance and biblical orientation as well as alternatives. To revert to the question posed in the beginning of this section, I read to help make a connection between the lived reality of contemporary society and the Lukan narrative. This connection I argue can be established by a deep contextual exploration of real-life issues confronting contemporary society. As I have tried to show above, a deep exploration of poverty and the political-economic context of the *aiga* in Samoan contemporary society is relevant for my contextual biblical reading of Luke.

Some Assumptions to Explore in the Text

From the perspective of a *tautai seu*, by deeply engaging and situating myself within the political-economic context of the PICTs and the issue of poverty in Samoan society, I come away with a rich contextual understanding of some of the institutional constraints and significant drivers shaping and influencing the context of the *aiga* in Samoan society. Poverty is multidimensional and merits exploring the institutional constraints embedded within the social environment of the family. These could be cultural, social, and ideological influences. Moreover, the contours and landscape of the political-economic context have much to do with the relational dynamics surrounding family life. From the perspective of a *tautai seu*, this deep and rich contextual understanding of family life in contemporary Samoan society provides a juxtaposition to help in my own contextual biblical reading of the context of the ruler in the Lukan narrative. This leads me to three basic assumptions that could be useful for situating and locating my contextual biblical reading of the Lukan narrative.

1. That there is a possibility the behavior and response of the rich ruler could be discerned by exploring the social, cultural and ideological aspects of his contextual environment.
2. That an emphasis on the institutional constraints and political-economic context can also help to illuminate nuances in the biblical text that otherwise would not be clear.
3. That a deep and rich contextual approach to a particular issue in contemporary society can also guide and inform my own contextual approach to reading the Lukan account of the ruler.

Tools of Sociorhetorical Exploration

Drawing upon the wisdom of the *tautai seu*, I situate and locate myself with what is needed to engage successfully in the process of fishing. Similarly, my approach to this contextual biblical reading is guided by sociorhetorical criticism. Admittedly, I am not able to utilize the full arsenal of sociorhetorical exploratory tools. However, one of the strengths of sociorhetorical exploration is the fact that one can use tools based on the nature of the questions and assumptions one brings to the text. That is, the questions and assumptions I bring to the text, borne of my own contextual approach to the political-economic context in Samoa, shape the design of my research and the tools I use. In this regard, I can confidently make the claim that by exploring just the social, cultural and ideological textures of the text, I should be able to explore evidence of the "institutional" constraints that may have influenced and shaped the contextual environment of the ruler's household. These could be rules, norms, traditions, beliefs, cultural values, social relations, and underpinning ideology embedded in the Lukan narrative.

Political-economic Context

One of my pet peeves about what one might call "traditional biblical interpretation" is that it has not given me space to incorporate some of my previous learning about the world in which I live into my reading of the biblical text. Therefore, my present attempt to explore the "political-economic" context of the Lukan text about the rich ruler is a welcome challenge and an undertaking that could prove liberating and transformative. I am please, therefore, to have read a similar attempt in Alex Hon Ho Ip's exploration of New Testament economics using the New Institutional Economics (NIE) (2020, 101).

Ip also starts from his social, cultural and economic location, Hong Kong. Known as one of the richest economies in the world, Hong Kong provides the platform for Ip to explore the institutional aspects of first century Roman society and bring this to his interpretation of the New Testament. As Ip writes

> My location, both geographical and social in Hong Kong, provides me with the incentive to investigate the institutional aspect of an economy, both contemporary and first century Roman, and to explore how we could bring the institutional aspect of the Roman economy into interpretation of the New Testament. In light of this concern and motive, I found the interpretive analytic of sociorhetorical interpretation (SRI) to be a perfect platform to help me bring my concern in economics into New Testament interpretation. The most important reason is that SRI

provides a systematic but not closed way to investigate a text. (Ip 2020, 104)

While Ip's emphasis is on economic aspects, I am also interested in the overall ramifications on systemic interactions among the various institutions. That is, I am intrigued by the interactions of the social, cultural, ideological, political and economic aspects of the "ecological" environment surrounding the rich ruler. Multiple sources of influence shape and reorient discernment of the biblical text. Moreover, my engagement with the text is shaped by questions I bring from my own social, cultural and diasporic view of a real-life issue in Samoan society. The challenge though is to find the right tools and interpretive analytics to explore the biblical text. In this regard I, much like Ip, find the interpretive analytics of sociological explorations useful to read the influence of the political-economic institutions on the Lukan narrative of the rich ruler.

In his search for economic texture, Ip claims that it is very much like the analysis of other textures. It is noteworthy that texture is a metaphor that comes from "weaving a tapestry" and presupposes that each "strand" of the weaving contributes to the overall texture of the tapestry (Robbins 2016, xxiv). Thus, an economic texture presupposes an economic strand added to the overall tapestry of meaning and meaning effects that the interpreter can explore. I would add also that since economic aspects are embedded within the social, religious, cultural and political aspects of society, it is difficult to ascertain what is strictly economic. It is for that reason that I claim a more systemic approach which allows for the plausibility of locating the political-economic aspects of the text. I find that the strength of sociorhetorical exploration is being able to set up a programmatic and systematic process for analyzing the text. But as Ip suggests, one of the concerns is to avoid the problem of mirror reading. It is for this reason that a sociorhetorical exploration encourages interaction and communication between the different textures. Thus, "the exact meaning of the economic texture, however, depends on findings from both inner texture and intertexture. The inner texture and intertexture may help to define what problem is addressed in the economic texture. This is important as it avoids the problem of mirror reading of the text" (Ip 2020, 108). In this study though, discernment of the political-economic context is also shaped and influenced by ascertaining the various institutions and the relational dynamics among them.

SUMMARY

In sum, the focus of this chapter has been to explore the political-economic context of the PICT's and in particular poverty in Samoa. Using the analogy of a *tautai seu*, I situate and locate information that both guides and informs my contextual biblical study of the Lukan narrative. More significantly, doing so also helps in my re-situating or recontextualization of the biblical text. This re-situating is enabled by blending aspects of sociorhetorical analytics and New Institutional Economics (NIE). Moreover, the approach and design of my contextualization blends my interest in government policy and public affairs with a worldview that is borne of my location as someone "in-between" my homeland and diaspora. It also engages my desire to ground reading in the lived reality of Pacific Island people, in this particular case, poverty in Samoan society. Vetting the scholarship on poverty and weaving it together with my own personal story sets up the platform from which I draw certain assumptions about the Lukan narrative. Drawn from my social locations, these assumptions form the basis for the questions that I asked of the Lukan narrative on the rich ruler. These assumptions and questions also help the design and approach of the study framing my own reading and discernment of the Lukan narrative on the rich ruler. It is not to dominate nor impose my understanding of these political issues. Rather, it is to situate and locate my contextual biblical reading of Luke within the lived reality of the people. As the *tautai seu*, the next chapter situates and locates my contextual biblical study within the scholarship on Luke.

4

Steering and Situating the Lukan Narrative

INTRODUCTION

DRAWING UPON THE WISDOM of the *tautai seu*, I situate my contextual biblical study within the scholarship on the Gospel of Luke in this chapter. From the perspective of a *tautai seu*, I survey the scholarship on Luke to situate myself better and also to set up the theoretical foundation for a deep contextual exploration of the social, cultural, and ideological textures of Luke 18:18–31 in chapter 5 and the political-economic context in chapter 6.

Furthermore, this chapter reflects my intent to highlight the need for Pacific Island biblical hermeneutics to not only exist as a particular area of study but also to engage in continual dialogue with the overall Lukan scholarship. From this perspective, Pacific Island biblical hermeneutics is not metaphorically just a fixed island floating in the middle of the Pacific Ocean but a "sea of borders" (Havea 2014, 7) that is fluid in content and serves as the connecting pathway to other interpreters in other cultures and contexts.

I begin the chapter by surveying early approaches to Luke up to about two decades ago. This is important to paint an overall picture of the history of the interpretation of Luke. Then the following section examines more recent works during the last twenty or so years that bring the reader closer to current scholarship. The section after this shifts the focus to studies that emphasize Luke's social context, a more immediate subject for this study. The purpose of this is to bring some finer nuances of the study of the social and cultural world of Luke into view. Then the discussion turns more specifically to the political and economic context of Luke. A summary of the findings concludes the chapter.

EARLY APPROACHES TO LUKE

As a *tautai seu*, I begin with Anthony C. Thiselton's (2005) brief but very helpful synopsis of the history of interpreting the Gospel of Luke.[1] I situate myself with the idea that during the nineteenth century, Luke was known mainly as a "compiler and arranger" of documents (3). His reputation as a reliable historian improved among many scholars during the early twentieth century. Still, some interpreters expressed skepticism toward his historical knowledge about the area where Jesus lived. For the most part, Luke was considered void of theological underpinnings and only communicated "flat didactic axioms about the love of God and the brotherhood of humankind" (Thiselton 2005, 4). In this context, some scholars highlighted the likelihood of a connection between Luke and Paul. Luke was associated more with the voice of Paul than his distinctive voice and theological point of view (Green 2010, 1). Others claimed that Luke did not have close, personal knowledge of Paul (Bock 2011, 36).

A pivotal moment in the scholarship on Luke came with the publication of Hans Conzelmann's work in the 1950s (1961). For Conzelmann, the aim was not so much on investigating the historical facts and possible sources, but rather to "elucidate Luke's work in its present form" (9). In doing so, the focus shifted from sources to the literary features of Luke's work (12). As Talbert observes, Conzelman's contribution lies in the methodology he proposed to ascertain Luke's tendency—what came to be known as redaction criticism (Talbert 2003, 11). Rather than exploring the sources from which Luke obtained his materials, the focus shifted to the discrepancies between the Lukan text and his sources. In Conzelmann's view, Luke is "confronted by the situation in which the Church finds herself by the delay of the Parousia, and her existence in

---

1. For a more detailed history of the interpretation of Luke, see Charles H. Talbert's essay on *Reading of Luke and Acts* (Talbert 2003, 1–18).

secular existence" (Conzelmann 1961, 14). The motivation appears to be related to new developments facing the church. In the words of Thiselton, Conzelmann "portrays Luke as a creative theologian, and Luke–Acts as formative for the transition in the very nature of the church" (Thiselton 2005, 6). This is not an attempt to deny that Luke is historiography, but Conzelmann places Luke within the development and transitioning of the Church, which appears to be aligned with a mission-oriented purpose. According to this perspective, the Church appears to be in need of re-orienting its narrative within the course of history. Luke's Gospel therefore reappropriates the existing Jesus tradition to fit the context. Conzelmann writes,

> What distinguishes him [Luke] is not that he thinks in the categories of promise and fulfilment, for this he has in common with others, but the way in which he builds up from these categories a picture of the course of saving history, and the way in which he employs the traditional material for this purpose. (Conzelmann 1961, 13)

Consequently, and more importantly, Conzelmann shifts the focus of the discussion. Green asserts that Conzelman "paved the way for what would become first composition—and then literary-critical analysis of Luke—and set the interpretive agenda in ways that would open the door to a wide array of other, especially social-scientific and political, approaches to reading Luke" (Green 2010, 1–2). It is important to note, though, that what Green means by "literary-critical" might be different from what Conzelman had in mind fifty years ago. Nevertheless, the importance of Conzelman as Green points out is in shifting the discussion to allow more space for other approaches.

From a *tautai seu* perspective, since the shift inaugurated by Conzelmann, the majority of approaches to Luke have been eclectic and for the large part have emphasized its literary aspects. The post-Conzelmann era, according to Thiselton, has witnessed "an increasing concern with literary theory, especially with narratology, together with a diversity of theological emphases and further debates about faith and history" (8). This gave rise to the utilization of other methodologies including the use of narrative criticism. Robert C. Tannehill (1986), for example, utilizes narrative criticism to explore the overarching purpose that ties together the narrative in Luke and Acts. To do this, Tannehill focuses on "major roles in the narrative, understood in the context of the comprehensive purpose which is being realized throughout the narrative" (Tannehill 1986, 1). The author of Luke–Acts "consciously understands the story as unified by the controlling purpose of God" and therefore "wants readers to understand it in the same way" (2). Claiming that the realization of God's purpose is pivotal to the unity of Luke–Acts, Tannehill argues that it is a unified plot because God's unifying purpose is "behind the events which are narrated" and externalized in the actions of Jesus and his witnesses (Tannehill 1986, 2).

In this new context, R. Alan Culpepper (1995) in a commentary on the Gospel of Luke, emphasizes the literary and theological treasures, the narrative characters, structure, connections with Old Testament Christology and the place of Luke within the development of various Gospel themes (3). Culpepper also offers reflections on various interpretations of specific passages for church and contemporary readers, and for contemporary situations. Despite a broad focus on the literary aspect, Culpepper overall seems to emphasize the historical context of Luke. In particular, the portrayal of Jesus as "compassionate, and a friend to outcasts" (4) connects Jesus to "the history of Israel, the Scripture, contemporary world history, and the unfolding of God's redemptive purposes in human history." Jesus is portrayed as the "Savior sent to seek and to save the lost." In this manner, by relating Jesus to the "history" of Israel, Culpepper appears to place Luke within the category of history writing (Culpepper 1995, 4).

The question of genre remains prominent in the scholarship on Luke. The overall nature of the debate underpins the question of whether Luke is a historian. Pivotal to this debate is the evidence drawn from an emphasis on Luke's preface which places it within the literary category of ancient historiography. In this context, Loveday Alexander's (1993) seminal work on Luke's preface is an influential and pertinent voice. Her thorough exploration of historical Greek prefaces seeks to examine whether Luke's preface follows the literary convention of Greek historiography. From this exploration, Alexander postulates that Luke follows a different literary tradition with its own preface conventions. The weight of the evidence suggests parallels within the scientific tradition. By scientific tradition, Alexander suggests a "long and multiform tradition of technical and professional prose" outside of the "normal canon of classical literature" (Alexander 1993, 21).

Joel B. Green challenges the conclusion of Alexander, claiming that any similarities between Luke's preface and "scientific tradition" disappear when "moving from the substance of the scientific tradition to the narrative of the Third Gospel" (Green 1997, 4). Moreover, the "affinities between Luke and the scientific tradition" do not "negate the identification of Luke 1:1–4 and Luke–Acts with the tradition of Greco-Roman historiography" (4). And just because Luke–Acts "does not match in every instance the formal features of Greco-Roman historiography," Green adds that it should not be an issue as "the genre itself was loosely defined" (4). Evidence shows also that Luke is heavily influenced by the Old Testament and Jewish historiography "especially with respect to the use of historical sequences to shape a narrative theology" (4). Green though proffers that the prototypes for Luke could be found in "the early Greek histories of Herodotus and Thucydides" (Green 1997, 4).

Others like Charles H. Talbert (1988) contend a closer connection between Luke and Greco-Roman biography. From this perspective, the narrative of Luke–Acts seems to follow the storyline of particular characters—Jesus in the Gospel and the apostles in Acts. The purpose of the "Christian appropriation of the biographical tradition" then "was to supply a controlling context for the interpretation of the Jesus traditions that would avoid both the subversion of the gospel and reductionism" (Talbert 1988, 67). By "subversion of the gospel" Talbert describes a poignant historical issue that hypothetically could have underpinned the writing of the canonical Gospels. That is, to confront heretical tendencies to "take material out of its canonical context in order to give it a meaning other than what it had within the gospel narrative" (Talbert 1988, 63). Given also the predilection to misinterpret individual traditions, Talbert reasons that a controlling context was warranted. Similarly, a considerable disagreement existed in terms of how Jesus himself was perceived. Within this setting, Talbert reasons that the canonical gospels were "attempts to avoid the reductionism of seeing the presence of God in Jesus only one way" (67). Subsequently, one gets the sense that from Talbert's view, Luke as a biographical narrative fits the events that shape the historical context of the writing of the canonical gospels. The question of genre is seemingly connected to the social context of the gospels.

Green, however, counters on the grounds that "biography grew out of historiography and, like it, has an historical referent(s)" (Green 1997, 5). The claim and appropriation of Luke–Acts as a biography is not easy to sustain, especially in light of the Acts of the Apostles. Acts seems to encompass multiple stories that all share an aggregate level of events and actions whose emphasis is "on God and the fulfillment of God's ancient purpose" (5).

Further refuting the biographical angle, Richard B. Hays notes that the design of Luke–Acts highlights "God's purpose in fulfilling the promise of redemption for his people of Israel" (Hays 2016, 233). One can make the argument, then, that Luke's account of Jesus' life underpins a larger scheme to emphasize the fulfillment of God's purpose. Jesus functions within a larger framework. David P. Moessner (2016) adds support noting that the sayings and actions of the Jesus as a character are part of the larger framework. It is difficult to see Jesus situated outside of his historical context. Rather, Jesus is situated within a Jewish setting in first century Galilee and Judea. Thus, it is imperative to recognize Jesus' relationship to the people of Israel and his ultimate significance in the larger process of the events of God's salvation for the whole world. Unlike Talbert, Moessner qualifies these as part of an "external framework, an outer husk which serves the greater purpose of allowing telling glimpses into the enduring character traits (ἤθη) of Jesus" (Moessner 2016, 41–42). While Luke appears to be "thoroughly biographical," Moessner argues that Luke is a demonstration of biographical information dovetailed into "the greater story of the fulfillment of Israel's salvation for the whole world" (46). In other words, the Lukan narrative appears to be about the fulfillment of God's plan, one that clearly pivots around the life of Jesus. Jesus is better understood as part of a larger story and connection with an historical people (Moessner 2016, 46).

Let me digress for a moment. While claims of Luke as a biographical narrative rest on uneasy grounds, I am anxious about the theological implications. Namely, the notion of Jesus as the manifestation of God's purpose could be compromised by claims of a controlling context or even shifting the emphasis to focus on the works of the apostles. More pressing are my own contemporary interpretive concerns about the apparent tendency to categorize and classify the Lukan narrative according to certain standards and within particular boundaries. I find this tendency to restrict opportunities and spaces for movement and maneuverability. On the contrary, I welcome the use of a multi-method approach.

Utilizing a multi-method approach appears to resonate with Green who sees Luke's narrative as consisting of a series of event-accounts. The events are to be treated in relation to each other, rather than in isolation. Echoing Mark Alan Powell (1990), Green notes that interests in certain aspects of the text including characterization and setting are important to the reading of Luke (Green 1997, 11). In this regard, Luke as a literary text represents values and contexts from which the text was generated. As a corollary, ascertaining this world of the Lukan text is important.

From a *tautai seu* perspective, I locate myself with Green's view of the text, which parallels my own predisposition towards sociorhetorical analytics. Information embedded in the text is externalized in the textures of the text (Robbins 1996a). The idea that the text embodies certain data underpins Green's assertion of Luke as a "cultural product" (Green 1997, 11). By implication, to read Luke merits the use of tools that are "cultural-critical sensitivities" to capture much of Luke's "cultural presuppositions."

Green moreover, underpins a critical aspect of exploring Luke. By cultural presuppositions, Green seems to prefer something more than the implied social setting in the text. One that is "more than the world available to us only through the narrative viewed as a closed system, but less than the world often represented to us by historical-critical inquiry" (Green 1997, 12). In this statement, I detect a multi-method approach to be desirable for exploring the Lukan narrative, and in particular Luke's context. Such an undertaking as Green clarifies warrants looking at "the socio-historical realities of the Lukan text" which includes the "world of Palestine in the first decades, C.E." and the "wider Greco-Roman world of latter decades" (Green 1997, 14). In order to understand Luke, one has to recognize how Luke engages the cultural assumptions of his world by means of the Lukan text. This warrants navigating between the use of historical-critical and literary-critical tools of analysis, an important consideration and the methodological basis for my attempt to explore the political-economic context in Chapter 6.

Regarding tools for exploring Luke, Green is guided by two important questions:

1. the order in which the events are placed "to serve a particular teleology"; and

2. how "Luke's model readers will have heard and been shaped by the episodes of which he has given an account as well as by his narrative understood as a whole" (Green 1997, 12).

To adequately respond to these questions, I would argue for a systematic approach, one that incorporates a multi-method, interdisciplinary program of analysis. While I may agree with Green that there is value in capturing the cultural aspects of Luke's social setting, and that social-scientific tools can be utilized, I propose, given the multi-variant nature of such an undertaking, that sociorhetorical criticism is a better fit. A systematic program where various components of the analysis are able to engage with each other is warranted. Moreover, I argue that there is space for bringing in one's own social context and cultural values to engage with the Lukan narrative; both would be transformative not only for the text but also for the reader.

MORE RECENT APPROACHES TO LUKE

More recent studies of Luke include an eclectic array of ecological, postcolonial and feminist approaches, to name a few. Michael Trainor (2012) connects Luke with ecological concerns of the contemporary global world and highlights how biblical and theological studies can raise awareness about personal and communal care for our planet.[2] For Trainor, his approach enables him to engage the Lukan narrative from the perspective of his presuppositions and sensitivity to ecological issues. Moreover, Trainor holds that "there is something fundamentally truthful" about Luke's encounter that can "influence" how one lives in the world and with creation and the people around (4).

Let me digress for a moment. That the Christian Bible can be brought to bear on one's own life setting is an undergirding purpose of my study and an affinity shared with Trainor. My own study seeks to engage Luke's treatment of the poor and needy in society, which is perhaps the most prominent treatment of this issue in the New Testament. As one of the dominant strands throughout Luke's narrative of the Jesus story, Luke's treatment of the poor and rich enables an interpretation that reappropriates Lukan emphases within the political context of the Pacific Island Countries and Territories (PICTs) and enables an engagement with my own preconceptions about the political-economic situation in the Pacific region.

---

2. I find a great affinity between Trainor's response to the modern ecological crises and N.T. Wright's (2020, 12) reflection on how Christians should respond to the COVID-19 pandemic. For N.T. Wright, it is not to ask "why?" but rather to ask "what?" Both Trainor and Wright are important as they provide insights needed to bridge the space between biblical interpretation and real-life issues facing people in contemporary society. It is to analyze and visualize a response to some poignant issues in one's context. This is something that I hope to do, connecting the Lukan text to the political-economic issues among the PICTs, issues that are reflected in the PCC's Island of Hope document.

Situating myself with Trainor, I read Luke with certain preconceptions. For Trainor, these preconceptions are framed around what he calls eco-justice hermeneutic principles. They include "intrinsic worth, interconnectedness, voice, purpose, mutual custodianship and resistance" (Trainor 2012, 5). In bringing these principles to engage with Luke, Trainor recognizes the need to not impose one's "environmental sensitivity" on the text. Rather, it is necessary to maintain respect for the cultural divide between the world in which the text was composed and our current situation (6). Drawing upon the wisdom of the *tautai seu*, I find this to be an important reminder. *"Seu le manu ae taga'i le galu"* (catch the bird but watch for the waves) is a constant reminder to be restraint in our biblical interpretations.

In this recent context of interpretation, Raj Nadella (2011) attempts to explain particular divergent views in Luke. Using insights from Mikhail Bakhtin[3], including polyphony and dialogism[4], Nadella lends evidence to the claim that Luke is polyphonic. The implicit corollary is to read Luke for what it is, one that enables all voices to participate in the dialogue. Because Luke, according to Nadella, is polyphonic, the divergent views inherent in the text are not to be taken as a critique. Instead, Nadella sees the polyphony in the text as a fitting way to celebrate Luke's skills and creativity[5]. In particular, the divergent views inherent in Luke are an outcome of Luke bringing together multiple viewpoints, and even contestations.

Christy Cobb (2019) also builds on the notion of multiple voices in Luke. Like Nadella, Cobb follows Bahktin's notion that truth can be ascertained from multiple voices engaging in dialogue, but with an added element. Utilizing a feminist hermeneutical angle, Cobb explores the intersection between "slavery, gender, truth, and power" (10). Cobb also appears to use a literary element of the Lukan narrative as her point of

---

3. Iosefa Lefaoseu (2018) uses Mikhail Bakhtin's polyphonic concept to create a Samoan indigenous multi-strandic method to read the Book of Job.

4. Nadella gives a definition of both terms. According to Nadella, polyphony "refers to many aspects of the polyphonic novel, but it primarily signifies the presence of disparate voices and their mutual interaction as equals" (23). Dialogism usually refers to "an active interplay and exchange of ideas between two or more divergent voices including that of the narrator, in a literary space" (23).

5. See the "Introduction" in Culy and et.al (2010) for an elaborate discussion of Luke's skills and some of the literary tools and devices he utilizes.

entry. For example, in the analysis of the slave girl in Luke 22:47–62, the Greek word παιδίσκη is central. The relationship between the slave girl and other main characters in the narrative becomes the focal point of analysis for Cobb aided by a feminist hermeneutical lens and Bahktin's polyphonic concepts.

Like Trainor, Cobb also employs intertextuality[6]. But while Trainor draws from his preconceptions, Cobb looks at Luke 22, Acts 12, and Acts 16, engaging them with ancient literature including "Greek novels, the Apocryphal Acts of Apostles, and evidence from material culture as exhibited by ancient funerary monuments" (Cobb 2019, 3). This affinity for the use of intertextuality to evaluate Luke is also shared by Richard Hays (2016). His exploration of Scriptural influence on the Gospels leads to his claim that meaning in Luke, and for that matter the New Testament, can be better ascertained by reading "retrospectively" (Hays 2016, 419). In essence, Hays highlights the intertextual connection between the Gospels and the Scripture writing that "all human discourse includes elements of intertextuality" (28). This is an important point for my contextual biblical reading of the Lukan narrative. Hay's claim is also a reminder to keep the overall Bible in view. While it is important as a *tautai seu* to re-situate my reading of Luke within my particular context, it is nonetheless a reminder to maintain respect to the deep and rich contextual relations within the context of the biblical text.

STUDIES OF THE SOCIAL CONTEXT OF LUKE–ACTS

From a *tautai seu* viewpoint, I situate myself with studies that explore the social context of Luke. Many such studies underpin a methodological slant towards ideas and perspectives from social sciences including anthropology, sociology, economics and so forth (Esler 2007, 337). Questions concerning Luke's social system, typical economic system, relations between the city and countryside, populate this methodological construct (Talbert 2003, 13).I begin with Phillip F. Esler's (1987) groundbreaking monograph, which pursues a correlation between the reality of the intended community and the underpinning theology of Luke–Acts.

---

6. For further reading on intertextuality see Julia Kristeva (1980), Graham Allen (2011) and David M. Carr (2012). Vernon Robbins also adopts this into SRI adding to the innertexture, socio-cultural texture, ideological texture, and sacred texture. The result is a multi-method approach that encourages dialogue and engagement across the various textures.

Challenging Conzelmann's assumption that Luke's theology and his view of how the Church could respond could be distinct and separated, Esler proposes that the theological, social, and political realms were "interrelated" (1). In particular, Esler asks whether the "social and political exigencies played a vital role in the formation of Luke's theology, rather than merely constituting the areas in which it was applied" (1). Taking a redaction-critical angle, Esler argues that Luke has re-oriented the "gospel traditions at his disposal in response to social and political pressures experienced by his community" (2).

A point of digression is in order. I find Esler's statement above to be a bold assertion given that the previous focus had been on the gospel traditions and Luke's sources. What is significant is the increasing awareness that Luke's purpose is shaped not only by religious aspects, but also by "the social and political realities of the community for which it was composed" (2). In this respect, Esler echoes Peter Berger's[7] view of a dialectical relation between religion and society (Esler 1987, 2). To gain clarity of meaning, one must engage with the historical realities of the intended audience in the text.

While Esler certainly paves the way forward, there are potential dangers. For one, it is easy to assume from Esler's viewpoint that Luke is speaking directly to a specific and particular community. Thoughts of the Gospel of Matthew speaking to a Matthean community[8] come to mind. The risk in limiting Luke to a specific and particular community is that it restricts and confines meaning. Focusing on a particular setting and its social and political realities could easily fall into the danger of specificity and singularity, ignoring more nuanced complexities embedded within the text and its meaning.[9] Nevertheless, Esler's claim is significant in broadening

---

7. Esler cites from Peter Berger's *The Social Reality of Religion* (1969, 48).

8. For some of the discussion on the Matthean community see J. Andrew Overman (1990) and Boris Repschinski (2000). Both Overman and Repschinski view the Matthean Community in relation to a "formative Judaism" movement, a term that signals the reconsolidation and regrouping efforts of Judaism after the destruction of the temple.

9. See Richard Bauckham's (1998, 10) convincing argument of the possibility that the Gospels were intended for a wider circulation and not for a particular Christian audience. In making his claim, Bauckham challenges the view of the early Christian community "as a self-contained, self-sufficient, introverted group, having little contact with other Christian communities and little sense of participation in a worldwide

the scope of reasonable variables to take into account when ascertaining the impact the text may have on the readers, be it intended or otherwise.

The shift in Lukan scholarship at this point also coincides with an emerging methodological trend among biblical scholars which challenges the more prevalent historical-critical paradigm. A number of biblical scholars have been bringing in ideas and methods from the social sciences for the purpose of constructing a systematic understanding of biblical meaning. The edited work by Jerome H. Neyrey (1991), for example, brought together scholars who shared this methodological approach to engage in an exploration of the social world of Luke–Acts. While the primary interest is to engage the conversation on methods and models for the interpretation of New Testament writings, more pertinent for this study is the exploration of Luke–Acts for its relevancy to contemporary situations including, inter alia, "its concern with rich and poor, roles of women, and inclusiveness of outsiders" (Neyrey 1991, x). In this case, it is fair to envision that rather than being critical of historical criticism, the aim is to expand on it. The difference in approaches is practical though. The expressed concern within the essays is to explore the "social and cultural patterns and processes, manifest and latent, that were primary concern to those who first heard of the Lukan narratives" (Neyrey 1991, xii). Questions were asked of the "typical institutions of Luke's society" including "the family, politics, the city, the countryside, patron-client relations, and the health care system" (Neyrey 1991, xiii).

Of particular interest is the institutional slant—including, among others, family and politics—in Luke–Acts. In his essay, John H. Elliott (1991) focuses on how Luke–Acts, in comparison with other writings in the New Testament, gives more details for the purpose not only to give background to an "independent message," but more significantly, "to give that message concrete content and shape in space and time and human interaction" (221). In this regard, Luke is seen both as a "historiographer and theologian" whose aim is "to convince his Christian audience of the certainty of the things they have been taught (Luke 1:1–4) so as to strengthen faith and commitment" (Elliott 1991, 221).

To "concretize" his message, Luke, according to Elliott, utilizes two main "institutions of Judaism and early Christianity"—the "Jerusalem temple and the private household" (221). Quantitative evidence is provided comparing the number of references to both institutions in

---

Christian movement" (20).

Luke–Acts and the rest of the New Testament. For Elliott, contrasting the roles these institutions played in "Luke's social concretization of the gospel" raises the question of Luke's motive. That these are two different institutions symbolizing "different and opposed forms of social organization, identity, and allegiance" is clear from the examples Elliott selects from Luke–Acts (230). The question is for what purpose and reason.

Borrowing from Bruce Malina's model of ancient social relations[10], Elliott applies this to Luke–Acts. From Elliott's view, the temple in Jerusalem in Luke's narrative symbolizes a "centralized, politically controlled redistributive system" (235). The household on the other hand, symbolizes a communal life that is marked by "the reciprocities of kinship, friendship, and domestic relations" (236). Taken altogether, Elliott argues that the temple provides the central focus for Luke's Gospel, while the household "frames and marks the chief focus of Acts" (238).

A point of digression. This is an important aspect that I hope to explore in my study as I attempt an argument that even in Luke's Gospel the household motif/institution plays a vital role in the narrative. In particular, a fuller appreciation of the rich man's response in Luke 18:18–30 is facilitated by considering him not as an individual but as a dyadic individual within the household. This subject is discussed in the next chapter when I do the analysis.

The importance of institutional and social analysis in the approach to Luke is reflected by Elliott writing that the "temple and households are linked with basic Lukan emphases and contrasts" (238). Moreover, "the social and economic system centered in temple, Torah, and purity failed in terms of just redistribution" and "it became for Luke a negative foil with which to compare the social and economic relations of the household as the arena of justice, mercy, and koinonia and as the sphere of the Spirit's presence" (Elliott 1991, 238–39). Thus, a more holistic and systematic approach to reading Luke unveils some of the embedded

---

10. See Bruce Malina (1986) in *Christian Origins and Cultural Anthropology: Practical Models for biblical Interpretation*. Briefly, Malina proposes a model to analyze different forms of social relations and interactions of societies and groups in the Bible. According to Malina, "human relations are normally mutual relations and hence avoid the extremes of utter individualism and agglomeration" (99). Thus, Malina places reciprocity on one extreme of the spectrum and agglomeration on the other, while centricity is situated in the middle. Reciprocity according to Malina "is a vice versa movement between two parties, individuals or groups" Moreover, it is a 'between' relation of back-and-forth movement marked by action and relation of two sides or distinct social interests" (99). Agglomeration is akin to a monopoly while centricity suggests redistribution by a central figure, or locality (100).

relationships in the text, which merit incorporating aspects of social and institutional analysis.

Elliott, therefore, illustrates how social scientific methods could be utilized to engage with the text of Luke–Acts. In particular, much can be gained from exploring the relationship between the political and social realities of the intended audience and the Lukan narrative. An important question emerges though. How can we measure the correlation between the social context and the Lukan narrative? In other words, how could we measure the influence or relationship, if any, between the social world of the intended audience and the shape and design of the narrative?

In examining the social location[11] of the implied author of Luke–Acts, Vernon Robbins (Robbins 1991) points out the difficulty in attempting to trace the correlation between social context and authorial thinking. A more plausible approach would be to identify a range of alternatives or to demonstrate that certain ideas are unlikely in a particular situation (306). For this reason, ascertaining the social location of the implied author[12] is pertinent.

Robbins, utilizing the works of T. F. Carney and John H. Elliott, produced a two-part model to analyze the social location of the implied author of Luke–Acts. In one part are nine basic arenas of a social system and in the second part, narrative functions described as intratextual phenomena (Robbins 1991, 309). Applying the model[13] to Luke–Acts,

---

11. According to Vernon Robbins, "social location" is a "position in a social system which reflects a world view or what Peter Berger calls a 'socially constructed province of meaning': a perception of how things work, what is real, where things belong, and how they fit together" (Robbins 1991, 306).

12. Note that at this point I have not discussed the author of Luke–Acts. For the purpose of this study, my approach to the issue of authorship is identical to Michael Trainor's (2017). I take the person named "Luke" as the author of Luke–Acts without any biographical claims. A comprehensive exploration of the many scholarly views of this subject is beyond the scope of this study. For a detailed reading on the issue of authorship, see Darrell L. Bock (2011). I am aware also that there is a rigorous discussion regarding the controversial issue concerning the Gospels as stories of eyewitnesses or products of oral tradition. To learn more about the dynamics and nuances of this discussion see the works of Richard Bauckham (2006) and Bart D. Ehrman (Ehrman 2016).

13. As described by Robbins, the nine basic arenas of social system include: previous events, natural environment and resources, population structure, technology, socialization and personality, culture, foreign affairs, belief systems and ideologies, political-military-legal system. One the other hand, the four narrative functions are: character/audiences, narrator/narrative, inscribed author/inscribed reader, implied author/implied reader (Robbins 1991, 311). The lack of any mention of economic or material aspects is conspicuous. The closest it gets is the political-military-legal system

Robbins goes through the nine basic arenas in detail, with the help of the intratextual functions. The result is a rich description of data and alternatives made accessible through and via the text of Luke–Acts. In conclusion, Robbins offers encouragement writing that there is much to learn from systematically analyzing the social location of the implied author of Luke–Acts, a text crafted in the Mediterranean area during the time of the Roman Empire (Robbins 1991, 331). Moreover, by applying this model, we are also able to place certain historical events mentioned in Luke–Acts in a timeline, allowing for better placement and insight into the social location of the implied author. This is an essential piece of information for the purpose of this study. Given that I will be exploring the various textures of the text, and especially the political-economic context of the Lukan narrative, the placement of the story within the historical environment, although implied, is critical.

THE POLITICAL-ECONOMIC CONTEXT OF LUKE

From the perspective of a *tautai ama*, my sense is there is a need to engage the scholarly material with specific focus on Luke's political-economic context. For that purpose, Rohun Park's (2012) survey of the eclectic reading strategies utilized to construct the economy at work in Luke provides a good starting point. After taking the reader through a list of interpretive model-constructs that include historical, literary and sociocultural interpretations, Park settles on an alternative, one in which "Luke's economy discourse transforms power and representation and promotes liberation in contemporary contexts where real readers are located, either cultural or social" (Park 2012, 95–96). Park's approach appears to shift the locale of meaning to bear directly on the context of the contemporary reader. Meaning resides with the reader. Moreover, Park underpins a radical perspective that sees the Lukan narrative as embodying a "vision of life, a living reality, in this world." Such a vision is "embedded in a new economy" according to Park (96). The underlining principle is a "changing" economy construct, one that is "subject to reconstitution" or "transformation." Park's argument draws from the postcolonial view of literature which in essence perceives the text as shaped by the "experience of colonization." The corollary is of writings that "asserted themselves by

---

which according to Robbins "stood in a close symbiotic relationship with socio-economic affairs" (Robbins 1991, 328–29).

foregrounding the tension with the imperial power, and by emphasizing their differences from the assumptions of the imperial center (sic)" (Ashcroft, Griffiths, and Tiffin 2002, 2). Luke's economy discourse therefore suggests something that traverses time and space to be brought to bear on the context of the contemporary reader. Park elects to use intercultural criticism to enable the crossing of Luke's construct of economy to contemporary locations. Among many reasons, the primary argument for intercultural criticism is that it can provide the tools to enable the reader to analyze the first-century biblical world and project the results onto "the contemporary experiences of colonialism/imperialism in a specific historical, cultural, geopolitical, geoeconomic location" (Park 2012, 98).

In conclusion, Park writes that

> Luke's discourse is directly related to the creation or restraint of life and life-together under the Empire and opens the possibilities for perceiving an economy without regard to property. Beyond the alleged value of individual assets and their utilitarian appropriation, such as trickle-down (from the top) economics, Luke's considerate and nuanced approach is directly related to the transformation of political economy. In this regard, political economy is a space in which one finds the most sacred social and political ideals as well as the greatest fears and anxieties, and, thus, potentially deeper hopes and visions of well-being and conditions of life and life-together. (Park 2012, 98–99)

Park, therefore, describes Luke's discourse on economy as considerate and nuanced. Defining political economy as a space of the sacred, social, and political ideals, Park further sheds light on the nature and dynamics of the Lukan discourse on economy that bring into prominence elements of hope, life-affirming conditions and solidarity. Moreover, Luke represents a discourse that prompts a transformation of existing institutions.

Peter Santandreu (2018) is more concerned with the question of whether Luke is pro or anti-empire. After presenting views on both sides of the debate, Santandreu concludes Luke is not only sympathetic to Greco-Roman culture but employs it to convey his message that God's revelation is in the person of Jesus Christ. Compared to other Gospel writers, Luke is more accepting of the Roman Empire. Looking at Santandreu's approach to Luke, a certain affinity for the function of the political, social and cultural context, as well as institutions, is implicit. As Santandreu writes,

> While Luke–Acts cannot be claimed as a 100% pro-Roman document or apology, there are several instances where the Empire is viewed in a positive light. At the end of the day, the Empire composed the reality in which Christianity existed and the government structure with which the church had to contend. Luke–Acts avoids easy temptations to pit the Jesus movement against the dominating imperial power of Rome. In fact, if one read Acts, it is because of the Roman Empire that the church survived the first few decades. While it does critique the way in which Rome uses its power, it nowhere suggests that the Empire is on its way out, or that it must be (actively or passively) subverted by Christian believers. (Santandreu 2018, 12)

For Virginia Burrus (2009), Luke's economic and political views are ambiguous. Attempting to survey the political and economic context invoked by Luke, Burrus situates her reading of the third Gospel within the context of empire and resistance. In this, Burrus explores the possibilities of reading Luke as postcolonial literature based on its ambiguities and ambivalences.

Taking the position of other postcolonial critics, Burrus suggests that Luke's ambivalence towards the "cultural authority of the colonizer" is not only a postcolonial condition but also its source of power (Burrus 2009, 134). The treatment of Herod's relationship to Jesus is explored as an example. Herod's response when he first heard of Jesus is quite intriguing. At a crucial point in the narrative, when Herod receives Jesus from Pilate, his questions suggest someone who is more curious than condemning. This ambiguity in the narrative is heightened with Jesus' non-verbal response, which is indicative of a preference for "noble silence" (Burrus 2009, 136). The overall impact of this event is to create a cloud of ambivalence and ambiguities. Throughout Luke–Acts, one can find other evidences that the Lukan narrative treats Roman representatives ambiguously.

Burrus also claims that Luke's economic views are equally ambiguous. That Burrus finds Luke's view of economic relations ambiguous is intriguing given that a cursory reading of Luke's narrative reveals a strong sense of sensitivity towards the poor and needy in society. Indeed, Burrus agrees that "the problematic relation between the rich and the poor and the crushing weight of poverty on both the urban and rural populations are recurring themes" in Luke's Gospel. Even in Acts, certain event-accounts suggest a narrative that is aimed towards those in possession, the primary source of wealth, to distribute according to need. The overall characterization is that of an "advocate of justice for the economically exploited" (Burrus 2009, 142).

Burrus argues though that despite depicting a more radical Jesus compared to the other Gospels, Luke responds more pragmatically "to the realities of economic patronage that structure the socio-political relations of the ancient Roman world" (144). Luke at times appears to be "centrally concerned merely with securing the right patrons and with converting those patrons to new levels of generosity in the age-old competitive pursuit of social honour." Moreover, Burrus highlights sufficient evidence in Luke–Acts of "relations of patronage" raising the possibility that Luke perhaps is "more paternalistic" in his economic view and attitude towards the poor. This claim is important as one can envision perhaps that Luke's attention is directed towards the patrons, the elite in society. From this perspective, perhaps the Lukan narrative exhibits a growing awareness of the need for better distribution of resources, one in which the patrons are expected to give to the poor and needy.

Other scholars in some variation, make similar claims. For example, Luise Schottroff and Wolfgang Stegemann (1986, 68) observe that Luke–Acts is filled with instances in which Jesus and the apostles frequented the homes of rich and important individuals. Even rich women have a role to play for example in Luke 8:3 and Acts 16:14. The implication is of a Lukan narrative that in all likelihood is aimed towards the "philanthropic rich" (Burrus 2009, 142).

That Luke's political stance in relation to the Roman Empire is ambiguous is also advanced by Yong-Sung Ahn (2006). Seeking clarity, Ahn draws upon his reading of Luke 19:45—23:56, emphasizing the conflict between Empire and the Reign of God. From this reading, Ahn argues that Luke describes Jesus in conflict "with the inseparable religious/political system of Empire, a system to which both Roman and Jewish authorities bear allegiance" (2). Luke is ambiguous as it is neither pro-Roman compared to the Romans 13, nor is it anti-Roman compared to Revelation 13. Luke's narrative rather represents a third way, one that Ahn argues "is not a simple middle path, but a complicated position that is characterized both by a counter-hegemonic discourse and as a colonial product" (Ahn 2006, 2).

In contrast to Burrus and Ahn, Seyoon Kim (Kim 2008) stresses a positive relationship between Luke and the Roman Empire. In an analysis of Luke's portrayal of Jesus' redemption, Kim argues that Luke's presentation of Jesus' redemptive work does not seek to alter extant political-economic structure, or even the social structure to engender political freedom, justice, or even economic prosperity. Luke's focus is not on challenging imperial rule or changing existing institutions. Rather, Kim sees Luke as more interested in bringing relief to the poor and the oppressed. Luke therefore, according to Kim, "limits his concern" to "creating the community of love and service, without thinking through further to the changes that can be brought to the political, economic, and social system of the Roman Empire" (Kim 2008, 112).

A point of digression is merited here. Kim's argument reflects a Luke with limited concerns. However, if his argument is based on the assumption that Luke has a universal vision of the growing Jesus movement and Christian community, then there is reason to suggest a more radical proposition. It is reasonable to argue that perhaps Luke also anticipates the need to alter existing institutions and structures in order to bring about the realization of God's redemption through the church. The need to create a community of love and service, using Kim's words, could only be realized by bringing much needed changes to the existing institutions and way of life that continue to constrain against the realization of God's redemption.

While there appears to be a lack of studies on Luke's political stance per se, a few focus specifically on Luke's political-economic context. Eben Scheffler (2011) for example provides helpful guidelines for such an undertaking. First, the economic context of Roman society in the first century should not be considered as homogenous. While Roman imperial rule may have dominated the world, Scheffler argues that it did not have the means to enforce economic policies across the empire (118). This implies the difficulties in simplifying the multi-dimensional nature of the Roman political economy.

Second, Scheffler revisits the question of context in relation to Luke's situation. In particular, Scheffler writes:

> To my mind Bauckham's view of Luke's universal vision should be conceded, without underplaying the context-related circumstances in which his writings originated and were addressed. It also stands to reason that if he wrote his Gospel in Rome, the contingent prevailing circumstances would have influenced him, even if only on a subconscious level. To investigate the prevailing Roman economic context during the time of his writing is therefore fully justified. (Scheffler 2011, 118).

The above statement underscores the difficulties facing attempts to explore Luke's situation, and in particular its political-economic context. Nevertheless, from a historical perspective, the claim that Luke has a universal vision merits an extensive look at the ancient economy in Roman-Palestine and Greek-Hellenistic contexts.

A third consideration according to Scheffler relates to the hierarchical nature of contemporary Roman society. Disputing scholarly consensus regarding economic classes, Scheffler cleverly shows that the emphasis on the rich and poor, or patrons and clients, risks simplifying the very complex composition of ancient society. There were seven economic classes across different levels including imperial, regional, municipal, and subsistence levels (Scheffler 2011, 119).

The fourth consideration for Scheffler involves questions pertaining to Luke's intent. In particular, when Luke talks about the πτωχοί (the poor) which economic layer is he talking about? This leads to the question of which economic layer Luke addresses.

Scheffler posits that Luke's Gospel was intended for the lowest economic class in society which consisted of the bottom 25 percent of the economic scale. Luke intended, according to Scheffler, to mobilize "the other economic layers of society (even those who merely survived) to cater for the dying or 'begging' poor" (Scheffler 2011, 120). In conclusion, Scheffler has this to say about the poor in Luke and Luke's intent:

> It can be concluded that for Luke 'the poor' (whether expressed by the term πτωχός or in other ways) are not a spiritualised concept but refers to real people living in this world, people who are not only eschatologically blessed (6:20) but whose this-worldly needs also have to be satisfied. The fact that people are called to beware of greed (12:15; cf. also 3:14) while simultaneously doing charity is an important feature of Lukan soteriology. Liberation of the poor will come about not just through God's ultimate action, but especially through human pity and sharing (which equals richness towards God, the receiving of his kingdom and heavenly treasure). The injunctions to renounce possessions *(Besitzverzicht, Armutsforderung)* and practice charity *(Wohltätigkeits-paränese)* are juxtaposed dialectically and should not be contrasted (contra Horn 1983:186–88). The main thrust of Luke's argument is that the lot of the poor should be ameliorated. (Scheffler 2011, 129)

Let me digress for a moment. Scheffler's argument seems to suggest that Luke's emphasis is on the poor. This suggests that even in the first-century Mediterranean world it is inconceivable to argue for a Luke that stops short of asking for some kind of changes to the institutional system that perpetuates the condition of the poor. Liberation of the poor will require changing the institutions that continue to constrain against the economic well-being of the many while the few enjoy the benefits. These include the way of life for that particular context including social, cultural, ideological and religious beliefs. Moreover, the way of life of any society is also a function of the way its political-economic context shapes and influences how people make decisions in life. To say that Luke's focus is limited to the welfare of the poor misses the more radical underpinnings that could be assumed from the argument. This is the line of argument I hope to pursue in my study.

From a *tautai seu* perspective, Scheffler seemingly demonstrates straddling different locales of meaning. On one hand, Scheffler's analysis of the word πτωχοί (the poor) helps to illuminate the emphasis within the Lukan text. The ensuing discussion of the poor and the different economic classes in first-century Roman society supplements our understanding by presenting history behind the text. The outcome is of an approach that oscillates between two locales of meaning that add clarity to our understanding by establishing an ongoing dialogue between the Lukan text and the social, cultural, and economic world in which it was written and in which it functioned.

SUMMARY AND PROPOSITIONS

As a *tautai seu*, my goal in this chapter has been to steer through the deep *moana* of Lukan scholarship. In particular, I situate and locate my contextual biblical reading within the contour and landscape of the scholarship on Luke. From the above review, there are certain aspects of the literature that are noted here.

First, the literature shows a trend that underpins a shift from the heavily historical critical approaches of earlier years to the more recent literary critical emphasis. The outcome is a shift in strategies for finding meaning and the subsequently eclectic choice of tools for analysis. Nevertheless, there appears to be a need to blend the different approaches to fully utilize both historical and literary-based data in our approaches to reading Luke. This is where I hope to explore bridging the social, cultural, and ideological textures of the text with data on the political-economic context of ancient society. Such an undertaking is enabled by the use of some SRI tools, blended with knowledge from the New Institutional Economics (NIE).

Second, the above discussions also shed light on the dearth of studies that focus specifically on the political-economic context of the Lukan narrative. Exploring the political-economic context sheds light on the institutional constraints that shape and influence individual responses and decisions in society. While it is reasonable not to over speculate on the mindset and rationality of the person in first-century Mediterranean society, examining the political-economic context can shed light on several relationships and potential factors and variables.

Finally, the scholarship on Luke, despite the different approaches of interpreters, demonstrates that Luke exhibits a certain degree of pragmatism, a sensitivity to the issues of the day. Luke seems to show a particular awareness to connect his story and narrative with his historical world. This is cleverly done by weaving together and blending the literary aspects of the narrative with a certain sensitivity to the historical world embedded within the text as well as the world that is represented by the text.

As a *tautai seu*, this chapter steers my contextual biblical reading towards the deep *moana* of Lukan scholarship. Scoping the contours of the Lukan scholarship helps situate my own contextual biblical reading of Luke 18:18–30. As a *tautai seu*, I am also cognizant of the need for this undertaking to be guided by a deep and rich contextual understanding of the Lukan scholarship, hence, to learn from the works and wisdom of other steersperson. Being from the Pacific Island region, my own attempt to carry out a biblical reading drawn from my own context necessitates engaging in perpetual dialogue with other steersman in Lukan scholarship. As a *tautai seu*, once I situate and locate my context within the Lukan scholarship, I then turn to begin the art of *tautai ama*, my contextual reading of the text without allowing other possible alternatives to distract me from my mooring point.

PART TWO

Tautai Ama

5

Social, Cultural, and Ideological Texture

INTRODUCTION

AS A STEERSPERSON OF the deep *moana*, the *tautai ama* navigates the waves and currents of the sea, negotiating its crests, troughs and flow, meanwhile, always alert to sudden changes in wind velocity and climatic conditions that may deter from the determined path. In a similar manner I steer my interpretive canoe to engage Luke's story of the rich ruler, yet always careful not to be diverted from getting the day's catch. I negotiate and circumnavigate the boundaries and possibilities in the world of the text and the world behind the text while partially conscious of other things in the context which should not distract from the major focus that I want to catch.

The story of the rich ruler is a familiar one. Preserved in the Synoptic Gospels (Matthew 19:16–30; Mark 10:17–31; Luke 18:18–30) it has garnered various interpretations and remains fertile ground for research. For Gerald McKenny (2020) there are two distinctive interpretive tracks: one interprets Jesus' demand to sell everything as an allusion to doing more than simply keeping the commandments; the second is an exposition on the rich ruler's failure to keep Jesus' directives (McKenny 2020, 59). Some scholars see Luke's version as an illustration of the Third Gospel's emphasis on wealth and possessions (Murphy 2017, 11; Culpepper 1995, 12). Others draw attention to Luke's showcasing of alternating responses to Jesus. The response of the disbelieving rich ruler is contrasted with Zacchaeus' trust in Jesus (Lioy 2017, 125). Some see the Lukan version of the rich ruler narrative through the prism of status reversal (Green 2003, 1888). Moreover, others refer to it as an illustration of Luke's intertextual use of the Old Testament, in particular the theme of justice and the socio-economic setting in first-century Palestine (Hays 2012, 43).

In many of these and other interpretations, the prevailing interest has been on the ruler's apparent refusal to give up wealth and possessions (Johnson 1991, 277). Such readings have cast a negative light on the ruler. The outcome is a text that is intolerant towards the "others." As a *tautai ama* navigating the possibilities, I argue that the text needs de-centering. Rather than focusing on the ruler's response, I argue for a contextual biblical reading. Such reading explores the text for any possible evidence of institutional constraints in the social, cultural, ideological, and political-economic context of the text. The assumption is Luke's depiction of the ruler is much more nuanced and complex. In this I intend to show that the ruler represents a negotiation of a situational space between the community of believers and their lived reality. In his contextualization of the Gospel tradition, Luke massages the Gospel narrative to re-situate it within the extant institutional reality of the day.

I begin the analysis by looking at the innertexture of the rich ruler story, followed by exploring its placement within the Gospel of Luke. This is an important step in locating the passage within the overall outline of Luke. Following the text placement, a close reading of the text is offered followed by a discussion of the social and cultural aspects of the text. For the social and cultural aspects, I propose potential scenarios for the contextual refurbishment of the text. I explore the possibilities and implications of the ruler as shaped and influenced by institutional constraints, a member of other subgroups, and his relationship with his family and others. The intent is to capture as much as possible various aspects of the social and cultural environment of the text. Given those social and cultural aspects, I then explore some of the underpinning ideologies. The chapter ends with some general observations and final thoughts.

THE INNERTEXTURE OF LUKE 18:18–30

There are several possibilities to approaching the text for analysis and interpretation. Like the *tautai ama* maneuvering the waves of the deep *moana*, I focus on a key aspect of the innertexture of the biblical text, its opening-middle-closing texture (Robbins 1996b, 50), to steer a path for my interpretive canoe. Luke 18:18–30 showcases a clear strand of opening-middle-closing texture: opening in verses 18–21; middle in verses 22–25; and closing in verses 26–30 (see Table 5.1). My intent is to correlate the analysis of the opening, middle, and closing subunits with the analysis of the overall passage "to define their function in relation to one another" (Robbins 1996b, 50). In the process of correlating, I am also able to steer my interpretive canoe to engage other possible intertextual materials.

The opening subunit begins in verse 18 with the ruler enquiring about eternal life and ends with him giving a positive response in verse 21. In the middle, Jesus says that "God alone is good." But then as Jesus proceeds, he ends with the commandment to "honor your father and your mother." As a *tautai ama* steering a path across the deep sea, I am drawn to the possibility that the ruler is trying to live out this commandment—honoring one's father and mother. This critical aspect of the text also resonates with my own personal journey. My decision to enter the ministry was motivated by "a desire" that God will somehow save my mother. Steering my biblical reading towards that direction, it is reasonable to conjecture that the ruler may have situated "inheritance" of eternal life with "honoring one's father and mother."

Opening

[O] 18 A certain ruler asked him, "Good Teacher, what must I do to inherit eternal life?"

[M] 19 Jesus said to him, "Why do you call me good? No one is good but God alone.

20 You know the commandments: 'You shall not commit adultery; You shall not murder; You shall not steal; You shall not bear false witness; Honor your father and mother.'"

[C] 21 He [the ruler] replied, "I have kept all these since my youth."

Middle

[O] 22 When Jesus heard this, he said to him, "There is still one thing lacking. Sell all that you own and distribute the money to the poor, and you will have treasure in heaven; then come, follow me."

[M] 23 But when he heard this, he became sad; for he was very rich.

[C] 24 Jesus looked at him and said, "How hard it is for those who have wealth to enter the kingdom of God! 25 Indeed, it is easier for a camel to go through the eye of a needle than for someone who is rich to enter the kingdom of God."

Closing

[O] 26 Those who heard it said, "Then who can be saved?" 27 He replied, "What is impossible for mortals is possible for God."

[M] 28 Then Peter said, "Look, we have left our homes and followed you."

[C] 29 And he said to them, "Truly I tell you, there is no one who has left house or wife or brothers or parents or children, for the sake of the kingdom of God, 30 who will not get back very much more in this age, and in the age to come eternal life." (Luke 18:18–30, NRSV)

Table 5.1: The opening-middle-closing texture of Luke 18:18–30

In the middle subunit, Jesus shifts the topic to the ruler's wealth in verse 22 and then adds a call to the discipleship of "following." This is a critical juncture in the conversation. The changing of the subject concerns an uncertainty about a tenet or institution of Jewish belief (eternal life) for a person who is wealthy. Following the wisdom of the *tautai ama*, I steer my interpretive canoe around the dominant negative perception of the ruler by asking whether Luke may have had in mind someone like Abraham. In this regard, I find possible intertextuality in the Testament of Abraham. Blessed by God with "a large livelihood and many possessions," Abraham "is very rich. But above all others he is righteous in all goodness, (having been) hospitable and loving until the end of his life" (T. Ab. A1.5.). I ask then whether the ruler may be trying to live out a form of discipleship that "honors one's father and mother," possibly by trying to continue to live responsibly with the wealth he has acquired and perhaps inherited through the stewardship of his parents and himself.

In the closing, the people who overhear the conversation move the discussion decisively back to "being called into special discipleship of following" in verse 22, and Jesus confirms that this "special" kind of discipleship does indeed promise eternal life. I ask then, where this leaves the ruler. Is there no possibility of his being a responsible disciple in the context of not giving everything away? What about the prosperous Christian? Could this be part of Luke's overall message regarding the confluence of political economy, household (family life) and faith? Steering around and circumnavigating other possibilities and alternatives in pursuit of the day's catch, I ask whether Luke's "re-situating" of the rich ruler is better understood in connection to other stories like Zacchaeus in 19:1–10 and Jesus' sermon on the plain in 6:35.

Let me digress here. Some interpreters have pointed to Zacchaeus in Luke 19:1–10 as fulfilling an alternative form of "responsible discipleship with wealth." He represents a "rich person who has understood something of Jesus' ministry and message and concern for the poor and the cheated" (Fitzmyer 1985, 1222). In this regard, the Zacchaeus story possibly provides one kind of answer for the political-economic aspects pursued in the story of the rich ruler. In the rich ruler story, Jesus does not say it is impossible for those who have wealth to enter the kingdom of God. Rather, he emphasizes that it is very, very difficult (v. 24). Is it possible to think that Luke could have envisioned the ruler as living another way of responsible discipleship with his wealth? Perhaps the rich ruler is sad (v. 23), because he now faces the reality that there is no easy and sure way for him to keep his wealth and receive eternal life. He must now commit himself to multiple ways of leading a responsible life with his wealth in order for there to be a possibility of receiving eternal life. It will be as difficult as a camel going "through the eye of a needle," but perhaps it will not be impossible in a world where "what is impossible for mortals is possible with God" (18:27). Perhaps there is a possibility that the rich ruler might be saved, just as Zacchaeus presented an alternative form of responsible discipleship with wealth by giving up half of his wealth and Jesus proclaims that he is saved "because he too is a son of Abraham" (Luke 19:9 NRSV).

Joel Green's assertion that Zacchaeus, unlike the rich ruler, "does not employ his wealth so as to procure honor and friends" and that he is also a "social outcast who puts his possessions in the service of the needy and of justice" (1997, 672), may add additional clarity to this situation. From a *tautai ama* perspective, I ask whether Luke in both stories may be steering a "re-situating" narrative on "following" for a "son of Abraham." Thus if, as Green claims, Zacchaeus is vindicated because he is a son of Abraham, namely one of "those whose lives (dispositions and behavior) are oriented toward God" (673 n216), then for the same reason perhaps there is vindication for the rich ruler. Luke in the rich ruler story is possibly showing a different form of discipleship by trying to live responsibly with wealth that honors his father and mother. But if this is the case, how then can we make sense of the call to sell everything?

The controversial conversation between Zacchaeus and Jesus in Luke 19:8 (Wolter 2016, 347) helps to shed light on Jesus' demand for the rich ruler to sell everything and give to the poor. Weighing the possibilities, I side with the claim that the present forms of δίδωμι (Luke 19:8 UBS4) and ἀποδίδωμι (Luke 19:8 UBS4) in the Lukan text have iterative meaning and that Zacchaeus is defending himself before Jesus. Zacchaeus does not say that he "will in the future" give and pay back, but he says that he regularly does give half of his possessions to the poor and when he discovers he has defrauded anyone of anything he pays them back four times as much. Understanding the context in the Zacchaeus story in this way may provide helpful information for us to expand our understanding of the story of the rich ruler. In other words, the greatest need may be for better distribution of resources and sharing of wealth. Perhaps Jesus is describing for the followers of Christ the notion of living responsibly with wealth as an acceptable form of discipleship, as well as a mode of leaving everything and following him.

Drawing upon the wisdom of the *tautai ama*, I steer around looking for other possibilities to ask whether this "responsible view of wealth" is present also somewhere else in the Gospel of Luke. I find another possible context in Luke's account of the sermon on the plain. It looks reasonable to think that the idea of "lending" and "expecting nothing in return" in Luke 6:35 makes best sense if the lender is rich. People who have given everything away would not be in a position to "lend" something to the poor. This is perhaps another moment when Jesus provides a responsible way for the wealthy to live a responsible life of discipleship in society. And perhaps this way of "living responsibly with wealth" is present in the "political-economic aspects" of the story of the rich ruler. Surveying the movement and flow of the analysis so far gives me a sense that I need to situate myself with Luke's purpose and intent. While I am aware of the issues associated with attempts to situate and locate authorial purpose, I maintain my focus that this path may lead to the day's catch.

NEGOTIATING WITH LUKE'S INTENDED PURPOSE

Attempting an examination of the author's intended purpose usually begins with the question of audience. In this case, who is Luke's audience? Luke Timothy Johnson (1991) describes Luke's audience as Gentile Christians. While there may have been Jewish readers, the more vigorous thrust of the narrative is directed to non-Jewish readers (9–10). Johnson's observation echoes much of the scholarly consensus regarding Luke's audience, although there are also claims of a Jewish Christian audience (Forbes 2000). The scholarly argument on both sides is inconclusive. One thing appears to be without much dispute—Luke-Acts was addressed to a situation external to Palestine (Forbes 2000, 322).

Some of the claims have signaled an apologetic nature that is at the core of much of Luke's writing. Those claims have pointed to historical events to provide support—events such as the expulsion of Jews from Rome in 49 CE, and Nero's accusation in 64 CE that the Christians started the fire that burned most of Rome. Claims based on historical events though call into question the date of writing which is also debatable. One of the most common claims, although not without objections, places the date of writing post-70, after the destruction of the temple (Bock 2011, 39; Dicken 2012, 25). Those who have argued for an apologetic purpose often emphasize the significance of the historical events of the time. The general purpose of Luke was to appease and respond to questions that have emerged as a result of these events having taken place. David Wenham (2005) summarizes Luke's reasons as follows: a) Luke was writing "to correct historical misperceptions"; b) Luke wanted to show that "Christianity was not a novel religion, but that Jesus was the fulfillment of the Old Testament and of God's purposes for Israel and the world" (101). From Wenham's perspective, the events of the time provide the context for understanding Luke's purpose and audience. It is noteworthy that views of an apologetic Luke vary between a formal apology and demonstrating that Christians are not politically subversive (Forbes 2000, 308).

The strong correlation between genre and purpose is also emphasized in the scholarship. From the perspective of those who emphasize the biographical aspects of Luke, the purpose of Luke's Gospel revolves around the character of Jesus, his role and function within the Lukan narrative. In other words, Luke's purpose, which is to re-situate the story of Jesus as the fulfillment of God's purpose, shapes the genre of the Third Gospel. Thus, the emphasis on historical things in the context is most likely to underscore a purpose that is closely related to the historical events of Luke's time.

Randy J. Hedlun (2013) suggests that the social conflict of the time as a result of widespread historical events in the Mediterranean world provides the motivation for Luke. What is appealing in this view is the suggestion that there is a connection between the social context of the text and its purpose. While the historical events are significant, the underlining purpose involves a "legitimatization" of a new social world surrounding the Jesus movement. Borrowing from Berger and Luckmann (1966), Hedlun writes that Luke utilizes historical events to provide a socially "legitimating" element for the emerging community:

> A new social world was emerging around the person and life of Jesus. Beliefs and behaviors grounded in a particular perception of reality were forming in conflict with the macro society within which it was residing and identifying itself. Theophilus represents the 'subsequent generation' who must be convinced of the legitimacy of the Jesus group's version of reality. (Hedlun 2013, 230)

What is important for me is the idea that Luke's narrative contains evidence that reflects its social world and context. Extracting or ascertaining meaning from the text warrants exploring the social world and context embedded in the text, which is an important aspect of my study.

Another intriguing response to the question of purpose is presented in an article by James Edwards (2017). Comparing parallels in Luke and Acts, Edwards highlights a common feature of Luke's style—the use of repetitions. These are repetitions observed in the perspective of style, vocabulary, and common themes. Edwards concludes, inter alia, that the story of Jesus in Luke's Gospel provides the model and pattern for Jesus' followers in the Book of Acts (499). Luke–Acts overall presents a master-disciple paradigm in which the story of Jesus in Luke sets the prototype for his followers in Acts.

Greg W. Forbes' (2000) claim of an evangelistic motive is also worth mentioning. Claiming that the most likely audience could be non-Christian, Forbes argues that these non-Christians would share certain traits including some knowledge of "the worship of the God of Israel in the synagogue; an appreciation of the authority and content of the Old Testament (in Greek); and some knowledge of the Christian faith." From Forbes' view, Theophilus could be "representative of a wider group of

God-fearers that Luke wanted to reach." Luke's narrative then appears to be motivated, not only by a desire that it be used for discipleship and for apologetic reasons, but also for evangelistic intentions (Forbes 2000, 327)—to spread the Gospel to non-Christian communities.

After surveying the scholarly literature, I engage the possibility that Luke's primary audience necessitates steering a narrative that breaks down institutional constraints prohibiting the sharing of resources. As a companion of the apostle Paul in his trips to many urban cities across Roman provinces, Luke must have witnessed the hospitality of rich and wealthy hosts and as a result developed a certain affinity for what the rich could do to benefit the emerging Christian community. Shaped by this lived experience, Luke depicts the rich ruler as a person obedient to God's commandments who is in a position to help the emerging community of faith by sharing resources with the less fortunate. In particular, Luke's re-situating of the rich ruler implicates traditions, beliefs and certain ways of doing things that are creating institutional constraints against the sharing of resources between the rich and the less fortunate in society. The rich ruler is part of Luke's attempt to re-situate the Gospel tradition within his context.

PLACEMENT OF LUKE 18:18–30 IN LUKE'S NARRATIVE

From Luke's intended purpose, I steer my interpretive canoe to negotiate the placement of the rich ruler passage within the larger context of the Third Gospel. In this regard, I am mostly intrigued by Joel Green's claim that Luke highlights the "centrality of God's purpose to bring salvation to all" (Green 1997, 21). Green writes that "in the conflicted world of the first-century Mediterranean, not least within the larger Jewish world, it is not difficult to see how this understanding of God's purpose and its embodiment in the Christian movement would have been the source of controversy and uncertainty" (21). This suggests a sense of uncertainty and need for resolution. Against this backdrop, Green reasons that "the purpose of Luke–Acts would have been to strengthen the Christian movement in the face of opposition." Luke's purpose is to encourage the Christian movement "in their interpretation and experience of the redemptive purpose and faithfulness of God" and in their "continued faithfulness and witness in God's salvific project" (22). More significantly, Green sees

Luke as "primarily ecclesiological—concerned with the practices that define and the criteria for legitimating the community of God's people, and centered on the invitation to participate in God's project" (22).

I resonate with this last quotation, although I would add that Luke also accentuates the need to explore rules and traditions, institutional aspects shaping and influencing individual responses to the call to be part of God's community. Being "primarily ecclesiology" I argue underpins a concern for the structural aspects of God's community including its functions, constitutions and institutions. As an emerging community in "liminal space" (Bhabha 1994, 4), there is much uncertainty as it grapples with its faith in light of the surrounding environment. Thus, Luke 18:18–30 gives a sense of the conundrum confronting members of the community as they attempt to navigate the nexus between their new faith and the old ways of doing things. Green brings clarity about the function of the Lukan narrative when he writes:

> Behaviors that grow out of service in the kingdom of God take a different turn: Love your enemies. Do good to those who hate you. Extend hospitality to those who cannot reciprocate. Give without expectation of return. Such practices are possible only for those whose dispositions, whose convictions and commitments, have been reshaped by transformative encounter with the goodness of God. Within the Third Gospel, the chief competitor for this focus stems from Money—not so much money itself, but the rule of Money, manifest in the drive for social praise and, so, in forms of life designed to keep those with power and privilege segregated from those of low status, the least, the lost, and the left-out. (Green 1997, 24)

The idea that certain institutions—"rule of money" and "drive for social praise"—are competing against the transformative goodness of God is explicit. In a similar vein, Randy J. Hedlun contends that Luke's historical narrative offers a "legitimation of the Jesus movement and that movement's social constructs" (2013, 227). Within this conception, the "conflicts behind the text drive the legitimation and should inform our understanding of why Luke included specific pericopes, structuring them as he did, and should guide our apprehension of their meaning" (Hedlun 2013, 227–28).

For me, it is important to understand that Luke's purpose is not solely focused on legitimation. Rather, legitimation is part of a larger process of "re-situating" that is taking place within Luke's faith community as it tries to find its ways and means especially in light of the surrounding dominant imperial system. This means that legitimation is an aspect of the "re-situation" process taking place. This is where my lived reality of "re-situatedness" comes in. I sense there is a similar re-situatedness taking place in the contemporary world in which I live and the world in which the early Jesus movement lived.

Table 5.2 below adapts Green's outline (1997, 25–29). Based on Green's outline, the rich ruler is situated in Luke's narrative on Jesus' journey to Jerusalem. As Jesus makes his ascension to the final geographical location of his ministry, he engages his followers in stories concerning various topics including "following," wealth and power, and family life. As Green notes in another publication "wealth is intricately woven together with issues of power, status and social privilege" (Green 2003, 1888–1889).

1. The prologue (1: 1–4)
2. The birth and childhood of Jesus (1:5—2:52)
3. The preparation for the ministry of Jesus (3:1—4:13)
4. The ministry of Jesus in Galilee (4: 14–19:50)
5. On the way to Jerusalem 9:51—19:48
5.1 Discipleship: hearing and doing the word (9:51—10:42)
5.2 The fatherhood of God (11:1–13)
5.3. Jesus' behavior questioned (11:14–54)
5.4 Vigilance in the face of eschatological crisis (12:1—13:9)
5.5. Who will participate in the kingdom? (13:10—17:10)
5.6 Responding to the kingdom (17:11—19:27)
    5.61 Gratitude from a foreign leper (17:11–19)
    5.62 Faithfulness at the coming of the son of man (17:20—18:8)
        5.621 When is the kingdom? (17:20–21)
        5.622 Where is the kingdom? (17:22–37)
        5.623 Faithfulness in anticipation (18:1–8)
    5.63 How to enter the kingdom (18:9—19:27)
        5.631 A parable concerning the self-possessed (18:9–14)
        5.632 Receiving children, receiving the kingdom (18:15–17)
        5.633 The problem of power and wealth (18:18–30)
        5.634 The enigma of Jesus' suffering (18:31–34)
        5.635 The irony of blindness (18:35–43)
        5.636 Who is a son of Abraham? (19:1–10)

5.637 Those who refuse the King (19:11–27)

5.7 Jesus arrives in Jerusalem (19:28–48)

6. Teaching in the Jerusalem temple (20:1—21:38)

7. The suffering and death of Jesus (22:1—23:56)

8. The exaltation of Jesus (24:1–53)

(Green 1997, 25–29)

Table 5.2: Outline of the Gospel of Luke

Luke's story of the ruler, inter alia, epitomizes constraints associated with power and wealth. Notwithstanding the influence of power and wealth, I argue that the passage offers an opportunity to explore the nexus or connection between two sets of institutional systems—kingdom of God and the reality of society. The story exhibits Luke's contextualization of the Gospel story to fit the shifting currents of social, political, economic and cultural environment. As it does this, it can bring us to a more nuanced and complex approach and attitude towards Luke's re-situating of the Gospel narrative within the dominant imperial system (Miller 2014, 342). Moreover, I argue that it serves as an illustration of the uncertainty within the emerging community itself with regards to its own Judaic heritage. I am conscious of how the Judaic heritage may play an important role. Nonetheless, my focus in this study on the political-economic context necessitates setting up the analysis in a manner that may not show well how the Judaic heritage functions. To show well how the Judaic heritage functions may require a different approach, outside the scope of this study.

LUKE 18:18–30 AS A CHALLENGE-RESPONSE

Guided by the wisdom of the *tautai ama*, I am conscious that there are other things that may be important but could divert from my focus to bring home the catch of the day. In this regard, I steer my reading with the aim of re-situating the ruler in a positive light. Based on my attempt to re-situate the rich ruler story, the flow and progressive texture of the text strongly suggests that the overall dynamics of the encounter between Jesus and the ruler from verses 18–25 resemble that of a challenge-response[1] social communication (Malina and Neyrey 1991b, 51).

---

1. I find Vernon Robbins's (1996a, 80–82) description of the "challenge-response" social communication very instructive in my analysis of the encounter between Jesus and the rich ruler.

The ruler in verse 18 first enters into Jesus' space by issuing a challenge. The challenge sets the framework for explicating some of the institutional rules, norms, beliefs, and even social constraints that "govern" and "guide" admission into God's Kingdom. I am not totally convinced that the intent of διδάσκαλος ἀγαθός in verse 18 is flattery as some have suggested (Fitzmyer 1985, 1199) or some contention that Luke is following a common Hellenistic salutation (Wolter 2016, 330). I associate myself with Kenneth Bailey's line of argument cited in James Metzger (2007, 162). The text reflects a certain convention of communication in the Oriental world. More importantly, it gives support to the claim that the ruler's demeanor and behavior exhibits someone knowledgeable and well instructed in the rules of communication as well as conducting formal conversations and conversations with superiors. From that perspective, I argue that the undertone of the text suggests a decentering of the individual. Neither the individual character nor the psychological aspect of the ruler is central to the passage, but rather there are more nuanced interactions in the text that are reflective of society. The story of the rich ruler has more to do with social interactions and relationships in society than with a particular response.

That this is a positive challenge is signaled by the ruler seeking a "benefit" from Jesus. Utilizing institutional knowledge, I argue that the challenge seeks resolution to an institutional dilemma. While it is obvious that the ruler's challenge puts Jesus on the spot (Malina and Neyrey 1991b, 52), I add that it is also Luke's less conspicuous way of telling another story. That other story anticipates the conundrum confronting members of Luke's faith community. When the "new way of doing things" as a result of "following" Christ comes face-to-face with the lived reality of society, the outcome is often a sense of uncertainty and bafflement. It is uncertainty and bafflement about a tenet or institution of Jewish belief (eternal life) for a person who is wealthy. I am interested, therefore, to add more contexts to the reality implied in the narrative for the social location of the implied author. For this purpose, I revert to Vernon Robbins's description of the implied author's social location. Describing the thought implied in the Lukan narrative Robbins suggests that

> It is advantageous to adopt a stance of respect that evokes a social location slightly below but in communication with people who have higher status in the social structure. Thus, although the thought of the implied author is near the artisan class, and holds no disdain for artisan labor, there is a social posture of

communicating upwards in the social order rather than downward to artisans or peasants. (Robbins 1991, 322–33)

This quotation suggests a more nuanced thought process reflecting a social location that warrants navigating multi-relations. In other words, the thought process implied in the text suggests an interaction that is more dyadic and multi-relational than individualistic.

One important aspect of the challenge in verse 18 stems from the use of κληρονομέω. In most instances in the New Testament, this verb is associated with eschatology or something in the future (e.g., 1 Cor 6:10, 1 Cor 15: 50, Gal 5:21—kingdom of God; Heb 1:14—salvation). In 1 Peter 3:9, however, the blessing that is inherited underpins something of material value, bounty or gift. I am not saying there is a direct connection between 1 Peter and Luke 18, but I think it is plausible that this could be the meaning intended here. As a ruler—someone with authority, status, and legal standing within the political economy—the challenge he puts to Jesus includes a concern about things of material value, namely, economic blessings. As such, the ruler's challenge reflects a concern with human capacity, meritocracy.

Based on this assumption, it is compelling for me to think that the meaning of κληρονομέω in this story includes inheriting, acquiring or coming into possession (BDAG s.v. κληρονομέω). The meaning has a double connotation, referring to things both inherited and acquired. On one hand, acquiring something suggests a reliance on the action or deeds of the doer. On the other hand, someone who inherits suggests someone who does not have to earn. Thus, there is a contradiction in the ruler's inquiry (Craddock 1990, 213), someone who inherits yet suggests someone earning.

More significantly, the use of κληρονομέω underpins a conundrum that differentiates between "insiders" and "outsiders." Perceived in this way, perhaps the narrative embodies the conundrum of someone on the "outside" looking "in." From this perspective, the ruler shares some similarities with the rich man in Luke 16 who disregards Lazarus in that he belongs more to the "outside rich than to the village" (Moxnes 1988, 57). As a result, the story of the ruler suggests an interface in Luke between groups divided by boundary markers[2] with distinctive sets of institutions that divide one group from another.

---

2. To understand the notion of boundary markers I consulted the works of Gupta (2013, 279), Dinkler (2016, 349), Ehrensperger (2019, 106), Gasper (2004, 320), and Cohick (2010, 74).

Jesus's rejoinder is compelling for the fact that he replicates a subset of rules and institutional means from the Ten Commandments which mainly have to do with social interactions or relationships with other people (Lioy 2017, 2). The fact that the ruler has kept these since he was young intimates that these are rules and traditions that have become institutionalized over time and have shaped and influenced the ways things are done in the community. Derivatively, the passage suggests an exploration of the institutional system, perhaps also Luke is calling for a re-situation of the boundary markers that set apart those on the inside and those on the outside.

I am aware of James A. Metzger's assumption that due to the presence of the postpositive particle γάρ, verse 25 is viewed as expanding on the general observation in verse 24 (Metzger 2007, 167n26). After surveying the possibilities, my sense is it is too simplistic to assume the rich as the sole referent. Rather, I am swayed by the evidence that the passage is of a nuanced purpose. By focusing on institutional influence on relationship and social interactions, the passage underpins systemic ways of interactions and relationships, dynamics within a community. More than wealth and riches, the passage underpins a concern for other institutional aspects of society including certain ways of doing things that separate and divide people.

Concerning the analogy of the camel and the eye of the needle the majority of interpretations often place emphasis on the rich. Even though many have attempted to soften the impact of the hyperbole, the corollary has been to highlight the impossible task confronting someone rich and wealthy (Phillips 2003, 167; Hellerman 2000, 143). The two images "represent the impossibility of the wealthy entering into the kingdom" (Stanley 2006, 49 footnote 20). Weighing the possibilities, I am not quite convinced of the suggestion that the intent of the passage is to focus solely on the wealthy. When the ruler is introduced in verse 18, he is described as a certain person. The crucial description πλούσιος σφόδρα is only introduced in verse 23. It is reasonable therefore to assume that the intent of the passage is more nuanced and multi-valent, rather than a singular focus on the rich and wealthy. This is also matched in the subsequent shift of focus to ἴδιος in verse 28 and the ensuing Jesus monologue from verse 29–30. The shift intimates the significance of family and relations or the lack thereof as suggested by Peter. That to me is a decentering of the text. Rather than a singular focus on the individual, the passage warrants a more holistic exploration of the situation of the text as implied also in the argument that there are also other unknown hearers in verse 26 (Wolter 2016, 328). This resonates also with the contention that Luke carries a certain attitude towards wealth (Fitzmyer 1981, 248).

More significantly, I argue that at the heart of this passage, Luke is concerned with the rules, regulations, traditions, and beliefs that have institutionalized disparity and poverty in society. The story of the rich ruler is a challenge to the overall system that perpetuates boundaries and social barriers. These boundaries have constrained the rich from sharing their wealth and being "hospitable" to the "others" in society. The challenge for followers is to be "responsible with wealth." As postulated above, Luke himself may have been an eye witness to the good that the generosity of the rich and wealthy patrons could bring to the emerging community of followers. Even without patrons, it is possible given that the "typical" Christian in Luke's context would be "a free artisan or small trader." Some would have been wealthy and rich enough to have "had houses, slaves, the ability to travel, and other signs of wealth" and they would provide "housing, meeting places, and other services for individual Christians and for whole groups" (Meeks 1983, 73). Yet, because of institutional constraints, this may include as a result of social, cultural, ideological and religious aspects, that equal distribution of wealth and sharing of resources between the rich and poor is untenable. Luke, therefore, is cognizant of the conundrum facing the community of faith, especially if the universality of God's salvation is to include people of all nations (Thompson 2010, 322). Weighing the possibilities, my sense is that it is by exploring the social, cultural, and ideological situation of the text that we begin to appreciate these other telling aspects of the narrative.

SOCIAL AND CULTURAL ANALYSIS OF THE TEXT

Vernon Robbins (1996) provides a systematic approach that allows for exploring the social and cultural situation of the text. Such an innovative undertaking allows space for the interpreter to isolate the social and cultural situation of the text using "sociological and anthropological theory" (71). The corollary is to engage the text in search of the social and cultural "location of the language and the type of social and cultural world the language evokes in us" (71). Thus far, I am interested in the institutional aspects and the underpinning ideologies of how and why people do things in a certain way. Just as the *tautai ama* circumnavigates the crests and troughs of the waves, I situate and locate meaning with the social and cultural textures of the text.

The ἄρχων and Social Features of the Text

Looking at the literary features of Luke 18:18–30, there are certain words and phrases that provide clues which may be reasoned as indicative of the social and cultural features of the text. Bruce Malina sheds light that "it is the meanings of first-century Mediterranean social systems that are realized by means of words in texts from that time and place" (1987, 358). In this regard, I find that the word ἄρχων in particular appears to be an important signifier. It is used 8 times throughout Luke (See Table 5.3). With the exception of Luke 11:15 (in which some of Jesus' opponents were saying that his power to cast out demons was by Beelzebul, the "ruler of the demons"), ἄρχων is exclusively employed to signal human agents, and to some extent it is closely associated with authority and status. It follows then that the ἄρχων in Luke 18:18–30 is highly likely to be a person in a position of authority and status. He could be someone who has access to resources and hence has better than average financial means, someone who is not considered poor in the first century.

More significantly, he may very well be someone who plays an important role in the management scheme of the household, someone who plays a key role in its decision-making (Dyck 2013). The ἄρχων would be in a position with authority to shape the allocation and distribution of goods and services within his household if not the jurisdiction over which he holds authority.

Luke 8:41	Just then there came a man named Jairus, a leader of the synagogue. He fell at Jesus' feet and begged him to come to his house,
Luke 11:15	But some of them said, "He casts out demons by Beelzebul, the ruler of the demons."
Luke 12:58	Thus, when you go with your accuser before a magistrate, on the way make an effort to settle the case, or you may be dragged before the judge, and the judge hand you over to the officer, and the officer throw you in prison.
Luke 14:1	On one occasion when Jesus was going to the house of a leader of the Pharisees to eat a meal on the sabbath, they were watching him closely.

Luke 18:18	A certain ruler asked him, "Good Teacher, what must I do to inherit eternal life?"
Luke 23:13	Pilate then called together the chief priests, the leaders, and the people,
Luke 23:35	And the people stood by, watching; but the leaders scoffed at him, saying, "He saved others; let him save himself if he is the Messiah1 of God, his chosen one!"
Luke 24:20	and how our chief priests and leaders handed him over to be condemned to death and crucified him.

Table 5.3: Luke's use of ἄρχων

Walter Wink's (1984, 13) profile of the use of ἄρχων in New Testament writings suggests that it refers to "human power arrangements" and "incumbents-in-office." While power is sometimes understood in ancient societies as a confluence of both spiritual and material aspects (Wink 1984, 3), I argue that the ἄρχων in Luke 18: 18–30 approximates a human agent and an incumbent in office.

Regarding the social surrounding of the ἄρχων in Luke 18:18–30, there is not much information available. While Joseph A. Fitzmyer identifies the ἄρχων as a Palestinian magistrate, no further information is given on what that may have meant (Fitzmyer 1985, 1198). One can only assume as I mentioned above that the ἄρχων is someone in a position of power and authority.

From the perspective of a *tautai ama*, I engage the possibility that the ἄρχων is a member of the Sanhedrin (Danker 2000, 140) or as I. Howard Marshall suggests, a leader of the synagogue (1978, 684). It is reasonable to argue that Luke surely would have mentioned if the rich ruler were a member of the Sanhedrin or a leader of the synagogue. The greatest likelihood is that he is a regional magistrate, which was enabled by ownership of land, which in Jewish circles usually pointed to membership in a priestly family line. The strength of this argument is buttressed by the fact that the ἄρχων is clearly learned in the Torah and exhibited as a devout adherent at an early age. And while there is no direct description of the social situation in the text, we can still gather enough evidence from the literature to make some observations about institutional aspects of social and cultural life in first-century Mediterranean society.

The best argument, in my opinion, is that as a wealthy Jewish ruler the ἄρχων is a landowner. And as a Jewish landowner, he probably is a member of a priestly family, because ownership of land was assigned and then inherited by priestly families. As a wealthy Jewish person who is a "ruler," namely a regional magistrate, he can most surely be identified as a Jewish *paterfamilias*, which may seem to be a strange confluence of terms, but I think may accurately describe what Luke has in mind in the story.

That the ἄρχων is treated "sympathetically" (Marshall 1978, 684) reaffirms the claim that the emphasis is not so much on the rich ruler as on his social environment. Moreover, this would also resonate with the notion that the first-century Mediterranean person "was not individualistic" but rather "dyadic or group-oriented" (Malina and Neyrey 1991a, 72–73). By addressing the social, cultural and ideological environment of the ἄρχων one can begin to appreciate some of the contextual relational dynamics in the text. In general, the ruler is primarily a function of the social environment and systemic institutions. The corollary is that the behavior and response of the ἄρχων correlates with the institutions around him. This resonates with the claim that Luke is also concerned with the "typical institutions of [his] society" including "the family, politics, the city, the countryside, patron-client relations, and the health care system" (Neyrey 1991, xiii).

I am always aware of the possibility of other things taking place in the text. Nonetheless, my aim is to maintain focus so that I am not distracted from the catch of the day. In this regard, the overall evidence leads me to make some general observations concerning the story of the ruler. First, there is reasonable evidence to suggest that the ἄρχων is a Jewish *paterfamilias* who is evidently a ruler over a district. This would mean he very likely is a member of a priestly family. While some may have suggested in the scholarship, the evidence is not clear enough that he is a member of the Sanhedrin. It is very likely also that the ἄρχων would have also been exposed to the imperial system of rules, processes, structures, and organizations that were institutions that guide decision-making and individual responses. In this regard, the ἄρχων externalizes the effects of an imperial institutional system that demarcates boundary markers that create conflict among people of the community.

Second, the ἄρχων externalizes the contrast between the poor and the rich in society. In a society where honor and shame are critical, I conjecture that the ἄρχων plays a rather influential role in the dynamics of social relations. With status and influence, the ἄρχων could be someone who has wealth and possibly has financial relations within society. Based on this assumption, I argue that the text offers a contrast between two contrasting life styles, between the ἄρχων and those living on the margins of society—the poor, the women, the children, and the needy. Reading this through an institutional prism, we get a glimpse of two different institutional systems for those on the inside and those on the outside—those on the periphery and those in the center of society.

Moreover, the ἄρχων is often portrayed as someone with a self-interested mindset. His response is interpreted as of a type of mindset that "asks not on behalf of all in the crowd or for their benefit but for himself alone" (Metzger 2007, 161). Like a *tautai ama*, I steer my interpretive canoe around other things represented in the text and focus instead on my experience as a Samoan father and member of the *aiga*. From this perspective, I have a strong sense that it is implausible to think someone of the nature of the ἄρχων is not free from the influence of other institutional constraints. Even for someone rich, there are always constraints that have to be taken into consideration. In light of this, I conjecture that the text represents an exploration of the mindset merited by an emerging community of believers in Christ.

ἄρχων and Lack of *Aiga* (Family)

As a result of the previous exploration, I ask if it might be possible to learn something about the ἄρχων and his *aiga* from my Samoan context and also from what I have learned from the scholarship on Mediterranean society in the first-century. In this regard, I envision someone in the capacity similar to the *matai sa'o* (primary chief) in the Samoan context. Despite the lack of explicit mention of family, I ask whether the text already presupposes the reader will be familiar with the social environment of the ἄρχων. As mentioned above, this is inferred from the use of ἴδιος in verse 28 which has within its range of meanings, home or possessions (BDAG s.v. ἴδιος). By referring to "our homes," Peter clarifies and concretizes the social situation surrounding the ἄρχων. While there is no mention of family in the rich ruler story, I am also buoyed by John H. Elliott's claim (1991) that part of Luke's emphasis is on human interaction. His purpose is not just to give background to an "independent message," but more significantly, "to give that message concrete content and shape in space and time and human interaction" (Elliott 1991, 221). Luke is a historiographer as well as a theologian whose aim is "to convince his Christian audience of the certainty of the things they have been taught

(Luke 1:1–4) so as to strengthen faith and commitment" (221). For these reasons, the ἄρχων should be treated not as an isolated individual but as a person who has relations and interactions with others, possibly within a family.

It is also revealing that many attempts to draw parallels between the ἄρχων and Zacchaeus in Luke 19:1–10 (Hays 2012, 60) seem to overlook a familial element in the analysis. Bruno Dyck's correlation between the ἄρχων and the οἶκος is compelling (2013, 56). The word οἶκος is significant in Luke's Gospel, with variations in its usage appearing more than 50 times in Luke. This emphasis on the οἶκος places a great premium on organizational management (Dyck 2013, 4), which includes not only managing relationships within the household but also relationships between one's own οἶκος and other people's households. Dyck notes that:

> In the first century, this arena of management was regulated by the norms and customs associated with patron-client relationships. In simple terms this meant trying to develop long-term relationships so that other *oikoi* would become subservient to your *oikos*. For example, if a peasant *oikos* received a loan from an elite *oikos*, the peasant *oikos* would thereby become the long-term client of the richer patron. (Dyck 2013, 5)

This statement adds further context to the relationship between the ἄρχων and the οἶκος. Also, it calls attention to the importance of rules, norms and customs that mold and determine intra-household and inter-household relationships. Re-situating these relationships and interactions appears to be at the heart of the conundrum confronting members of the emerging community of faith.

While the story of the rich ruler does not explicitly exhibit the relation of this ἄρχων to his οἶκος, the story of Zacchaeus does. Indeed, Jesus implicitly insists on participating in Zacchaeus' family when he says "it is necessary" (δεῖ) for him to stay in his house with him (19:5). Here the Lukan narrative seems to include explicitly the requirement of the ἄρχων to navigate the perpetual interface between his own household and the growing faith developing community among those who follow Jesus. It may be that the emphasis in the Zacchaeus story is on the rich tax collector's repentance from the idolatry of Mammon (Kim 2008, 142). In contrast, the story of the rich ruler may offer yet another form of "following" Christ, one that is possible by living responsibly with wealth, even within the context of *aiga*. In particular, the rich ruler story shows how institutional systems are precluding better distribution of resources and sharing of materials in emerging communities who claim to follow Christ faithfully.

ἄρχων—A Member of a Subgroup

The notion that the story of the ruler underpins an alternative view of institutional systems leads me to explore the subject of group formation. This is important to lend support to my argument above. As discussed earlier, I am assuming that the Lukan narrative is also dealing with "re-situating" the emerging community of faith in an environment that faces the challenge of fulfilling discipleship within family and community structures rather than leaving these structures to participate in an itinerant mode of discipleship. The question that the ἄρχων puts to Jesus demonstrates an attempt to be re-situated in this new environment. In this "re-situating," I am drawn to the possibility that in the rich ruler, Luke is navigating the uncertainty about the tenet of Jewish belief that focuses on honoring one's father and mother. Among other responsibilities, this includes the special challenges facing rich and prosperous Christians who now must live responsibly with wealth in the emerging community of followers.

In this regard, I find resonance with Brawley's claim that Luke's intent is to revisit the notion of inclusion and exclusion (Brawley 2016, 251). In particular, Luke's story of the ruler adds to the context in which an emerging faith community takes form and shape. I would imagine that in light of Luke's community of first-century Christian believers, especially in a society of honor and shame, there is much to learn from ascertaining elements of group development dynamics.

To explicate this claim, I find Bruce J. Malina's (2012) work on group development instructive. First, Malina starts with an explanation of some common truisms in the social sciences. These social science "truisms" according to Malina are largely a product of "the mid-twentieth century" (2012, 4). They include the notion that "human beings are socialized and encultured in a specific social system, at a given time and place" (4). As a result, they are able to share meanings with others in their social group through the expression of "language, gesture, artifacts, and the like." Subsequently, this shared meaning expresses "the social system at a given time and place, into which the persons communicating have been enculturated." Thus, "whatever persons perceived, they perceive according to the social presuppositions they bring to the events they perceive" (Malina 2012, 4).

The final presuppositions listed by Malina deal with the historical Jesus. While the analysis of the historical Jesus is outside the scope of this study, I am including the two presuppositions as further evidence of how first-century people are characterized as group oriented, hence, the process of socialization and enculturation are significant.

First, Jesus "was socialized and enculturated in hellenized Israelite peasant society, hence influenced by what we today call Hellenism as it was assimilated in Israelite peasant village life in that section of the Roman province of Syria called Galilee" (Malina 2012, 4–5). And second, Malina holds that Jesus "was socialized and enculturated into a high-context society." A high-context society "produces sketchy and impressionistic documents, leaving much to the reader's or hearer's imagination and common knowledge" (5).

Malina's description of the above social science truism offers support to my earlier claim. That is, the individual is situated within the relevant social system. Through an institutional prism, the ἄρχων also represents a social system, social and cultural institutions. To read the story of the ἄρχων simply as an individual response misses the nuances and complexities merited of the passage.

Following his description of the above social science truism, Malina then provides a sketch of the life of Jesus using the pattern of group development. There are two types of groups according to Malina, task group and support group. Jesus' faction in Malina's assessment is a task group, to proclaim "the forthcoming theocracy to Israel" (2012, 10). Accordingly, as a task group, it has five phases: forming, storming, norming, performing and adjourning. Forming "occurs when the group is put together" (12). Groups are put together to either "accomplish some extragroup task or for intragroup support." For example, the group Jesus recruited "was a group with an extragroup task to perform" (12)

The second phase is storming. In this phase, those invited are engaged in some form of competition "jockeying for position and ease into interpersonal stance" (Malina 2012, 12). Members "become more assertive, and each tries to change the group's purpose to satisfy personal needs" (12). It is intriguing that Malina locates the Lukan version of the rich ruler narrative within this phase, interpreting it as part of a "general concern for reward" (12). This portrays the ἄρχων as representing Luke's claim of those members who are "competitive" in nature and think only of themselves.

The third phase norming, is "marked by interpersonal conflict resolution in favor of mutually agreed upon patterns of behavior" (12). This involves negotiating "clearer guidelines" to resolve conflict (Malina 2012, 13).

The performing phase is when group members "carry out the program for which the group was assembled." Members have been able to resolve their conflicts and "work together productively." The final phase in group development is adjourning in which "group members gradually disengage from activities in a way that reflects their effort to cope with the group's approaching end" (Malina 2012, 13).

The usefulness of Malina's description of group development is it adds perspective to the possible relations that are guiding and framing the context of the ἄρχων in the passage. One of the possibilities is the dynamics with other group members in the rich ruler story reflects a movement beyond the storming phase into the norming phase. In this regard, I conjecture that the ἄρχων is very much in the same grouping as the disciples. It is a group whose dynamics are still forming and developing. From this perspective, I ask whether the ἄρχων also represents a particular "subgroup" in Luke's re-situating of the text. He and Peter are similar in that both are standing on the outside looking in. The contrast is in wealth. The text seems to suggest Peter is poor and the ruler is rich. But when Peter asks Jesus about leaving their families, he speaks not only for the other disciples but also for the ἄρχων. They underpin the norming phase, negotiating relational conflicts borne of the interface between the emerging Jesus group and the two conflated institutional systems they were more familiar with: an externally imperially-induced system of relations, and an internally Judaic system of interactions.

The ἄρχων Underpins a Reformist Narrative

The basis of my argument so far for a fresh look at the passage is instead of emphasizing the rich and wealthy ἄρχων perhaps there is more to gain from conceiving a systematic overview of his contextual environment. It is my humble opinion that the passage underscores a certain view of social and cultural institutions in society. Vernon Robbins's (1996a, 72) description of the specific social topics is instructive. Subsequently, I argue that the text of Luke 18:18–30 underscores the social rhetoric of a reformist.

A reformist according to Robbins "views the world as corrupt because its social structures are corrupt. If the structures can be changed so that the behaviors they sanction are changed, then salvation will be present in the world" (73). More importantly, "this response then assumes that evil may be dealt with according to supernaturally given insights about the ways in which social organization should be amended" (73). Finally, "investigation of the ways of the world and recommendations for amending it are the essential orientation" (Robbins 1996a, 73).

The above description fits well with the basic assumption that guides my steering as I approach the text from an institutional perspective. By having the ἄρχων challenge Jesus, Luke 18:18–30 opens up a window of opportunity to propose a different form of discipleship that "honors one's father and mother," possibly by trying to continue to live responsibly with wealth. Moreover, it opens up an opportunity to challenge the "structural arrangements" or institutional aspects of society that encircle social relations in society. The ἄρχων then plays an important role in the social rhetoric of the text. He is a simple cog caught in the confluence of various institutional systems in society. As a strict adherent of the Ten Commandments, as a member of the imperial institutional system, and as a leader of his household, we see in the ἄρχων the externalization of these constraints.

Jesus's demand to sell everything and give to the poor challenges the lived reality of the ἄρχων that demands a drastic systematic institutional reform. Could it be then that for Luke, Jesus' imperative challenges even the rules and traditions governing relationships and interactions within the homes, the family? More crucially, rather than ignoring families and one's responsibilities at home, instead it calls for an expansion of the concept of family, of the *aiga*. This in turn warrants breaking down boundary markers and institutional constraints that have led to the division between those who have the means and those who do not within the emerging faith community.

From the perspective of *tautai ama*, my goal is to steer a biblical reading that puts the ἄρχων in a more positive light. For it is through him that Luke challenges the institutional constraints impeding people in society. It is only by asking about eternal life that space is provided in the text to explore the negotiation taking place between one's faith and lived reality. It is a rubber meets road moment in the Lukan narrative, re-appropriating the Gospel narrative within the reality of imperial rule.

The ἄρχων as a Dominant Culture Rhetoric

Cultural location according to Vernon Robbins "concerns the manner in which people present their propositions, reasons, and arguments both to themselves and to other people" (1996a, 86). Perusing the five types of cultural rhetoric identified by Robbins, I find reasonable support for the argument that Luke's account of the ἄρχων exhibits elements of a dominant culture rhetoric. The challenge-response between Jesus and the ἄρχων underpins an institutionalized "system of attitudes, values, dispositions, and norms . . . supported by social structures vested with power to impose its goals on people" (86). That there are two contrasting systems is suggested by the ἄρχων "on the outside" asking Jesus the question of how to inherit eternal life. Jesus' rejoinder acknowledges the existence of a system that is grounded in the Ten Commandments. The ἄρχων in response clearly accepts this as the dominant culture. His submission that "I have kept all these since my youth" (Luke 18: 21 NRSV) substantiates claims of a "meticulous record of law-keeping" leading to a "sterling reputation" (Lioy 2017, 129). As alluded to above, it is plausible that the ἄρχων's pedigree is an offshoot of a particular culture. As someone working "under the authority of the Roman government and exercised judicial as well as administrative responsibilities" (Lioy 2017, 129), there is reason to believe that part of the ἄρχων's constitution is shaped and molded by an imperial cultural system.

Just like any other cultural system, an imperial cultural system is supported by institutions including rules, traditions, and norms. The ἄρχων all his life lived through that system, those institutions. I am intrigued therefore with the observation that the ἄρχων in asking Jesus about eternal life perhaps is anticipating a "scrupulous observance of edicts" (Lioy 2017, 129). In the ἄρχων there is a manifestation of a system with clear boundary markers defining groupings of people, shaping and influencing individual behavior and attitudes. It is a system that breeds a dominant culture with the mindset of exclusivity and of holding on to one's possessions and relationships. The individual therefore is captured within that dominant culture with its institutions breeding exclusivity and self-aggrandizement.

Moreover, the ἄρχων's question also reflects a cultural system that perhaps sees eternal life as based primarily on meritocracy. The ἄρχων evidently sees eternal life as a commodity, something that can be "transaction-ed" and acquired through strict observation of the existing system's rules and regulations. Could it be possible then that Luke is offering a counter or alternative culture. It is not an undoing of the existing Mosaic cultural system, but rather a re-situating of it. This resonates with Robbins's statement about counterculture that it's "underlying theme is the hope of voluntary reform by the dominant society of an alternative, better way of life" (1996a, 87). As such, the demand to sell everything and give to the poor offers a glimpse into the type of institutional reform warranted for a re-situation. Based on the observation that eternal life is about a relationship with God (O'Day 2003, 1942), I argue therefore that the imperative to sell everything and give to the poor underpins an expression of a new institutional cultural system. This offing re-situates existing boundary markers that have created and contributed much to the unequal distribution of resources and the demarcation between those on the "outside" and those on the "inside" of society. This also supports part of my argument that in the ruler Luke is offering another form of discipleship, one that lives responsibly with wealth.

Drawing upon the wisdom of the *tautai ama*, I circumnavigate other things to look for evidence of liminal cultural rhetoric in the text. Robbins writes that "liminal culture exists among individuals and groups that have never been able to establish a clear social and cultural identity in their setting" (1996a, 88). The nature of the text indicates a "dialectic of culture and identification that has neither binary nor hierarchical clarity." Jesus' public declaration regarding the impossibility of human wealth finding its own way naturally toward eternal life serves as not only a warning against wealth and power but also the dissolution of a cultural system that prioritizes possession and status. In this regard, the text exposes a cultural system that uses wealth and possession as a boundary marker. Instead, the text encourages a re-situation of relationships and interactions based on new rules and institutions that are moored in the practical life of society.

Peter's reaction most of all underpins the "liminal" rhetoric of the text. His query in verse 28 and Jesus's response in verse 29 underpins a re-situation of one's home, possessions, and relationships. This necessitates a re-situation of one's mindset to adjust to one's new and emerging social and cultural environment. Moreover, it merits re-situation of one's own sense of identity.

IDEOLOGICAL ASPECTS OF LUKE 18:18–30

To gain more perspective, I situate meaning with my social location. I steer around other things to engage with the social location implied in the text. I see ideological analysis as space for such dyadic interaction. In other words, it provides space for my context to engage with the ideological context of the text. More importantly, it gives space for other interpreters to engage in my interpretation of the text (Robbins 1996a, 95). As a reader, I bring an ideological agenda to the text (Piotrowski 2016, 21). I explore how the text of Luke 18:18–30 could have been symptomatic of first-century readers' worldview and derivatively how that worldview speaks to contemporary society. In this regard, I agree with the contention that the text's so-called "ideological power" is "ultimately imposed from without" or in other words from my interaction with the text (Metzger 2007, 46n226). Subsequently, I begin with my own worldview. I explore the text from my social location, my situation and my subsequent interaction with the text. I read by pushing the boundaries of the text meanwhile keeping focus so that I am not diverted from the process of catching.

My Situation

Living in the U.S. for more than twenty years changed how I see myself. As intimated earlier, I resonate more with the notion of a Samoan "living in-between." The lived reality of "living-in-between" shapes and influences my worldview. Again, it is not to dominate nor is it my desire to impose my worldview on the text. Nonetheless, my ideological stance is largely a function of my lived reality. By the same token, my lived reality reflects also my ideological tendencies.

Working on Capitol Hill could be demanding at times. Nonetheless, I was buoyed by optimism knowing that I was doing the work of the people. I also made some friends on the Hill and crossed paths with all kinds of people, including people from other States, of other races, ethnicities, and of various political orientations. I learned golf and became a weekend golf player, an important cultural aspect of Washington D.C. in addition to its historical monuments and statutes.

Meanwhile, I was still keeping touch with my Samoan culture and Christian faith. As a member of the Samoan Church Community attending *lotu* (worship service) at the Fort Myer U.S. Army chapel, an inter-denominational church made up of mainly current and retired

Samoan military personnel and federal government employees, I enjoyed singing in the church choir and attending monthly prayer meetings. My favorite activity without a doubt is the regular Sunday *toonais* (feast, lunch) where the sometimes-partisan discussion covers matters of politics, economics, and sports, as well as timely commentaries on the news from the Samoa Islands.[3]

Through annual events like the Pacific Fun Day and to some extent the Cherry Blossom Festival, the Washington, DC, Samoan community became involved with other Pacific Island and Asian communities. There were also many collaborative events hosted by the Office of the American Samoa Delegate to the U.S. Congress that called for the participation of the Samoan community. Overall, I found myself in a socially-diverse as well as culturally rich situation.

When I left the U.S. in 2013 to enter the ministry at the Malua Theological College in Samoa, I did it mainly for personal interest. My prayer was for God to save my mother and in return I would give up everything and go into the ministry. She was stricken with cancer and at 82 years old she did not have the will to go through rounds of chemotherapy. As the youngest of her seven children, and seeing my mother's strength slowly ebbing away, I desperately wanted to do anything to save her out of my own naivete. It did not matter that I just bought a house in the nice comfortable urban setting of Virginia with the security of federal government employment and good friends. All I thought of at the time was to fulfill a promise made to my mother but most of all for God to save her. Yet, the day I entered the ministry was the day my mother passed away.

Reflecting on my personal journey, the story of the rich ruler continues to haunt my imagination, my rationale. I find the narrative on the ἄρχων unsettling and perplexing. I find that there is often some disconnect between one's faith and the practicality of life. The demand to give up everything appears to be the requisite for most religious beliefs. That has become the rallying call to muster blind devotion and faithful

---

3. The Samoa Islands historically consist of one people sharing the same language, culture, faith and almost everything. It was not until the Washington Convention of 1899 that an agreement was reached between Britain, Germany and the United States whereby the Eastern Islands of Samoa consisting of Tutuila and Aunu'u were ceded to the U.S. while Germany gained control of the western islands including Upolu and Savaii (Lebowitz 1980, 229). Manua was later ceded to the U.S. in 1904. Tutuila, Aunu'u and Manu'a became American Samoa, an unincorporated and unorganized territory of the United States, whereas the western islands, after gaining independence in 1962, later became the Independent State of Samoa. When I speak of myself as a Samoan, I see myself as part of a people, not a political entity.

commitment. Yet, taken literally, it underpins a total disregard and ignorance of one's situation and relations including children, wife, and family. This to me is perplexing and something I struggle with. It is an apparent disregard for the practicality of faith (Carter 2015, 466).

The more I read the story of the rich ruler, the more I identify with his social and cultural location. When I started theological training in 2013, it was a tremendous challenge having to re-situate myself in a new social and cultural reality. After living in a totally different environment of "climbing the corporate ladder," returning to Samoa was not easy. I struggled not only with having to re-start at the undergraduate level of theological training, but also with the college's monastic life style. This is not in any way serving judgment on the institution. It is only to reflect on the divergence in worldview that often leads to some difficulties and perhaps a conundrum that even the present-day believer still wrestles with. To get re-situated warrants resetting of the mindset and adjusting to the rules and traditions, the norms and beliefs that constitute the institutional environment. It is in a lot of ways a decentering of one's epistemological center and peripherals. Yet, navigating this re-situating also necessitates perpetual reconciliation and adaptation to changes in one's lived reality.

Life at MTC underpins collective responsibility. The individual is expected to live within the confines of the rules, norms, traditions, and value system—institutions that underpin a communal or collective interest. Individuality is often suppressed to the point of marginality. Coming from the U.S. where the rights and freedom of the individual are religiously and constitutionally protected to a society where communal interest takes precedence, negotiating the boundary and space in between can be challenging. This negotiation in my opinion could have been an alternative understanding of the ideological conundrum in Luke 18:18–30.

Rich Ruler and Society

I read to liberate the ruler, yet always cautious that I am not diverted from what I desire to bring in as the day's catch. I argue that the text does underpin a worldview grounded in lived experience. The story of the ruler conveys a sense of navigating some disparate systems of institutions. For an emerging church community, the story of the ruler reflects the ideological conundrum confronting a growing and multi-faceted community. There are external and internal ways of doing things or rules of the game. Institutionally, the presence of the imperial system of institutions is a significant consideration (Santandreu 2018, 11; Tanzer 2017, 632). Even an individual in an emerging faith community in the course of a lifetime of service has the opportunity to acquire wealth and power (Fiensy 2014, 196).

Within the developing community of believers itself, there is also a demarcation between those on the inside and those on the outside. Navigating and negotiating these boundary markers underpin the story of the rich ruler. Overall, while I agree with some of the contentions that Luke seems to oscillate between a pro-empire and an apologetic stance, I argue for something far more delicate. As stated above, I am not fully content with the argument that Luke sees the story of the ruler as only about wealth and power but about constraints. Much more than this, I argue that the story of the ruler embodies part of the conundrum facing Luke: how to re-situate the story of Jesus in an environment that is becoming more diverse and much more complex. As Luke Timothy Johnson writes, Luke is "more than a minituarist" (1991, 4). He is like a story teller forging short stories "into a single narrative which draws the reader imaginatively from the mists of antiquity all the way to a rented apartment in Rome, and in the short space of 52 chapters communicates an impressive sense of historical movement" (4). For Johnson then, Luke's main contribution to Christian literature "was connecting the events of the early Church to those of Jesus' ministry, and to the whole story of God's people, indeed of humanity, all the way back to Adam" (4).

Wealth and power are only part of the systemic problem that is causing much uneasiness in the emerging community of faith. More significantly, there are other boundary markers, both endogenous and exogenous factors, which continue to constrain and restrain people in society. The Lukan worldview therefore conveyed through the story of the ruler in my view reflects someone who is exploring the nexus between institutional systems. On one hand, Luke is navigating a fine line between a developing community of faith and the practical life of an imperial system. Moreover, even within the developing community of faith, Luke also calls attention to the needed re-situating of an institutional system with rules and conventions influenced by its Judaic heritage in order to meet the social and cultural challenges of the day. Perhaps this is demonstrated in the fact that scholarly debate on Luke's political view is differently manifested. As Rohun summarizes in his dissertation,

> The scholarly literature have often seen divergent interpretations of Luke's political stance with regard to the Roman Empire, whether it is a compromise (apologetic about the church or the Empire), legitimization (assuring believers and legitimating their faith with allegiance to the Empire), contradiction (presenting believers as contravening social patterns supported by the Empire), or of no interest (uninterested in the politics of the Empire). These proposals have put Luke's Christian community and Rome in binary opposition. (Park 2011, 180)

But while the above quotation refers to the connection between Luke and the political, economic, and religious conditions, I argue that these conditions are shaped and framed by the institutional dilemma facing Luke.

Let me digress for a moment. That both my mother and sister died around the same time I entered the ministry haunts me with many questions regarding my own faith. Death came upon my mom and sister despite my many prayers and pleadings with God that I give up everything to enter the ministry. In retrospect, perhaps I was putting too much faith in myself thinking that God responds to meritocracy, to human deeds. Reflecting on my personal journey and Luke 18:18–30, I ask myself whether there was a similar ideological underpinning in Luke's story of the ruler? Perhaps Luke is also seeking answers concerning the rich ruler. Could it be that in the rich ruler, Luke shows another form of following, one that is demonstrated by "honoring one's father and mother" through "living responsibly with wealth"? Perhaps the "distressed" ruler exemplifies a sense of uncertainty and bafflement among members of the community, especially the rich Christian patrons. Jesus's overall instructions only exemplify the absolute sovereignty of God. Trying to grapple with God only accentuates the fragile and temporal nature of our institutions, our systems of knowledge, our ways of justice, our humanly existence.

SUMMARY

In steering around the various possibilities and navigating the crests and troughs of the text, I maintain focus on the catch of the day. What I have learned so far from my contextual exploration of the biblical text leads me to consider the following implications. First, the things the rich ruler says are conventional things he has learned to say. This means the reader must not try to get "serious meaning" out of his speech because the rich ruler is simply trying to have a *talanoa* or conversation with Jesus to show the reader of the story some deeper dimensions of the political and economic realities about wealth in the relation between the Jesus movement and broader Roman imperial society.

Second, it is important not to apply the actions or the responses of the rich ruler at the end of the story to any "personal character traits" of this particular ruler, because this rich ruler is simply an "actor on the stage of Lukan theater." This means that the ruler serves to show the audience how many rich rulers would not be able to find it possible to join the Jesus movement.

Third, if "social wealth" is the major character in this story, rather than "a particular rich ruler," the story is virtually an allegory about wealth. Put another way, if the rich rule were actually named "Wealth," then Wealth came to Jesus and said, "how can I inherit eternal life"? At this point we see that Wealth is a "Jewish man." This is evident in the way that he has remained loyal to the commandments. Perhaps it is also Luke's way of telling how its Judaic heritage is creating "uncertainty" within the Jesus movement. Perhaps also the major challenge for social interpretation of this story lies within its two-pronged social nature, namely that the ruler is both "rich" and "Jewish." If he simply were Roman, he wouldn't worry about eternal life. The problem in the story is that the ruler is concerned about eternal life and Jesus has turned the answer onto "his wealth."

Overall, the Lukan narrative on the rich ruler, therefore, underpins the struggle of faith coming face-to-face with one's lived reality. Luke in a sense is challenged with re-situating the Gospel narrative within the context of contemporaneous institutional systems which include the imperial institutional system. The rich ruler story represents a rubber-meet-road moment in Luke's narrative. The ruler exemplifies an existing set of institutions. He is someone who is in a position of leadership and very much part of the imperial system of institutions, ideology, and worldview.

Moreover, there is also a sense that even within the community of believers, there is also uncertainty and befuddlement. Their reaction to Jesus's call to discipleship is shaped and influenced by their existing way of doing things. Those ways of doing things are borne of existing religious convictions as well as social and cultural ways of doing things within their households, their communities, their personal relationships.

6

The Political-Economic Context and the Institutional Environment of the Household

INTRODUCTION

HAVING EXPLORED THE SOCIAL, cultural and ideological texture of Luke 18 in the previous chapter, I steer around other possible alternatives by simply focusing on where I sense to be other good fishing waters to find the catch. My contextual reading of the Lukan passage on the rich ruler compels me to look at institutional relations. Much can be gleaned from exploring the institutional relations shaping and influencing the context of the rich ruler. In this chapter I engage the political-economic aspects that shape and influence the institutional environment. It is part of my argument that a contextual biblical reading of Luke 18:18–30 also tells us something about the dynamics between and among the formal and informal institutions.[1] To highlight these relational dynamics I steer my interpretive canoe to focus on the household. My reason is to show that there is a possibility the context of the rich ruler is more nuanced and it is possible that there are institutional constraints in the institutional

---

1. For further reading on institutions and institutional analysis, see the following works by Carl Hampus Lyttkens (2013), Marc R. Tool and Paul Dale Bush, eds. (2003), and Douglass C. North (1990).

environment of the household. Surveying the possibilities, I am not distracted by the thrust of the narrative that seems to revolve around the interaction between Jesus and the rich ruler. And by all appearance, it is easy to assume the rich ruler is isolated and defined without social relations as often suggested in many studies of the popular passage. It would appear presumptive therefore to claim otherwise.

Be that as it may, I steer my interpretive canoe towards the conjecture that the rich ruler is part of a holistic relational framework which pivots around the household. As shown in the previous chapter, there is multiple evidence suggesting the plausibility that the household plays a critical role in the reading of the text. While it is not explicitly mentioned in the rich ruler passage, there are enough signs and movements in the passage that evoke images and pictures of a household. For example, Peter evidently appears startled after hearing Jesus' rejoinder towards the ruler. I get the sense that Peter is baffled by the idea of neglecting and leaving one's own house and extant relations and institutional environment. As a *tautai ama*, I ask then whether it is possible that Luke in the rich ruler passage is anticipating something more nuanced and an increasing level of complexities? While an emphasis on the character of the ruler is instructive, even more significant is an emphasis on the "dyadic person." That is, the individual is not isolated and is "always in relation with and connected to at least one other social unit, usually a group" (Malina 1996, 38). Yet groups are connected and bonded in relationships comprising of rules and conventions, both formal and informal. In this regard, I ask whether the passage is also about institutions with household as the basic unit of analysis.

Just as the *tautai ama* negotiates the crests and troughs of the waves, I explore boundaries in the text and its social environment, meanwhile, maintaining focus so that I am not distracted from the process of catching. Yet, it is only by crossing these boundaries that one can start to take account of the lived reality that gives rise to the text. To delve into a deep exploration of the political-economic context, I take a leap into the world behind the text to explore the lived reality in first-century society. And just as the *tautai ama* is always aware of any sudden shifts in the wind and changes in wave patterns, I am also conscious of the risk of anachronism in my contextual reading. Nonetheless, I maintain focus on doing a deep contextual biblical reading to shed light onto the lived reality that shapes and influences the text.

The outline of the chapter is as follows: I start by reviewing some of the intertextual sources regarding the study of ancient economy. This is followed by a discussion of how I blend elements of sociorhetorical (SRI) exploration and the New Institutional Economics (NIE). Following this, I look at some of the attempts to explore ancient economy. A brief overview of the household in ancient economy follows before I explore some of its internal makings and external influences on the household.

DEFINING WHAT IS POLITICAL-ECONOMIC CONTEXT AND LUKE'S SITUATEDNESS

Surveying the broader landscape of scholarly materials, I want to first situate my interpretive canoe with two observations that are critical at this point. First, in trying to engage the political-economic context of the passage, I situate myself with some of the classical thinkers of political economy. For Adam Smith, "political economy was the science of managing resources so as to generate wealth" (Weingast and Wittman 2008, 3). Karl Marx on the other hand understands political economy as "how the ownership of the means of production influenced historical processes" (3). More recently, political economy is viewed as the nexus between economics and politics while some refer to it as a methodological approach. But even the methodological approach is divided between the economic—emphasizing the rational individual behavior track, often referred to as public choice—and sociological, which orients towards institutional (3).I subscribe to a more blended approach, similar to Weingast and Wittman:

> In our view, political economy is the methodology of economics applied to the analysis of political behavior and institutions. As such, it is not a single, unified approach, but a family of approaches. Because institutions are no longer ignored, but instead are often the subject matter of the investigation, this approach incorporates many of the issues of concern to political sociologists. Because political behavior and institutions are a subject of study, politics also becomes the subject of political economy. All of this is tied together by a set of methodologies, typically associated with economics, but now part and parcel of political science itself. (Weingast and Wittman 2008, 3-4)

Thus, a political-economic framework situates the rational behaving individual within institutional relations and constraints. Exploring these relations and constraints and their influence on rational behavior involves a wide range of methods. For example, to borrow from Weingast and Wittman, the response of the ruler in Luke 18 is probably susceptible to modern economic methods of rational choice theory.[2] The ruler is constrained by the institutional environment of the household.

A slight distinction exists though in how I envision the relationship between the ruler, the household, and Luke's narrative. In my view, exploring the institutional environment of the household unravels some of the more subtle movements in the narrative. I approach the text with questions based on the assumption that people make rational[3] choices—choices that are shaped and influenced by their relationship with others. In light of this, the dynamics of the interaction in the narrative are a function of rational decision making, constrained by the political-economic context. Taken altogether, the text is not just about the individual's response or behavior. Rather, I argue that the Lukan passage on the rich ruler warrants exploring the institutional systems that shape and influence the behavior and response of the individual. By emphasizing the institutional systems, I am then led to the understanding that the text underpins an exploration of the interface between disparate institutional systems. By extension, I add that it explores the "re-situatedness" taking place and the level of navigation the reader in Luke's context has to engage with as a result of this interface between incompatible institutional systems.

A second important observation relates to Luke's "situated-ness." One of the challenges in engaging the scholarship on ancient economy is the fact that it is difficult to clearly define Luke's historical and social context (Robbins 2018, 115). With that being the case, I approach it with the understanding that we may possibly make hypotheses about the political-economic context of the text. As a result, I am encouraged to steer my interpretive canoe to engage other disciplines that could possibly assist

    2. For further reading on rational choice theory see James S. Coleman and Thomas J. Fararo, ed.(1992), Joe Oppenheimer (2012), Jon Elster (1986), and Jan de Jonge (2012).

    3. Rationality to me suggests that the person has clear goals and aims. The relationship between the goals and the means by which the goals are achieved is clear, and less inclined to feelings or emotions. In this case, I am making the claim that the ruler's reaction to Jesus' imperative to sell everything is a consequence of rational behavior.

in the process of catching. And as I stated in the beginning my focus is to carry out a contextual biblical reading of the Lukan passage on the rich ruler that can be extended to all centuries of interpretation of the Bible from antiquity to the present, sometimes using intertextual materials from various writers in intervening centuries.

There is much to learn from other intertextual sources. In particular, my focus is on the relational dynamics surrounding the household. The household throughout ancient society has been the basic unit of relations. Similarly, my own experience of the "*aiga*" (family) in Samoan society in chapter 3 provides a useful connection where the *aiga* occupies the basic level of the political-economic system in Samoan society. Thus, a particular focus on the formal and informal institutions that give shape and form to intra and inter household relationships helps in my attempt to populate the context of Luke's rich ruler. My aim, therefore, is to engage with the current scholarship on ancient economy and on the household in particular. It is not to be exhaustive but to ascertain enough competencies to populate and to reasonably interact with the political context of the passage.

It is also noteworthy that when I speak of ancient society, I am referring to a general understanding of Greco-Roman society in first century Christianity. Much of the literature available on ancient economy is broad in scope and purpose, some covering ancient Galilee, ancient Palestine, and Greco-Roman economies for example. Thus, navigating Luke's historical context within the vast scholarship on ancient economy merits some critical choices and decisions. As a *tautai ama*, I make this conscious decision on the basis that it is an important element in my contextual reading with respect to Luke's re-situating of the Gospel tradition. In doing so, I am also aware of the potential danger and risks of "rogue waves" in the process of catching.

Finally, then, let us turn to potential "rogue waves" as we steer and navigate a path across the abyss between literary-based exploration and historical critical approaches (Robbins 1996b, 12). This is the site where I call upon historical critical and literary critical evidences to engage one another. As a Pacific Islander interested in exploring the real-life political-economic context in the Pacific region in light of the Lukan narrative, I am oriented towards navigating boundaries. I look to bridge the social, cultural, ideological aspects of the literary text and its political-economic context. While the social, cultural and ideological features of the text draw upon the different textures of the text, I intend to investigate the political-economic context of the text using the household as foil for the relational dynamics driving the narrative. It is noteworthy not to expect the ideas, language and terms of political economy in contemporary society to be the same in Luke's day. As Michael Trainor suggests (2012, 297) in his engagement with the Lukan text, I do not expect Luke to be an economist as we understand in the twenty-first century. Luke is not writing about political economy in the way we understand in today's society. Be that as it may, I claim that we can engage the Lukan text from a contemporary political-economic context by enabling a sociorhetorical approach. Sociorhetorical inquiry helps facilitate the interrelational dynamics between the world of the text (literary construction of the text), the world behind the text (the historical context of the text) and the world in front of the text (my social location and my political-economic concerns). It is my hope that together with the integration of elements of the New Institutional Economics (NIE), SRI exploration will help steer my "interpretive canoe" to find a connection that bridges and engages these three interrelated dynamics.

Integration of SRI and NIE in a political-economic exploration of household

Drawing upon the wisdom of *tautai ama* helps me to become aware that my "fishing" so far has led me to the plausibility of an engagement to bridge text-based analysis and contextual analysis. The implications of such an undertaking warrants prudence. This is where I believe the value of SRI is critical. SRI is "grounded in the belief that the true nature of something is exhibited in how it relates to all other things" (Robbins 2009, 5). Distinguishing between a method and an interpretive analytics, Robbins clarifies the philosophical difference between the two as a "difference between a philosophy of essence or substance and a philosophy of relations" (5). The goal therefore is to "guide people toward a robust understanding of the relation of things to one another" (2009, 5). SRI therefore provides space for the interpreter to bridge between historical critical approaches and literary based explorations. By employing SRI, bridging the divide between the political-economic context of the text and literary based analyses is a possibility. The task is even made less challenging by integrating the NIE approach which shifts focus to the value of institutions in shaping the relational dynamics.

Recognizing the potential in the use of NIE in exploring New Testament writings, Alex Hon Ho Ip (2020) raises the value of language in speaking about economic issues. In particular:

> Economics does not create a new form of rhetoric, but a new need and new target for the rhetoric. In order to address economic issues, New Testament writers had to consider the nature of the problem they were addressing and generate specific ways to speak to various aspects of economic issues. In reading the rhetoric of the text in relation to economics, we can bring different layers of the economic texture into consideration and ask about the ways writers addressed them, which we might not notice without the awareness of rhetoric. (Ip 2020, 109)

Ip's enthusiasm appears to be about the potential for further explorations that integrate elements of the New Institutional Economics (NIE) in New Testament writing. The challenge is to find the rhetoric of economic texture.

From the perspective of *tautai ama*, I steer around other things in the context of the rich ruler to maintain focus on the household. In this regard, I argue that Luke in the rich ruler provides space to explore the institutional systems surrounding the household and its political-economic aspects. Subsequently, the household becomes the focus to engage a deep contextual biblical reading of the Lukan narrative on the rich ruler. This necessitates situating myself with the numerous intertextual resources available and the rich scholarly literature on early Christianity and ancient economy.

CAN WE APPROACH ANCIENT ECONOMY WITH MODERN ECONOMIC PRINCIPLES AND METHODS?

I start my contextual biblical reading of the political-economic context by asking the question, how does one navigate the vast and rich scholarship on early Christianity and ancient economy? Moreover, how does one blend the numerous existing intertextual resources? Like the *tautai ama* trying to circumnavigate the crests and troughs of the Pacific Island Ocean waves, there is no simple and straight forward approach to steering around the rich scholarly materials available on early Christianity and ancient economy. One particular question that keeps surfacing is whether we can apply modern economic principles and methods to ascertain features and elements of ancient economy. A prevalent fixture in ancient economy literature, Moses Finley's monograph (1985) appears to discredit the above question as unattainable. In that seminal work, Finley begins by compiling some lexicography of the Greek word οἰκονομία (20). The plausible intent is to shape and put in place how meaning and context of economy as a concept develops over time, in particular from ancient classical Greek through Hellenistic-Greek and eventually, to how it is understood in the modern world. Through this bit of history telling, the ostensible link between economics and politics emerges. For example, Xenophon the Greek classical historian coined the word οἰκονομία which based on Liddell Scott and Jones literally refers to managing the affairs of the household (LSJ s.v. οἰκονομία). Over time, οἰκονομία as a concept, according to Finley, has developed into something different and extended to other organizations and management, for example, state affairs. And because revenues are a major component of state affairs, the inevitable transition from the level of household to government materializes (Finley 1985, 20–21). Be that as it may, I argue that this cannot and should not lessen the role and value the household as an institution brings to the analysis on the political-economic aspect of society. The household remains a vital consideration in the study of ancient economy.

Given the understanding that the market is pivotal to the economic system, Finley postulates that in ancient society the notion of an integrated market economy is not pertinent[4]. For him, it is nonsensical to explore or "formulate laws of economic behavior (sic)" for something that did not exhibit any modern concept of economy (22). For Finley, "ancient society did not have an economic system which was an enormous conglomeration of interdependent markets" (22).

Another critical challenge to employing modern economic models and principles in a study of ancient societies is in language. For Finley, the use of modern economic language to describe ancient societies is problematic as they "tend to draw us into a false account" (23). Using the

---

4. It should be noted however that Finley's contention has been challenged by several scholars. Some of the pertinent works include the integration of the Roman economy by Alan Bowman and Andrew Wilson (2009, 3), the degree of integration Galilee plays in an integrated Roman economy by Mark A. Chancey (2005, 20), and an integrated wheat market system by Peter Temin (2013, 29).

example of wage rates and interest rates, Finley claims "the Greek and Roman worlds were both fairly stable locally over long periods (allowing for sudden fluctuations in moments of intense political conflict or military conquest)." Similarly, "no modern investment model is applicable to the preferences of the men who dominated ancient society" (Finley 1985, 23).

Further compounding the challenge is the implausibility of working with limited data, especially in relation to methods. The challenge of methodology underpins the lack of available data. Finley observes, "our problem is less one of devising new and complicated methods, which, given the available evidence, will of necessity remain simple, than of posing the right questions" (Finley 1985, 25). Thus, even if record and data keeping is important, for Finley, what separates antiquity from modern economy lies in the fact that reasoning by figures is more than counting in the ancient world. It "implies a concept of relationship and trends without which the categories that were counted were narrowly restricted, and what is equally important, few records normally retained once they have served their immediate purpose" (26). This is an important claim as it underscores the value placed on social relationships. Furthermore, it appears to be an endorsement of utilizing modeling design to moderate the lack of meaningful quantitative data. As Finley later adds,

> No historical or sociological model pretends to incorporate all known or possible individual instances. In the absence of meaningful quantitative data, the best that one can do is to judge whether or not a model, a set of concepts, explains the available data more satisfactorily than a competing model. (Finley 1985, 194)

One can read this as a less than enthusiastic approach by Finley towards the usefulness of modern economic tools that might provide space for innovation in our study of Luke's political-economic context. Without neglecting the degree of difficulty identified by Finley, however, we detect space for further engagement and movement.

Always cognizant of other possibilities, I am aware that Finley has his detractors. One of his contemporaries at Oxford, the Marxist ancient historian G. E. M. de Ste Croix (1981), labelled Finley's work as filled with "serious defects" (58). One of the "defects" is "a cavalier rejection of Marx's whole concept of class as an instrument of analysis." For Croix, Finley's rejection of class as an instrument of analysis constitutes a methodological flaw tantamount to findings that fall short of explaining economic behavior. While Finley's notion of a "spectrum of status and orders" is useful as a descriptive category, it fails however to offer any concrete explanation of economic behavior. Croix adds,

> The possession or lack of political rights would not of itself determine a man's class, in the sense in which I am using that term, so that in an oligarchy a man who had the civil rights of citizenship, but lacked the franchise and access to office because he had not quite a sufficient amount of property, would not necessarily, on my scheme, have to be put in a different class from his neighbour, a fraction richer, who just succeeded in scraping into the oligarchic politeuma (the body of those possessing full political rights). The non-citizen, however, the xenos who lacked even the civil rights of citizenship, would certainly fall into a different class, if he was not one of those rare foreigners who had been granted full gēs enktēsis by the State, for without this essential right of property he would be unable to own the one form of wealth upon which economic life mainly depended. (Croix 1981, 95)

The question of whether we can use modern economic methods to explicate ancient economy is also framed in the scholarship on ancient economy as pitting "primitivists" against "modernists" (Hollander 2017, 2). Primitivists claim antiquity as more agrarian while "modernists" argue for a closer relationship between ancient and modern economies. At the heart of the divide, David B. Hollander writes, is "whether the ancient economy is fundamentally different from the modern, market economy and therefore not susceptible to analysis with the tools of economics" (2). Exacerbating this division are plausible barriers that include but are not limited to "scholarly disagreement on the issue of demography," "concerns about economic growth," and "the question of economic integration" (Hollander 2017, 2–3). These are important issues that have not been resolved and Hollander suggests ways of moving forward. He also notes, inter alia, the recent increase in reliance on modern economic theory, in particular the emergence of the New Institutional Economics (NIE).[5]

A key criterion in NIE is looking at economic history as the exploration of "structure and performance." Structure refers to things that

---

5. For a detailed description of New Institutional Economics, how it started, its meaning and evolution into various strands within the field of economics, see Rudolf Richter (2015). For further readings see also Eric Brousseau and Jean-Michel Glachant, eds. (2008) and Douglass C. North (2005).

include political and economic institutions, technology, demography, and ideology, whereas performance are things such as production, distribution, output, and income (Hollander 2017, 4). In essence, NIE suggests that there is much to be learned about the performance of ancient economy by studying its institutions and their relation to transaction costs. Transaction cost in this case is ultimately about social relations. While societies in antiquity "may not have had economic thought in anything like the modern sense of the phrase" (Hollander 2017, 17), they would probably have some notion of important economic considerations that may include "wealth and poverty, the relative respectability of various professions, patronage and gift-giving, and household management" (17). Hollander adds that they would also have some notion "about how they conceived of risks and rewards" (17).

In a similar vein, Alain Bresson refutes any notion that the ancient economy was "primitive and irrational" as portrayed by the likes of Moses Finley and Max Weber (Bresson 2016, 62). For Bresson, it is legitimately possible "to analyze the economy of societies anterior to capitalism, and particularly the ancient economy" (62). While skepticism regarding the viability of applying modern economic methods remains, Bresson endorses the possible utilization of modern approaches.

Similar to Hollander, Bresson spends time also describing the upside to employing the New Institutional Economics (NIE) paradigm in exploring aspects of ancient economy. The potential value of the NIE paradigm, among other things, is its focus. While neo-capitalism focuses on individual choices, institutional relational perspective instead emphasizes contract, or the interactions among individuals. These interactions underpin social aspects that are often marginalized in a neo-capitalist paradigm. Like Hollander, Bresson adds that these interactions or transactions constitute the "social life" (2016, 52). Social life though from the perspective of the exchange of information is subject to "the domain of uncertainty" (52). That is, there is an asymmetry in the exchange of information involved in the interaction or the transaction.[6] To mitigate this, the goal of an institution is "to reduce to a tolerable level the uncertainty of transactions, so that the future is no longer a domain of unpredictable chaos, but rather one of reasonable forecasting" (Bresson 2016, 52). As Bresson's reasoning unfolds, ancient economic institutions were situated and engaged in constraints that were different from our context. These

---

6. For further reading regarding the connection between institutions and individual cognitive behavior see Jonathan Bendor (2010) and Alistair Munro (2009).

constraints are operationalized as "the reverberation among diverse institutional systems of politics (supervision of people), religion (symbolic image- repertory), human fabric (kinship), and material life (the economy)" (Bresson 2016, 63).

Like a *tautai ama*, I survey the scholarly materials to situate changes and disruptions in patterns and movement. From this perspective, the contours of ancient economy scholarship have changed somewhat with new claims based on recent findings. Finley's claim that ancient economies were primitive in comparison with the modern industrial world and that they lacked long-term planning and large-scale factory manufacture and commerce, while still valid, have been challenged by recent discoveries. The recent uncovering of more evidence of epigraphic and archeological information for example suggests the Roman economy as indeed sophisticated and complex (Rosenfeld and Perlmutter 2019, 13). Archeological, epigraphic, and papyrological findings suggest the Roman economy was capable of producing large quantities of products supported by "extensive commercial networks that brought these products to markets that were geographically far away from the place of manufacture" (Rosenfeld and Perlmutter 2019, 14). The implication of these claims is critical. While Finley's claim still holds validity, these new claims offer hope for the use of modern economic concepts and principles to explore certain aspects of ancient economics.

I am also aware of other aspects in the scholarly literature concerning the Roman Palestine economy. Nonetheless, my focus in particular is on "the question of whether or not socioeconomic relations were antagonistic in the first century CE" (Keddie 2019, 2). The corollary is the debate exploring whether the Jesus movement could be perceived as a resistance. Thus, on one side, the conflict model approach underpins the claim that "the Jesus movement and First Revolt may be understood as attempts to resist this situation of class exploitation." Proponents of this approach draw from Josephus and the New Testament as primary sources and archaeological and documentary as secondary sources. They "envision the "aristocracy" and "peasantry" as relatively homogeneous classes and their relationship as exploitative and extractive" (Keddie 2019, 2). The aristocrats, because of their close alignment with imperial Roman power and culture, are considered less indigenous. Having become assimilated into the Roman culture, they are therefore considered "more-or-less inauthentic Judaeans." The indigenous Judaeans and Christians are perceived however as the "pious victims, devoid of any agency except when mobilized towards justified strategies of resistance" (Keddie 2019, 3). From this perspective, imperial Roman power serves as the "stimulus for new or heightened forms of class exploitation that corroded the egalitarian nature of traditional subsistence-oriented communities" (3).

By circumnavigating other aspects in the scholarship on ancient economy, I shift focus to another interesting and prevalent feature—the concept of consumer city. According to Helen M. Parkins (1997) consumer city as a concept is derived from Max Weber's explanation of the ancient city. In general, the ancient city is typified by "the separation of town and country, and by the competition between the élites from these two different spheres" (Parkins 1997, 83). It is considered mainly a center of consumption in contrast with the medieval city, which is mainly a center of production (Garnsey et al. 2014, 76). This model of ancient city gives support to the central role of agriculture in ancient economy. As the site and base for many of the major landowners and some of the wealthiest residents, the city also became the locality of all their spending. Many of those spending "were funded in large part by their rural investments" (Garnsey et al. 2014, 76). While the concept of a consumer city underpins a view of the ancient economy as undeveloped as Finley suggests it is nevertheless useful to give us a fair description of the ancient city (Morley 2004, 10). That is, it is fair to describe the ancient city as resembling a consumer rather than a producer type (21).

One of the intriguing derivatives of the concept of the consumer city is it brings into focus the important role of the household, its sociopolitical and economic relationships. The outcome is to move beyond an emphasis on the city and to accentuate the institutional environment of the household. This is echoed by Parkins writing that

> What this suggests is that, in order to understand a city's 'economy', we should move away from the town/country division which, as already mentioned, has typically fuelled ancient historians' interest, and instead look at the ways in which the élite managed their economic relationships—under the organizational umbrella of the household. (Parkins 1997, 86)

Drawing upon the wisdom of *tautai ama*, I am aware that much has been said to set up the fishing process. Nonetheless, I argue that it is an essential part of navigating the wide ocean of scholarly materials on ancient economy and early Christianity so that I can focus on a particular fishing water. Overall, my contextual reading so far indicates a strong connection between modern economic tools and ancient society. In establishing and reaffirming the connection between ancient and modern economy, a certain appeal for institutional analysis emerges. Clarity on the dynamics and nature of how certain institutions function in ancient society is warranted.

HOUSEHOLD

In this section my focus is to "fish" in the ocean of available scholarly literature concerning household. As a *tautai ama*, I make the conscious decision to focus in particular on the literature on Greco-Roman society in the first-century. In doing so, I circumnavigate other possibilities and focus instead on what could possibly be Luke's context.

As stated above, the concept of οἰκονομία underpins the management of a household. But while it may have originated within the confines of household, οἰκονομία has since morphed into something extensive, not only in terms of how the "church fathers used the concept of economy to describe the manifestation of the divine in the world" (Leshem 2016, 30), but the more recent being state affairs. Nevertheless, at the basic level, οἰκονομία is very much associated with the affairs of the household.

Household Economy

From a *tautai ama* perspective, I find it necessary to first discuss the notion of household economy as it has been the subject of interest for many scholars. This is important to get a sense of the political-economic aspects of the household in ancient society. The household serves as both the primary unit of production and consumption (Tropper 2005, 189) in ancient society, and embedded within its political-economy (Oakman 2013, 147). For scholars like Halvor Moxnes, the household represents the basic economic unit in ancient society (1988, 31). One would assume from much of the scholarship on ancient economy though that this is not the case, mainly for the reason that economic activity is often perceived as "one of the activities of the household." The primary goal of the household economy appears to be for the elite to maintain status through "conspicuous consumption" and for the "satisfaction of their needs," which indicates political and even military bearings (31). Therefore, one can reason the household is significantly embroiled in political and power relations. The direct consequence is to lose sight of its economic aspect.

Nevertheless, the very notion that ancient economy was an "embedded economy"[7] gives merit to the claim that it was not a separate institution with its own rules as we understand it in modern days. Rather, it was "embedded in society and its power structure," situated "within the framework of the social organization of society as a whole" (Moxnes 1988, 29). While some have taken this to downplay any bearings the economic aspect may have (Malina 1987, 361), I beg to differ. The level of differentiation and degree of distinction between ancient and modern economy sanctions a balanced and nuanced approach. To consider ancient economy as embedded is to recognize the complexity of integration that is the consequence of relational dynamics in antiquity. But while we may think of the economic aspect as just another indicator to investigate in order to capture a holistic view of ancient economy, it is nonetheless critical in any profile of first-century society (Longenecker 2009, 243). As the basic institutional domain of the Greco-Roman political-economic system, exploring the institutional environment of the household (Oakman 2013, 154) brings clarity. This warrants exploring its relations with not only the political and economic aspects of society, but including among other things, culture, ideology and religion (Barclay 1997, 66).

For this reason, some clarity on the notion of economy in antiquity warrants looking at the systematic relations that govern the household. The household presumably is entangled in the political-economic dynamics of ancient society. Social status, economic, political and even imperial rule all have bearings on the relational dynamics of its institutional environment.

General Profile of Household in Greco-Roman Society

Household in ancient society represents something far more different than what the modern conception of family allows. Household in ancient

---

7. The term embeddedness is mostly associated with Karl Polanyi who in his critique of market economy notes that "it means no less than the running of society as an adjunct to the market. Instead of economy being embedded in social relations, social relations are embedded in the economic system" (2001, 60). Polanyi henceforth describes a double movement, between neo-liberal advocates and those seeking to prevent the dis-embeddedness of the economy. For further discussion of the concept of embedded economy see works by Walter Scheidel et al. (2008), Ed Noell (2007), and Joseph P. Hellerman (2000).

society basically includes a different designation that covers "slaves, former slaves or freedpersons, matrilineal and patrilineal ties and laws, and a series of obligations of one set of members to others" (Maier 2019, 134–35).

James S. Jeffers (1991) provides a helpful profile of the household in first-century Greco-Roman society. Defined by head of the family, the household is led by the oldest male in the blood line of the family who is known as *paterfamilias*. Perhaps similar to the function of the *matai sa'o* in the Samoan context, the *paterfamilias* holds legal authority over every resident of the household which may include relatives by kinship, women who married blood relatives, slaves, former slaves, and even livestock (Jeffers 1991, 81). Even the management of finances is under the control of the head of the family. While the wife may give advice, it is primarily the role of the *paterfamilias* to administer and control the management of household affairs. For example, he gets to decide the number of children and the level of education they would have and also who they marry. Even slaves "attached to the family were owned by him alone" and as a result, the *paterfamilias* has "the legal right to make any decisions involving them" (82).

A slave who is freed by the *paterfamilias* still owes him certain duties. Even as a freedman, the former slave now becomes a client with the *paterfamilias* as his patron. As a client also, the former slave owes the head of the family "duty and honor." In this capacity the head of the family is seen as one who unites "the members of the family in his roles as husband, father, master and patron" (Jeffers 1991, 82).

In a society where the general belief is in the inherent superiority of men and that the women are to be protected from sexual temptations, women are consigned to work in the house under the auspices of the head of the family. They are usually responsible for overseeing "the domestic slaves and other workers, as well as the nurture and education of their children" (Jeffers 1991, 82).

Village Communities

With respect to its place in the village setting, the household is part of a "larger social structure, the village; people come into the picture as relatives, neighbors (sic), friends, participating in one another's lives" (Moxnes 1997, 23). This is an important element in understanding the relational dynamics surrounding the household. Richard Horsley (2014, 37) aptly writes about the implications noting that "what is also often undetected or ignored by historians and historical sociologists as well as by New Testament scholars is local or locally based politics." While more attention is rightfully accorded to the political aspects given the "importance of the state and state formation" the relationships within the village communities have not been given enough consideration. Yet, Horsley argues that "before and well after the formation of the state in traditional agrarian societies, village communities (comprised of many households) continued to be the fundamental form of political-economic religious life for the ordinary people, the peasantry" (2014, 37). Implicitly, the emphasis also needs to be placed on the local setting to get a balanced view of some of the institutional dynamics surrounding the household.

Within this paradigm of household in ancient economy it is easy to see power dynamics emerging. Dependency and responsibility lay the foundation for power relational dynamics in a household. This is where I sense that a survey of some of the internal makings of the household can prove significant.

POSSIBLE INSTITUTIONAL CONSTRAINTS IN THE HOUSEHOLD

Like a *tautai ama*, my sense is much can be learned by focusing on the internal and external factors that may have bearings on the function and composition of the household. In this sub-section, I situate myself with some observations on plausible endogenous variables. It is noteworthy also that any attempt to explore the inner makings of the household is difficult, even more with the lack of quantitative sources. Exploring the inner doings of household has several challenges.

Although his interest in the household is within the context of gender roles in the household, Richard P. Saller's work helps identify some of the challenges facing studies on the internal dynamics of household (2008, 88). Despite the lack of quantitative data on ancient societies, Saller argues that this is no different from contemporary economies where "it can be difficult to document the dynamics of decision-making within the household." This makes it all the more complicated in antiquity with "the thin, male-dominated sources" (Saller 2008, 88). I anticipate therefore that the availability of sources regarding the ways of doing things in the household is often limited and slanted towards a male-dominated perspective.

Re-situating Discipleship as a Calling to be a Christ-Following *Paterfamilias* in Colossians and Ephesians

One of the significant ways of doing things in the household has to do with its rules. To this point Harry O. Maier notes that "the household rules reflect the patriarchal organization of Greco-Roman society" (2019, 136). These rules, or stipulations I refer to in formal and informal institutions, are known also as "codes"[8] that "reinforce the position of the male householder as husband, father, and—above all—master, and urge duties that preserve his authority" (136).

For example, in Col 3:18—4:1, we find instructions to wives to "be subject to your husbands, as is fitting in the Lord." Meanwhile, husbands are to "love your wives and never treat them harshly." In accord with this, instructions are given to the children to "obey your parents in everything, for this is your acceptable duty in the Lord" and in turn, "fathers, do not provoke your children, or they may lose heart." Rules also exist for slaves to "obey your earthly masters in everything, not only while being watched and in order to please them, but wholeheartedly, fearing the Lord." Moreover, "whatever your task, put yourselves into it, as done for the Lord and not for your masters, since you know that from the Lord you will receive the inheritance as your reward; you serve the Lord Christ. For the wrongdoer will be paid back for whatever wrong has been done, and there is no partiality." And finally, there are rules to govern the relationship between masters and slaves instructing masters to "treat your slaves justly and fairly, for you know that you also have a master in heaven." In all of these codes one gets a certain appreciation of the role of the husband as *paterfamilias* and observes their responsibility for a wife, children and slaves.

More examples of household codes and the emphasis on husbands as *paterfamilias* can be found in Eph 5:21–29 where the relationships to other members of the household is "out of reverence for Christ." Similar

---

8. I understand household codes to be rules or stipulations regarding the management of the household. Such biblical units are sometimes given the German name Haustafel in biblical scholarship. For further readings see J. Paul Sampley (1971), and more recently Sean M. Christensen (2016) and Lilly (S. J.) Nortje-Meyer and Alta Very (2016).

to the example above, rules exist for the relationship between husbands and wives "for the husband is the head of the wife just as Christ is the head of the church, the body of which he is the Savior. Just as the church is subject to Christ, so also wives ought to be, in everything, to their husbands." Meanwhile, husbands are to "love your wives, just as Christ loved the church and gave himself up for her, in order to make her holy by cleansing her with the washing of water by the word, so as to present the church to himself in splendor, without a spot or wrinkle or anything of the kind—yes, so that she may be holy and without blemish." In the same way, "husbands should love their wives as they do their own bodies. He who loves his wife loves himself. For no one ever hates his own body, but he nourishes and tenderly cares for it, just as Christ does for the church" (Eph 5:21–29 NRSV).

The result is an institution that reflects much of the issues and concerns confronting society. Household management underpins much of the institutional system shaping and influencing everything including social, political, religious and economic activities in society. Moreover, several examples from the New Testament provide access to other aspects of ancient society. Maier provides several examples including instructions to slaves in 1 Pet 2:18–25 describing circumstances in which slaves may be beaten even when they do right (v.20). In doing so, this particular example takes us into "the brutality of ancient household life" (Maier 2019, 137).

Maier also draws from Paul's teachings to assess the influence of formal and informal institutions, or codes, in household institutional relations. For example, Paul in 1 Cor 7:12–16 gives instructions to Christian wives making it permissible "to accept divorce from their unbelieving husbands" and as a corollary "offers a glimpse into possible tensions arising between partners who had differing religious beliefs" (136). The resulting outcome is "the question of how the household looked from the underside of Greco-Roman households" with recent explorations of "the lives of women, children, and slaves and their experiences, in Greco-Roman and Jewish households." By doing so, scholars are able to unravel "a multitude of people long shrouded by the darkness of patriarchal indifference" (Maier 2019, 137).

Some scholars have also noted the parallels between the New Testament household codes and the traditional understanding of household (Neufeld and DeMaris 2010). Exploring ancient works on this parallel, Margaret Y. MacDonald noted "a dual tendency" (2010, 32). On the one hand, "there is general consensus that the codes draw their origins for traditional expositions of the household management theme discussed by philosophers, and various political and moral thinkers from Aristotle onward" (MacDonald 2010, 32). On the other hand, some scholars claim that the traditional understanding of household management "is not fully replicated" by the New Testament writers (33). Nevertheless, two underpinning features emerge. First, the discussion of the two sets of codes appears to involve three key relationships in the household: slave–master, wives–husbands, and children–father. Second, both sets of codes appear to view "familial relationships as determinative of wider social realities, even theological conceptualizations" (32). An example is that of the "metaphorical comparison of marriage" to the relationship between "Christ and the church" (Eph 5:22–33 NRSV). In this case, "domestic relations here are used to articulate nothing less than the relationship between the human and the divine" (32).

Across the Greco-Roman world, some of the basic internal makings of the household are consistent. Monogamy appears to be the norm, although "divorce is permitted and available to both husband and wife" (Saller 2008, 90). Concerning marriage, it was not uncommon for aristocratic women to marry early, around their early to mid-twenties. The average age for marriage would be for a husband around his late 20's or early thirties and the wife in her early or mid-twenties. For men and women of lower status, they appear to marry at an older age (Saller 2008, 90).

Marriage also plays an important function in shaping the internal dynamics of the household, with political-economic underpinnings. This depends "on where the married partners were located on the socio-economic spectrum" (Longenecker 2020, 219). For example, arranged marriages are usually for those at a higher socioeconomic level. The intent is political and economic, with strong underpinnings of social status and honor. The marriage "usually tied together two households and enhanced the prospects of each extended family." In this regard, marriages "were expedient means of creating new households that reflected well on the households from which the two partners had come" (Longenecker 2020, 219). One could envision then that the goal for many households would be to improve their political-economic and social status. It could very well be the underpinning motivation in many of the Gospel narratives "wanting the best for members of their families" (223).

The decision for a married couple to embark on their own family or stay embedded within the household also has political-economic ramifications. The gains are usually in the form of freedom and autonomy and to establish profitable networks. These gains are mitigated by the notion that the household reduces risks for the married couple (Scheidel 2006, 6). To gain clarity on some of the risks confronting the household, David Fiensy (2017) building on Walter Scheidel's (2006) paper in the *Stanford/Princeton Working papers on Classics*, paints a picture of a "grieving" household. The infant mortality was estimated at 30 percent for the first year of life. Half of all people died before they had children which translates to the fact that death was as much a phenomenon of childhood as of old age. This suggests that the ancient population was necessarily young. The consequences on the socio-economic conditions were unfortunate: "destabilization of families"; "ubiquity of widows and orphans"; "disincentives to investment in education"; and the "disruption of trust networks that sustain commerce" (Fiensy 2017, 120).

Overall, a deep contextual reading of the household and its institutional environment renders a sense of the overall dynamics and relationships involved. These relationships reflect some of the issues and challenges confronting people in society. To render change to the institutional environment warrants a "re-situating" taking place. To bring about such "re-situatedness" necessitates the *paterfamilias* to become a "re-situated disciple" who is called to accept these responsibilities with actions guided by love.

Re-situating Discipleship into Service as a Deacon (*Diakonos*) or Bishop (*Episcopos*)

The focus on the internal makings of the household is also important with respect to indicating how a successful Christ-following *paterfamilias* may become a re-situated Christ-following disciple as a deacon or bishop. For example, in 1 Tim 3:1–15 there are clear instructions for whoever aspires to the office of bishop to be "above reproach, married only once, temperate, sensible, respectable, hospitable, an apt teacher, not a drunkard, not violent but gentle, not quarrelsome, and not a lover of money." The suggestions give a sense of someone who, among other things, must be hospitable and live responsibly with wealth. More significantly, a person must manage "his own household well, keeping his children submissive and respectful in every way—for if someone does not know how to manage his own household, how can he take care of God's church?"

Furthermore, "he must not be a recent convert, or he may be puffed up with conceit and fall into the condemnation of the devil" and "he must be well thought of by outsiders, so that he may not fall into disgrace and the snare of the devil."

Similar instructions for deacons also underpin the importance of relationships within the household as they "likewise must be serious, not double-tongued, not indulging in much wine, not greedy for money; they must hold fast to the mystery of the faith with a clear conscience. And let them first be tested; then, if they prove themselves blameless, let them serve as deacons. Women likewise must be serious, not slanderers, but temperate, faithful in all things." More importantly, the deacons must be married once and must show that they manage their children and their households well as those who serve well as deacons gain a good standing for themselves and great boldness in the faith that is in Christ Jesus. Towards the end of the passage the writer's instructions gives a sense that the relationships within the household reflect "the household of God, which is the church of the living God, the pillar and bulwark of the truth" (1 Tim 3:1–15 NRSV). This household of God comes into being through the actions and dispositions of people who accept the responsibilities to live their lives as re-situated disciples.

Similar instructions appear in Titus 2:1–10, which also suggest the importance of relationships within a household and the emphasis on managing the household.

> But as for you, teach what is consistent with sound doctrine. Tell the older men to be temperate, serious, prudent, and sound in faith, in love, and in endurance. Likewise, tell the older women to be reverent in behavior, not to be slanderers or slaves to drink; they are to teach what is good, so that they may encourage the young women to love their husbands, to love their children, to be self-controlled, chaste, good managers of the household, kind, being submissive to their husbands, so that the word of God may not be discredited. Likewise, urge the younger men to be self-controlled. Show yourself in all respects a model of good works, and in your teaching show integrity, gravity, and sound speech that cannot be censured; then any opponent will be put to shame, having nothing evil to say of us. Tell slaves to be submissive to their masters and to give satisfaction in every respect; they are not to talk back, not to pilfer, but to show complete and perfect fidelity, so that in everything they may be an ornament to the doctrine of God our Savior. (Titus 2:1–10 NRSV)

Finally, perhaps indicative of how society treats widows and elders with emphasis on the household, the instructions in 1 Tim 5:1–10 are instructive asking not to "speak harshly to an older man, but speak to him as to a father, to younger men as brothers, to older women as mothers, to younger women as sisters—with absolute purity." Similarly, the passage suggests generosity and hospitality to those who are really widows and that "if a widow has children or grandchildren, they should first learn their religious duty to their own family and make some repayment to their parents; for this is pleasing in God's sight." Importantly, taking care of relationship within the family takes prominence as "whoever does not provide for relatives, and especially for family members, has denied the faith and is worse than an unbeliever." In this regard, "a widow be put on the list if she is not less than sixty years old and has been married only once; she must be well attested for her good works, as one who has brought up children, shown hospitality, washed the saints' feet, helped the afflicted, and devoted herself to doing good in every way." Meanwhile, there are also those whose "sensual desires alienate them from Christ, they want to marry, and so they incur condemnation for having violated their first pledge. Besides that, they learn to be idle, gadding about from house to house; and they are not merely idle, but also gossips and busybodies, saying what they should not say." These guidelines show re-situated discipleship in its full maturity, with guidelines for living in households of Christ with fully developed guidelines for caring for everyone in the household with love and concern for one another. These guidelines also call for everyone to join in reciprocally with contributions that make the household a place where everyone cares for one another by accepting tasks they are able to do and helping others as they are able to do so.

Private and Public Space

The scholarly discussion on the notion of private and public space in the context of ancient society household underpins another element of a "re-situatedness" taking place, one that involves a re-situating between those on the "inside" and those on the "outside." In this regard I ask whether Luke in Peter's response in verse 28 about "leaving home" is steering the conversation towards certain aspects of institutional constraints. Searching for the day's catch, I steer around certain possibilities to locate and focus on certain aspects in the scholarly literature including the structural layout of the ancient household.

Bruce W. Longenecker (2020) notes that our twenty-first century understanding of public and private space is not the same with Christians in the first-century. Despite ancient households having a variety of structural layouts, they "were not devised simply to be private spaces for family members to retreat to after a long day in the public arena" (230). Rather, it appears that the notion of privacy as we understand it in the twenty-first century does not exist in the ancient households. As an example, Longenecker explains:

> For instance, in houses where the householder had a significant public profile, clients would congregate in the morning outside the residence's entrance and move into the house's atrium when invited to do so by a household slave (by instruction from the householder). As the clients waited to meet individually with the householder, they might pay their respects to the householder's deities displayed in an atrium shrine. When it was their turn to meet with their patron, they would be ushered into the tablinum (or office), where (after a few moments of submissive dialogue) they would present their request. They would then be told what was required of them (to enhance the householder's reputation) in exchange for his support. In these instances, the residence doubled as a place of business and politics, overseen by the household deities. Moreover, it was hoped that passersby would glance into the house and see how busy it was inside, thereby reinforcing the importance of its householder. (Longenecker 2020, 230)

Thus, the household is not just home to its residents but represents also other important aspects of society. In this sense, the household underpins the notion of "re-situatedness," a space where those on the "inside" and "outside" can be re-situated through the act of generosity and hospitality.

I am also reminded of how negotiating private and public space is a significant feature in the Samoan context, one that also impacts the role of the *sa'o*. For example, it is not uncommon for the *aiga* to have *fale-tali-mālō* (guest-house). As part of the infrastructure of the *aiga*, the *fale-tali-mālō* is accessible not only to visiting relatives but even passersby, strangers and anyone. Culturally, it is private space made accessible to accommodate outsiders, extending the span of the *aiga* to those beyond. More importantly is the value in establishing relationship with the visiting party, which is manifested through the space provided and the impromptu activities that followed as the family members play host to the guests. It is not uncommon for the host family to provide meals and care for the visiting party throughout their stay. In that manner, the amount of space and the extent of hospitality is culturally and socially significant with the *sa'o* as the primary benefactor.

Monica Trümper (2003) adds clarity on another element of the household in antiquity. In particular, there are clear demarcations, some of which are reflective of the society at large. For example, "the most important contrasts in Greek houses are often regarded as that between male and female space and that between patronal and servile space" (26). There is even a clear differentiation "between household members and outsiders, usually guests or visitors" (26).

While Trümper's work is particular to Greek society, the emphasis on polarization within the household significantly brings into focus some of the institutional constraints precluding against "re-situatedness" taking place. These are profoundly culturally contingent notions that would be considered important even in first-century society. Linking the private and public space of a household, Trümper writes, "the concrete layout of the 'public' spaces" would allow us to make "deductions about the character and importance of social life in a house." Subsequently, "the presence and extension of 'public' space in a house is usually taken as an indicator of its social meaning and the social status of its owner" (Trümper 2003, 26). Thus, the significantly close relation between the public and the private space of the household is undeniable.

The claim of a clear distinction between private and public space within the household is further attested to in Peter Lampe's chapter (2003) on social context. The reasoning follows that the mental construct of the ideal stands in contrast to its social reality. From there, one could envision some distinction between the mental construct borne of the internal activity, and the social context on the external.

From a *tautai ama* perspective, I ask then whether this could have any implications on Luke 18? Could it be that in the rich ruler, Luke intends to show this "re-situatedness" taking place, that of an institutional system borne of a new identity for the emerging faith community, and the social reality of its surrounding which includes the political-economic social context. Based on this projection, I conjecture that the ruler's response is indicative of the "clash" that resulted when two contrasting institutional systems come face-to-face. This is played out in the Lukan narrative between the rich ruler who represents a particular form of "following" by possibly living responsibly with wealth, and an institutional system with institutional constraints precluding against better distribution of resources and sharing of wealth. The underpinning of this claim is a community faced with conflicting sides. This image resonates with Lampe's observation on early Christians:

> The early Christians lived in two contexts and moved back and forth between them. Whenever they shifted from one to the other, the mental context became social—and the social became mental. It depended on which people they interacted with: fellow Christians or pagans. In my opinion, the constructivist instrument provides an adequate tool for describing the coexistence of the two realities that are hinted at in New Testament texts such as Galatians 3:28. (Lampe 2003, 80–81)

While this contrast of social context is quite prevalent in Pauline texts, could it be that perhaps the Lukan community also shared this conflicting manner and could it be possible that the surrounding institutional environment contributes much to this behavior? If this is so, then Luke in the rich ruler is possibly offering another form of following, especially for the rich and wealthy. It is one in which following is possible by living responsibly with wealth. Hence, the rich ruler in the Lukan narrative represents an apparent attempt to offer a form of "re-situated discipleship."

INCOME DISTRIBUTION AND HOUSEHOLD IN GRECO-ROMAN ECONOMY

From a *tautai ama* perspective, I explore the political-economic context of the rich ruler to look for other elements of "re-situated discipleship." Steering around other things in the context of Luke, I maintain focus on providing a deep contextual biblical reading which warrants a brief review of income distribution in Greco-Roman economy. To gain insight on this appraisal, I find two quite promising works. Steve Chang (2018) in his assessment of Paul's collection for the poor and saints in Jerusalem (see Rom 15:26), explores income distribution and inequality in ancient economy. Looking specifically at the Roman economy, Chang finds evidence of a society in which a small number of wealthy families dominates (211). The top 10 percent of the population controls about 50 percent of the total income. In contrast, 10 to 22 percent of the total population lived "below subsistence" (Chang 2018, 212). Based on the work of Scheidel and Friesen, Chang postulates a Gini coefficient[9] at 0.42—0.44 which is considered middle-of-the-road when compared to other pre-industrial societies.[10] Chang's assessment provides the likelihood of a not so "peasantry" society. Relative to today's standard, we are looking at an income disparity that was not as bad as often interpreted from the Gospel narrative.

Bruce W. Longenecker (2009) is similarly instructive. Building upon Steven Friesen's "poverty scale," Longenecker endorses a less "binary" view of investigating poverty in the first-century Greco-Roman world. In his view, a lot of Greco-Roman literature appears to advocate for a view of a world between the "elites" on one hand, while the rest of non-elites are collapsed into a broader category of "poverty" (Longenecker 2009, 246). The consequence is missing the more nuanced and complex socioeconomic levels. For this reason, Longenecker finds merit in David Friesen's scale of poverty which breaks down 7 levels of socioeconomic ranks. Occupying the top 3 percent are the "imperial elites" at PS1, "Regional or provincial elites" at PS2, and Municipal elites at PS3. Occupying the middle 29 percent are those with moderate surplus at PS4, and those just above subsistent living at PS5. At the bottom of the ranking, 68 percent of the population are at PS4 and PS3, those at subsistent level and those below the subsistent level. From this, one can envision a more nuanced income level distribution. In some way, it compels one to look at the political-economic situation in Luke's context in a whole new way.

The importance of the above contextual description is to reflect on the institutional constraints that merits Luke's offing of a new form of "re-situated discipleship." Living responsibly with wealth offers a more meaningful approach to combating the political-economic context that continues to render an unbalanced distribution of wealth and resources in society.

---

9. See explanation of the Gini coefficient by Scheidel and Friesen (2009, 86). Essentially, it is a measure of equality from 0 to 1 where 0 reflects equal income distribution and 1 maximum inequality of income distribution

10. To put things in perspective, based on a World Bank survey of Household income and expenditures, Samoa in 2008 had a Gini coefficient of little less than 0.44 (2017, 11).

HOUSEHOLD AND LANDOWNERSHIP

Focusing on household and landownership underpins other possible contextual framework for the carrying out of re-situated discipleship. Because of the growing population in the cities, the need for land grows with great consequences. Not only did the need for land further create an imbalance in power between cities and countryside, but according to Wayne A. Meeks, ownership of land became concentrated in the hands of fewer and fewer proprietors living in the city. As a result: "

The small, independent landowners living on their own land began to disappear, reduced to tenancy or slavery, gone to the city to subsist as laborers, or recruited into the army" (Meeks 1983, 14).Meanwhile there is also evidence that the cities were also facing political-economic issues as a result of "urbanization." Jinyu Liu describes these issues:

> There was a lack of stable employment to coarse diet and poor housing conditions, the lives of the poor in the Roman cities can be characterized by multidimensional deprivations—of resources, capabilities, choices, security, and power. This deprivation was embedded in the sociopolitical systems that organized the ownership of land, the ultimate form of wealth in the premodern, agrarian economy that was Rome. (Liu 2017, 54)

Wealth is land. As such, it is possible that the more land owned the wealthier and richer the households. However, the question is who really benefits from this as it is also clear in the scholarly literature that much of the wealth and profit from owning land went to the imperial rulers in the form of taxation. Taxes were paid not only to the emperor "who had immense land holdings" but also to the "large landowners, including the senatorial, equestrian, and local elites to support their social and cultural status and political careers" (Liu 2017, 54). This institutional setup is reinforced by the fact that these same privileged and powerful people were the ones instituting the laws. From a *tautai ama* perspective, I circumnavigate the evidence to postulate that it is quite possible Luke's context is shaped by a similar institutional system that continues to allow for the continued suppression of the poor and marginalized. And as a result, it could very well be possible that Luke in the rich ruler story provides a response to the problematic institutional system that is at the heart of many of society's problems.

> It was structural factors that caused and exacerbated poverty and rendered episodic poverty irremediable. These structural factors or variables included land-owning patterns, modes of resource allocation, (lack of) mechanisms of social mobility, gender relations dominated by patriarchal hierarchy, and so on. It is precisely because of the institutionalized inequality and limited space of structural chances that we hear more about episodic poverty, caused by individual, circumstantial "misfortunes" including bad harvests / high grain prices, unemployment, sudden illness, debt/insolvency, absent husbands, death of bread-earning spouses, divorce, and so on. (Liu 2017, 31)

Land ownership is even more critical in the rural villages. In agrarian societies, 85 percent lived in villages and engaged in some form of farming (Rohrbaugh 2017, 177). A large portion of arable land was owned by aristocrats, which suggests that the rich and the wealthy households were most likely to be connected to landownership in rural areas. The scholarly evidence also suggests the prominence of absentee landownership. Meanwhile, "absentee landowners were forced to employ tenant farmers, landless laborers, and slaves in producing their crops" (Rohrbaugh 2017, 177).

Could this have been Luke's context? By focusing on the household as the unit of analysis, I steer to conjecture that Luke, in his attempt to address the institutional constraints that continue to create inequality and limiting opportunities, offers a different model of discipleship that is possibly based on the notion of "living responsibly with wealth." Luke may have learned from a "patronal" relationship with Theophilus who is offering him his house and resources that enable Luke to write the story of Jesus. In this, Luke offers space for the wealthy patrons, like Theophilus, to be followers of Christ though it is a different model of "following" that also offers the wealthy in the emerging community of faith an opportunity to engage in living responsibly with wealth. It is in a way Luke's own attempt to resituate discipleship for the wealthy and rich in society.

PART THREE

Tautai A'e

7

The Mooring Point
Aiga, Church, and the Island of Hope

TAUTAI A'E—UNPACKING THE DAY'S CATCH

Tautai a'e! It is time to celebrate. It is time the sennit lashing is brought to a closure, the interpretive canoe to come home, to end. Yet, it is not a complete end, rather, a critical juncture to reconcile "the day's catch," to reflect, and ponder, anticipating that it is never an end in itself but an opportunity for possibilities. In this regard, it is a mooring point to anchor, to rest, but never in permanence. It is space provided to share "the experience" and "the catch" with other fishers, and steerers, underpinning a sense of responsibility not to dominate or impose. Rather wisdom is knowledge shared and made accessible. The *tautai a'e* welcomes the mooring point to find anchor and grounding to reflect, ponder the future, and find ways to continue the conversation. The findings from my contextual biblical reading of the Lukan text are guided by the questions I laid out in the introduction. They are as follows: What are some of the institutional and social constraints that could have shaped and influenced the context of Luke's rich ruler narrative? What other possible interpretations could this contextual reading of Luke 18:18–30 be amenable to?

The above questions are guided by the underpinning claim that the nuances of Luke's narrative warrant an exploration of its social environment, which includes its cultural, social, ideological, and political-economic context. Moreover, this contextual biblical reading also highlights my desire to ground biblical reading in the lived reality of contemporary society, to find the catch of the day in the reality of today's society. From the *tautai a'e* perspective, I celebrate the findings as well as recognize the critical task of self-reflection and anticipate the possibilities for future dialogue.

RE-SITUATED DISCIPLESHIP AS BENEFICIAL USE OF WEALTH

As a *tautai a'e*, I "celebrate" the rich ruler in Luke's story. I celebrate prudently, knowing the challenges and the consequences of such a motive. In fishing for the day's catch, I find myself becoming the "catch." In my own personal experience, my own personal journey, I find myself drawn to the rich ruler. Despite the many scholarly interpretations of the Lukan passage, I steer my interpretive canoe to focus on liberating the rich ruler. I read to liberate the rich ruler by asking whether it is possible that the rich ruler represents my own struggle to make sense of "following" Christ. To liberate the ruler, I ask whether it could be possible that Luke in the rich ruler, resituates eternal life by "honoring one's father and mother." And in doing so, Luke perhaps is showing us another form of following.

By doing a deep contextual reading of Luke, I get the sense that Luke, in his "re-situating" of the rich ruler story, is also drawing from his own lived reality. In his lived reality, including accompanying Paul in his many visits to various Roman provinces and cities, Luke may have seen and benefitted equally from the wealthy and rich patrons and householders in the Christian community. The question for Luke is how to resituate the Jesus tradition within his own context. As I argued above, the rich ruler represents Luke's intent to show another form of "following" by possibly "living responsibly with wealth." In this regard, the "Abrahamic" model of "following" comes to mind. That is, someone who is known to be "hospitable" and willing to "share his wealth" even with strangers.

Part of the catch is offering a reading of Luke with new eyes. Luke shows aspects and nuances of re-situated discipleship, stories, and verses that provide prosperous Christians a model for living responsibly with wealth. In the next section, I propose a brief overview of a reading of Luke 1–13 with eyes that look for generosity, wealth, and hospitality. As a *tautai a'e*, I celebrate with prudence, knowing this is only the beginning of more conversation.

READING LUKE 1-13 WITH NEW EYES

Luke 1:1-4: Theophilus as Patron

In the first four verses of the Gospel of Luke, the reader is introduced to a patron of the author of Luke who most likely had wealth. In my contextual reading of Luke, I steer towards this patron as a follower of Christ, a person who already is a disciple of Christ and receives further instruction from the writer of this gospel. As the writer of Luke composes his narrative, he resituates discipleship into a form of patronage that supports an author who is writing the story of Jesus. Theophilus is the first wealthy man, very likely a householder, mentioned in the Gospel of Luke. It seems very possible that the author of the Gospel of Luke is in a house supported and probably owned by this patron. It probably is a house equipped with writings such as the Septuagint and other compositions. And so, if we assume this patron to be a follower of Christ, we begin to see the worldview of the writer of Luke, who is experiencing generosity from a patron. In other words, Theophilus in the Gospel of Luke functions as a re-situated disciple patron. It seems natural, then, that sprinkled throughout the gospel of Luke, there are stories, parables, and verses here and there which show the reader glimpses of what it means to live in this re-situated discipleship, by living responsibly with wealth.

Luke 3:10-14: John the Baptist's Teaching of Generosity

From Theophilus, the Gospel of Luke moves to John the Baptist. While in the gospel of Mark John teaches a baptism of repentance for sins, in Luke, John teaches about generosity. The point in Luke 3:10-14 is not whether one has a lot of wealth. Rather it is about showing a re-situated model of discipleship where "whoever has two coats must share with anyone who has none, and whoever has food must do likewise." When tax collectors come to be baptized and ask John, "Teacher, what should we do?," he tells them not to extort money from anyone but instead to be generous. In other words, as the forerunner of Jesus John the Baptist teaches generosity and hospitality. He is the pre-teacher of generosity and hospitality, teaching those who come to him how to live responsibly with wealth.

Luke 7:41–43: Beloved Generous Creditor

Steering around the following few chapters, I find the next instance of living responsibly with wealth in Luke 7:41–43. It is the first dinner a wealthy pharisee offers, where a "woman in the city" comes in and washes Jesus' feet. While Jesus is talking to the pharisee about the woman, he translates love through an experience of generosity by a creditor. In verses 41–43, Jesus tells of a generous creditor who forgives a person's debt, and the response is love for that creditor. Thus, it is acting out of generosity that reciprocates the love. In other words, Jesus uses wealth, the giving of wealth, and generosity within wealth to translate the meaning of love. In this way, the story creates an experience of nurturing and learning about love through generously given or forgiven wealth. Luke, in a very special way, then, presents an interaction between Jesus and a wealthy Pharisee in this story that creates a particular instance of living responsibly with wealth in a way that creates love between a debtor and a creditor.

Luke 10:33–37: Generous, Caring Samaritan

Looking at the story of the Good Samaritan using the same lens, the narrative takes on a different sense. The Good Samaritan does not simply take care of the wounded man in the ditch by binding up his wounds and pouring in oil and wine. He also takes the man to an inn and tells the innkeeper that he will come back later and, if anything is owed, he will pay it. In this case, Luke re-situates wealth, generosity, and hospitality again. In the parable of the Good Samaritan, Luke offers a model for someone who has wealth, a model of re-situated discipleship, a model of what Jesus is asking people to do as a result of re-situated discipleship.

A point of digression is offered here. The Gospel of Luke, as noted earlier in the review of the scholarship, is perceived by many interpreters as a form of biography. One of the compelling aspects of Luke's writing is the presentation of models and "anti-models" for people in a manner that distinguishes virtue from vice. In this regard, the Good Samaritan, in my opinion, is an example story, a model of what I call re-situated discipleship. Later in this section, I show examples of Luke offering "anti-models."

Luke 11:5–8: A Friend Who Gives Bread

In Luke 11, as Jesus is describing giving in the Lord's prayer, he talks about going to a friend's house at midnight, explaining to the householder that a friend has come to visit, and telling him that he needs some bread to feed him. And so, though the friend gets up reluctantly, he gives him bread. Here Jesus is showing that asking is an action that enables other persons to give. And as people give, they act in the mode of a re-situated disciple of Christ. Thus, Luke shows multiple aspects of re-situated discipleship, including when a friend or someone with wealth has a household and some bread, and when another friend asks for some food, he is willing to give it.

Luke 11:42: Warning to Do Justice and the Love of God

Further in chapter 11, Luke tells of a second banquet that a rich pharisee gives. This is an important aspect of the Gospel of Luke exhibited when wealthy Pharisees give banquets in chapters 7, 11, and 14. In the midst of the second banquet, Jesus gives a warning in verse 42 to the Pharisees, "But woe to you Pharisees! For you tithe mint and rue and herbs of all kinds, and neglect justice and the love of God" (Luke 11:42 NRSV). This suggests that justice and love are enacted. They are actions a person does. In the Gospel of Luke, it is "these you ought to have practiced" (Luke 11:42 NRSV). In other words, love and justice are to be practiced "without neglecting the others" (Luke 11:42 NRSV).

Luke 12:15–21: Beware of Greed and Hoarding of Earthly Wealth

Later in Luke 12, in the context of not being "concerned about food," Jesus talks about all kinds of greed and then gives an "anti-model" of hoarding one's earthly wealth by putting it in storehouses, rather than making it available as food, or giving it to people who need food. As stated above, as Luke shows a model of discipleship based on living responsibly with wealth he also includes anti-models of people who hoard their wealth or are simply unwilling to share it.

MODELS AND ANTI-MODELS OF BENEFICIAL USE OF WEALTH IN LUKE 14–16

In particular, chapters 14 through 16 contain good models and anti-models of the beneficial use of wealth. As a *tautai aʻe*, I celebrate by proposing these as the catch of the day with my view that these are reasonable grounds for further research and discussion.

Luke 14:16–24: The Generous Inviter to Dinner

In chapter 14, Jesus is invited a third time to a banquet by a wealthy Pharisee. In the context of the banquet, Jesus tells a story about a host in a fantastic model of a wealthy man who regularly gives big dinners. The rich man is the owner of a house with slaves. While it is not mentioned in the text, it is reasonable to argue that he probably has a family and children as the paterfamilias or the matai saʻo in the Samoan context. When those who are invited to the banquet are so occupied with their wealth—like buying an extra farm or getting extra oxen—that they do not accept the rich man's invitation to come to the banquet, the wealthy host opens his household to others by having his slave go out and bring the poor, the crippled, the blind, and the lame to the banquet. His generosity and hospitality do not stop before he tells his slave to invite people to come in so that his house is filled. In this wealthy man, Luke gives a model of someone who is generous and hospitable, even to the lowliest of people living on the roads and lanes around the town.

A point of digression is warranted here about the kinds of people the generous host invites into his household. Discussion of purity laws in scholarly literature is usually associated with the elite priestly class. Anthony Keddie gives some insights into the political influence the priestly class could wield and the extent of their influence:

> As at other temples of the Roman East, the political influence of priestly elites in Jerusalem reached beyond the Temple. Not only were the high priests appointed by the Herodian kings and Roman governors, but some priestly elites also held municipal offices of various sorts. Families of priestly elites in Jerusalem were wealthy and owned land outside of the city, yet they still benefited from their privileged positions within Jerusalem's economy of the sacred. (Keddie 2019, 174)

It is clear that the privileged positions of the priestly class could lead to internal constraints involving the household:

> Priestly elites engaged in a distinctive class culture in which they competed for status. They are explicitly depicted as involved in the type of banqueting that would have taken place in the *triclinia* at the Banqueting Hall near the Temple Mount and in the Jerusalem mansions. The second is that these ruling men are cast as using their positions of power—they are distinguished leaders, they say they do things out of compassion, and they claim to be concerned with purity—in order to "eat the goods" of God's people. (Keddie 2019, 175)

As a *tautai a'e*, I celebrate with prudence asking whether part of this "concern with purity" involves hosting of invited guests. And if so, we begin to see a context in which the influence on the household may lead to a particular notion of what I can call "selective hospitality." The elite priestly householder can only be "hospitable" to those considered pure under priestly law.

This influence could possibly have spread outside Palestine as there is also strong evidence that purity laws are a prevalent feature even in the Jewish diaspora and throughout Greco-Roman society, including Luke's context. While many New Testament scholars "regard any indication of a concern with purity to be Pharisaic," E. P. Sanders provides evidence that such an argument "completely mispresents purity in the ancient world." Instead, Sanders notes that "all ancient people had purity practices" (2015, 39). Adds Amy Jill-Levine, "purity is of concern also to Greek and Roman cultures" (2003, 229).

By virtue of this, I ask whether Luke, in the story of the generous host, had this in mind. The conjecture is that Luke is challenging the problematic institutional system, including purity laws that have become constraints precluding "hospitable" wealthy Christians from "living responsibly with wealth." This could also be an underlying dimension of the story of the rich ruler. In other words, the question of "following" Christ in Luke's rich ruler story has substantial implications for the rich and wealthy in the emerging faith community. Luke's challenge would have significant implications on several political-economic issues, such as "adequate food, the disintegration of family, and the drain of economic resources to support the Temple and the empire at the expense of local needs" (Horsley 2014, 140).

Luke 15:11–32: The Generous Loving Father

In the story of the prodigal son, Luke once again provides a picture of a householder with wealth and children. It is reasonable to argue that this wealthy father may have acquired his wealth through inheritance. This story involves the division of what he inherited and cared for among his two sons. One of the sons asks for his share and then travels to a distant land where he squanders his wealth. And when the son comes back, the father is so generous with his son that he kills a fatted calf and gives him his best robe and puts a ring on his finger and shoes on his feet. His generosity and hospitality are concretized through the use of his wealth so much that his elder son complains about it. The underpinning sense is a merciful father who uses wealth to celebrate the homecoming of his son. In this we see a model of a re-situated disciple, a merciful father functioning as a disciple who uses his wealth generously to celebrate the homecoming of a lost son.

Luke 16:1–13: Manipulating Wealth to Serve God

If we continue to read into chapter 16 through the lens of re-situated discipleship, we may also get a different sense of the story and statements of Jesus about the people in the story than we usually do. The story again starts with a rich man who is probably a householder, someone with a family and very wealthy. In this particular case, the story has an additional element that the rich householder has a manager. Charges are brought to the householder that this manager is squandering his property. The householder brings the manager in, and as the story continues the manager freely takes actions within his power to rewrite the bills so that he becomes friends with the debtors. For these actions, the rich man commends the manager for acting shrewdly. The question then is what could make these commendable actions?

I conjecture that Luke is offering yet another aspect of being a re-situated disciple living responsibly with wealth. This time the story deals with the question of true riches and one's relationship to God. The overarching argument is that a person is either devoted to wealth or to God. In the midst of this, even dishonest wealth can be massaged[1] through

---

1. The idea of "massage" draws from the Samoan concept of *fofō*, particularly in birthing. The Samoan *fofō* (masseuse) *fofō* the belly of the mother so that the baby in the womb is aligned correctly. The idea is to negotiate and massage to make the birth

generosity in ways that can maintain a focus on true riches related to one's devotion to God. There are ways, then, in Luke's understanding of things to navigate and negotiate the intricacies of wealth for the purpose of serving God.

Luke 16:19–31: An Uncaring Rich Man as Anti-Model

Later in chapter 16, Luke tells of another rich man, one who is dressed in purple and in fine linen. In this rich man, Luke offers a vivid display of an anti-model, someone who is not willing to be generous enough even to offer basic hospitality to Lazarus, who lives a completely destitute life. When the story presents a rich man with a complete lack of generosity or hospitality receiving eternal torment in Hades rather eternal life, readers are seeing the opposite side of the rich ruler's goal, namely receiving eternal life. Is it unreasonable then to think that the implication of this story could be that if the rich man would have been generous and hospitable to Lazarus, he could have received eternal life of comfort alongside Abraham in Hades? Surely this anti-model implicitly offers an answer to the question the rich ruler asks Jesus two chapters later, along with the story of Zacchaeus we have already discussed above. If it is miraculous for wealthy people to be generous and hospitable, perhaps this is a miracle God is able to perform in some wealthy people. And perhaps it could be appropriate to think of this miracle as foundational for the context of re-situated discipleship within the emerging community of followers of Christ.

THE PRESUPPOSITION OF RE-SITUATED DISCIPLESHIP IN JESUS' RESPONSES IN LUKE 18:26–30

Reading the first 16 chapters of Luke through the lens of a re-situated disciple seems to offer a somewhat new view of how generosity and hospitality can be actualized through the use of wealth in this gospel. Luke shows different ways that wealth can be used responsibly to act out love and justice, aspects of a re-situated discipleship. These displays of re-situated discipleship reach an apex in chapter 18 when the ruler who comes up to Jesus turns out to be wealthy and wants to know how to receive eternal life. It is as if Luke at this juncture in his gospel attempts to address one

---

process safe and comfortable for the mother and baby. The idea behind *fofō* is to negotiate and manage challenges in the process.

of the poignant questions facing many members of the emerging faith community—how can wealth be re-situated within the Kingdom of God?

What Is Possible for God in Luke 18:27

When Jesus says that what is impossible for humans is possible for God, one may ask then, how is wealth possible within what God does? The text suggests that it is miraculous given how difficult it may be for a wealthy person to enter into God's Kingdom. I would argue however that this is the kind of miracle that takes place when a rich person becomes generous, hospitable, and loving, as witnessed in the models presented above.

Getting Very Much in This Age and Eternal Life in the Age to Come in Luke 18:29–30

Moreover, I argue that this view directly shapes and influences a rereading of the closing of the story of the rich man. When Jesus responds to Peter the second time and says in verse 29–30, "truly I tell you there's no one who has left house or wife or brothers or parents or children, for the sake of the Kingdom of God, who will not get back very much more in this age and in the age to come eternal life" (Luke 18:29–30 NRSV), the subsequent question is how the rich ruler is going to get back very much more in this age? I argue that this particular aspect of the text presupposes that there are re-situated disciples with wealth who are going to be hospitable and generous to those who have accepted itinerant discipleship.

Let me digress here. As a *tautai a'e*, I celebrate the day's catch knowing that there is much space for discussion and more conversation to continue. As such, I propose that when you have people who have given up their home and family and follow Jesus, they become itinerant disciples. In the context of the latter part of the first century and early second century, during the formative years of the Christian movement, the question is where are those disciples going to go? I argue that they are not just going out into mission where no one knows anything about Jesus. Instead, they are regularly visiting Christian households. The patrons of Christian households throughout the Mediterranean world to which these itinerant people are going are patrons who have re-situated discipleship from itineracy to generosity and hospitality as householders. Further evidence is found in the Didache where it warns that itinerants who come only have the right to stay three days in a household then they have to go on or they will abuse the discipleship generosity hospitality of those who run the households (*Didache: The Teaching of the Twelve Apostles* 2013).

FURTHER PROPOSITIONS

My deep contextual reading of Luke's passage on the rich ruler leads me to the following findings. From the perspective of *tautai aʽe*, I offer these not as conclusion, but instead as propositions for further dialogue. As such, I find reasonable evidence to infer the validity of the following propositions:

Proposition 1

The findings from this contextual biblical study provide evidence to suggest the validity of the argument that an exploration of the institutional system by way of examining the cultural, social, ideological and political-economic context of the story does much to add other possible interpretations of the rich ruler story.

Much has been said about Luke's purpose and attitude towards Rome. Some emphasize Luke's apologetic attitude. Against a backdrop of historical events that include the expulsion of Jewish people from Rome and the fall of Jerusalem (Bock 2011; Dicken 2012), the claim is for an apologetic purpose to appease and respond to questions that have emerged as a result of these events taking place. Others highlight Luke's ambivalence (Burrus 2009). A certain degree of uncertainty underpins a Luke that muddles a fine line between accommodating and resisting imperial Rome.

I do submit, as a *tautai aʽe*, that the scope of my contextual biblical reading would only allow me to "celebrate" a certain perspective on Luke's purpose. In this regard, the evidence of this study suggests that the encounter between Jesus and the ruler underpins an emphasis on lived reality. The encounter between Jesus and the ἄρχων would fit well with the notion that it seeks to undermine the existing institutional system that shapes and influences the lived reality of household or family life in society. From this perspective, I would further argue that this reading liberates the ruler and puts emphasis on the institutional system that put certain constraints on the household in society.

As a *tautai a'e*, I argue that Luke's re-situating of institutions warrants challenging the existing norm, or the existing way of doing things, which continues to perpetuate the demarcation of boundaries and creating divisions among people. These demarcations often create divisions between "outsiders" and "insiders." The re-situation therefore seeks to decenter an institutional system which is based on a colonized mindset and rigid traditions that continue to permeate and sustain injustice in society. It is a decentering of the epistemological center and its peripherals, not to dominate, but rather to celebrate and amplify the particularities of the many.

Let me digress for a moment. As a *tautai a'e* I celebrate the household especially as a metaphor for interconnectedness as well as relationality. Nonetheless, I celebrate with prudence. *Seu le manu ae taga'i ile galu* (catch the bird and watch for the wave) gives me the sense that the household as a metaphor can easily morph into a camouflage for imperialistic and colonizing means in the name of interconnectedness and relationality. As this study has suggested, it is imperative therefore that any discussion of household as a metaphor is to also recognize the lived reality within and the consequences of the rules, codes, and conventions that give shape and form to the interconnectedness and relationality within the household.

In Samoan society, household is captured within the notion of *aiga* with physical as well as metaphorical meaning. The evidence from this study demonstrates the *aiga* as fundamental to the lived reality of Samoan society. The relationship between the *matai sa'o* (chief administrator) and the members of the household are guided by formal and informal institutions including rules, traditions, and kinship. Yet, as I have tried to show in this contextual biblical study, the same institutions that give shape and form to the *aiga* could be suspect in their political-economic issues. Poverty in Samoa to a large extent is attributed to the institutional dynamics internal and external to the *aiga*.

A similar focus on the institutional environment of the rich ruler is instructive as well. The findings from this contextual biblical study therefore suggest the validity of the argument that an exploration of the institutional system by way of examining the cultural, social, ideological and political-economic context of the story does much to add other possibilities of interpreting the text. By exploring the social, cultural, ideological and political-economic context of the story, we can begin to appreciate other aspects of the text.

Proposition 2

The evidence from this contextual biblical reading suggests the validity of the notion that Luke in the rich ruler demonstrates the critical interface between faith and lived reality in society and offers a different way of following that is possible through living responsibly with wealth.

Exploring the social, cultural, and ideological textures of the text, there is evidence to suggest the validity of the notion that the story of the ruler demonstrates the messy and often frustrating intersectionality between faith and lived reality. Jesus's injunction to sell all and the subsequent reaction of the ruler and that of Peter and the disciples, highlights a critical moment in the growing faith of the Christian community. In particular, Luke in the rich ruler captures a conundrum facing the people of any community of faith. Peter's reaction and the subsequent discussion on family relations heightens the sense of anticipation of a "rubber meets road" juncture in the Lukan narrative. Such a moment is indicative of when faith comes into contact with lived reality of family life.

Luke also in this juncture of his gospel narrative suggests a strong challenge to the institutional system that continues to permeate the Christian community. It is a system that is embedded with institutional constraints that continue to separate and divide "outsiders" and "insiders." In the case of the rich Christians, Luke challenges the very way of doing things based on religious beliefs and customs that preclude "hospitable" Christians from engaging in a better distribution of resources and sharing of wealth with the less fortunate. In this regard, Luke in challenging the existing institutional system in the Christian community offers a different form of following that is possible by living responsibly with wealth.

I submit that this is a challenge that is also suggested in the Pacific Island of Hope report. Part of the economic problems facing people in the Pacific region is attributed to the church.

> Churches in the Pacific have also contributed to making the poor poorer. Because it is the norm to raise money for the church, congregations are continuously drawn into giving to the church monies needed to pay for their children's school fees, uniforms and text books. Although it is not obligatory to give money to the church, social and peer pressure usually make it almost impossible not to do so if one wants to remain in the good books of the village or the community. (World Council of Churches 2001, 119)

But rather than isolating the cause, the Island of Hope report only gives it peripheral treatment. Yet, I argue that this contextual biblical study has suggested the need for the church to find its mooring point in the issues that matter most to people. The apparent disconnect is a seemingly total disregard of the lived reality and total well-being of the family. For example, Samoan society is still guided by the institutional framework of the *aiga* and the institutions of the Samoa way of doing things—*faa-Samoa* (Samoan way of life). To challenge this way of life is to resituate the institutional systems that give shape and form to that way of life.

This contextual reading of the rich ruler offers another form of following that is relevant also for the church. It is a way of following that is possible by living responsibly with wealth. Rather than continuing to live by institutions including rituals and traditions that divide and separate, the church in its mission is to engage in reforming its institutional system to enable "living responsibly with wealth." This is to be demonstrated in church policies and rules that are "hospitable" to its members and that encourage the sharing of resources between the rich and the less fortunate and marginalized in society. It also calls for the church to be responsible for the lived reality of the people, to take responsibility for issues such as poverty that is creating further disparity in the quality of life for the rich and the poor in society.

Living responsibly with wealth also has significant implications for the political economy of the Pacific Island region. In post-COVID restrictions, the Pacific Island Countries and Territories (PICTs) are facing difficult challenges of a new norm. Coupled with the ongoing challenges of climate change and environmental crisis, PICTs are always at a disadvantage in the global context especially in view of economies of scale. Because many of the Island economies are based also on single-industry, it is almost imperative for the PICTs to engage in regional agreements for a reasonable sharing of resources and wealth. Living responsibly with wealth calls for a "hospitable" attitude that is based on the notion that the region is part of the Pacific *aiga*. And as such, each should have the mindset of being responsible to one another. This has to start with the rich economies in the region. Living responsibly with wealth warrants "lending" without any expected returns, the emphasis rather is to build trust and openness in dialogue and for a better distribution of resources and sharing of wealth in the region.

Living responsibly with wealth can also be an underpinning principle in the ongoing discussion at the global level on how to address the imminent threat of climate change. While the smaller Pacific Island nations like Tuvalu, Tokelau and Kiribati are literally sinking into the Pacific Ocean, the big economies including USA, China, and European nations could do a lot more for the sake of the global household by offering to live responsibly with wealth by reducing the over-exploitation of the environment and the pursuit of excessive profiting. New models of economic development that promote prudence and living responsibly with wealth could do much to help rein in the deterioration of the global ecosystem and the harm they may cause to our lived reality. This warrants a re-situating of the mindset and a commitment at the global level to undo some of the institutional constraints that continue to permeate the lived reality of the local communities.

As a *tauta a'e*, I celebrate with prudence. In this regard, I submit that this notion of living responsibly with wealth is filled with a lot of challenges just as Luke himself admitted that it is even more difficult than for a camel to go through the eye of a needle. Nonetheless, my contextual reading of Luke suggests perhaps a deep contextual review of our existing institutional systems as a first step. This calls for a conscientious review of those institutions that have become part of tradition, part of our belief systems, part of the conventional ways of doing things. Only then is a significant beginning to a possible outcome of living responsibly with wealth.

Proposition 3

The evidence from this contextual biblical reading suggests the validity of the claim that there is much to learn from grounding biblical interpretation in real-life issues facing society.

As a *tautai a'e*, I celebrate with much prudence my own attempt to contribute to the rich and growing scholarship on Pacific Island biblical hermeneutics. This is an attempt in contextual biblical reading to foreground real-life issues. The findings from my contextual biblical reading suggest the validity of the claim that there is great value in such an undertaking. In particular, grounding biblical readings in the lived reality of today's society is not only liberating but also transformative. It liberates and transforms the text as well as the reader.

This study has been an attempt at contextual biblical reading that demonstrates a desire to ground it in lived reality. It is my attempt to contextualize the story of the ruler moored in the lived reality of today's society, in this case political-economic issues and poverty in Samoa. I read therefore to liberate the ruler. I read to re-situate the ruler within his *aiga*. In this regard, it is an attempt to decenter the text. By decentering the text, I also create new peripherals, new limits, new boundaries. It is also in decentering the text that a "decentering" of myself is possible.

In decentering the text, I join the growing trend of Pacific scholarship that seek to cross boundaries and navigate the deep ocean of biblical interpretation. It is a growing field of tremendous contextualization with increasing indigenization of the biblical text. While the particularities and specificities of our Pacific Island context are bringing to life new permutations of exotic readings, the challenge remains to overcome institutional barriers that continue to disadvantage biblical studies in the region.

One of these challenges is to overcome the perception that contextual biblical reading lacks theoretical value. Because we are dealing with a specific context, this view holds that it is implausible to formulate theories that could be valuable to others in different contexts. With the valiant efforts of some of our prestigious Pacific Island steersperson, contextual Pacific Island biblical readings are slowly emerging as a voice to be heard in the larger context of global scholarship. Hearing Pacific Island voices in the cacophony of global scholarship is something to be desired, a goal shared also by other indigenous contexts.

As a *tautai a'e*, I celebrate the call to decenter biblical reading, to resituate a mooring point for biblical studies that is also conducive to the particular needs of the respective cultures and contexts. For the Pacific Island region, one of the distinctive aspects of Pacific Island life is the lived reality of Pacific Island people. We live in connection to the vast *moana* that serves as boundaries between us as well as pathways linking our islands, our people. Given the growing interests in the region in terms of geopolitics and global political economy, as well as the increasingly gloomy forecast of the impact of climate change, and given that the majority of its people identify as Christians, grounding biblical reading in the lived reality of the Pacific Island people is potentially a great fit.

Be that as it may, I think it is also important to bear in mind that by decentering biblical studies, I am also anticipating perhaps having multiple centers with multiple peripherals. Could it be then that value is established by having cross-centered discussions and deliberations? Thus, to re-verse and to de-center institutional barriers that marginalize the majority while prioritizing the few, the focus then is to create multiple centers talking and sharing resources with one another. To make this possible, though, would require the few with resources to have a "hospitable" mindset. This would also mean the willingness to "lend" without expecting anything in return.

MOORING POINT

The confluence of economics, politics, religion and family life is at the heart of this contextual biblical reading. As the world is becoming more interconnected, there is no denial that Pacific Island Countries and Territories (PICTs) especially are subject to globalization. It has certainly influenced and shaped the way of doing things in the Pacific Island region including our economic development models, political-economic context, as well as how we understand the Bible. For Pacific Island biblical reading in particular, a certain re-situating is needed. While our reading scheme and hermeneutical framings are fluid and dynamic, nonetheless, it is not to detract from but to celebrate our distinctiveness and indigenous contexts. Thus, a balancing act is warranted. This study through the *seu le manu ae taga'i ile galu* sennit lashing highlights a blending of skills associated with a steersman—*tautai seu*, locating and situating, *tautai ama*, navigating while maintaining focus on what is desired, and the *tautai a'e*, to celebrate and to reflect. It is not to demarcate nor separate as the deep *moana* bears no boundary and is constantly fluid and shifting with the ebbs and flows of the currents. Nonetheless, the aim is to frame a biblical reading within Pacific Island scholarship that is distinctive of our own particular context but also interconnected enough to be respected in the global context. But this also calls for a re-situatedness of the institutional system of biblical studies to celebrate and amplify the particularities of many. Meanwhile, there is also a sense of responsibility in doing biblical contextualization. That is to be responsive to multiple contexts and also to be responsible for the ways in which we engage these multiple contexts.

As a *tautai a'e*, I find space not only to celebrate but also to reflect. It is a mooring point for my interpretive canoe not only to celebrate the day's catch but also to ponder future dispersion. This contextual biblical study has research limitations which could possibly be mitigated with more trials and experience. These limitations are without doubt shaped by personal biases and predispositions. Moreover, my methodological approach that blends certain tools of SRI and aspects of the New

Institutional Economics (NIE) also include blending historical and literary critical approaches that could have easily led to biasness in the analysis. Nonetheless, the aim of my contextual biblical reading is to show and highlight how utilizing a multi-method approach can diversify our findings and analysis. Moreover, this contextual biblical reading is an attempt to also show how our analysis can possibly benefit from blending SRI with existing methods from other disciplines including economics and politics. In particular, integrating and interweaving also with our social location, indigenous context and lived reality, the possibility for Pacific biblical hermeneutics is endless.

IS THERE AN ENDING?

Tautai a'e! I close by returning to the beginning. This contextual biblical reading is at the core a testimony of my struggle trying to make sense of my "context"—my faith journey and the challenges of my lived reality. It took me a while to come to terms with the loss of my mother. Similarly, getting re-situated in my faith journey is taking longer than I anticipated, and I may never fully understand my purpose in all this. I may never become fully re-situated as context is fluid and watery. But I have learned perhaps this is what the ruler is teaching me—that faith warrants a "perpetual re-situation." In this regard, Luke underpins a story of navigating a world that is continuously becoming more diverse and eclectic. It is a world in which constant navigation and negotiation of boundaries and constraints is essential. Could it be that my vindication is knowing that my mother before she passed learned on the same day that I have been accepted for theological training at the Malua Theological College? Before succumbing to cancer, she may have been conscious enough to learn that her son stayed true to a promise made years before.

In the end, I find it fitting to end my story with the testimony of a corporate lawyer (rich ruler?) who in real-life took some time off to participate in an experimental monastic community run by the archbishop of Canterbury. In her testimony she writes about her own decision to join as a monk and reflect on this immersion, integration between theology and the lived reality of an attorney. Her story resonates with my own struggle to make meaning of this "re-situating" I experienced in my faith journey. I close by sharing with you an excerpt from her *Citizens of two realms*.

In the end, there was no triumphant metamorphosis: as it turns out, the work of transformation is messy, frustrating, and achingly slow. And yet, in the midst of the chaos, we seemed to unearth a deep, reverential awe—an awe that, it seems, resulted from full-bodied participation in the impulsive curiosity that has stirred our short-lived species from the beginning. (Skinner 2021)

Glossary

I. SAMOAN WORDS AND PHRASES

'afa	sennit
aiga	family, extended family, household
ali'i	lord, high chief
alofa	love
ama	to be focused, someone who is handy
faaaloalo	respect
faafaletui	sharing and discussing
faalavelave	family affair, family event
faa-Samoa	Samoan way of life, Samoan culture
fale-tali-mālō	Guest House
faletele	meeting house
fanua	land
fatua'iupu	keeper of tradition, myths and genealogy
fau'afa	sennit lasher
fono	council
itumalo	district
lagi	heaven
lagisoifua	life-justification proofs

mana	sacred
matai	chief
matai sa'o	head of household
Mau	Samoa independence movement
moana	ocean
nu'u	village
sa	ban
sa'o	literally the one who is straight
seu le manu ae taga'i ile galu	catch the bird and watch the wave
soalaupule	sharing of authority
sumu	name of a fish, name of a sennit lash pattern
taeao	morning, historical
talalasi	multiple versions of a story, big telling or telling big
talanoa	story, telling, discussing, conversation
taula	anchor, name of alcohol brand
taulaga	mooring point, capital, offering
tautai	steersman, fisherman
tautai a'e	celebrating with prudence, the act of grounding and reflecting
tautai ama	the skills of negotiating and navigating while maintaining focus on the goal of getting the day's catch
tautai seu	the skills of locating and situating
tautua	service
tautuaileva	service in between
tosi-lasi	multiple strands
tufuga	carpenter, artist
Tui Atua	one of the paramount chiefs in Samoa
tulāfale	orator

Upolu	second largest island in the Independent State of Samoa, location of the capital city of Apia, location of the seat government
usiusita'i	obedience
va-tapuia	relational, space in between
viiga	praise

II. TONGAN WORDS AND PHRASES

angafai	Tongan for way of doing, method, practice
fonua	Tongan for land
founga	Tongan for points of entry
lalava	Tongan word for sennit lasher
ma'ahi	Tongan word for wake
matua	Tongan word for gap
ngalu fakaofo	Tongan for the unexpected breaking of waves
takanga	Tongan for a sense of community
talanga	Tongan for orality, multivoicedness
tu'a	Tongan for commoner
tu'unga	Tongan for location, status or position

Bibliography

Abbott, David, and Steve Pollard. *Hardship and Poverty in the Pacific*. Manila, Philippines: Asian Development Bank, 2004.
Adamo, David Tuesday. "The Task and Distinctiveness of African Biblical Hermeneutic(S)." *Old Testament Essays* 28 (2015) 31–52.
Ahn, John, ed. *Landscapes of Korean and Korean American Biblical Interpretation*. International Voices in Biblical Interpretation. Atlanta: SBL Press, 2019.
Ahn, Yong-Sung. *The Reign of God and Rome in Luke's Passion Narrative*. Biblical Interpretation Series 80. Leiden: Brill, 2006.
Aiono, Fanaafi Le Tagaloa. *O Motugaafa*. Alafua, USP: Le Lamepa, 1996.
Alama, Samasoni Moleli. "Jabez in Context: A Multidimensional Approach to Identity and Landholdings in Chronicles." PhD diss., University of Divinity, Melbourne, Australia, 2018.
Alexander, Loveday. *The Preface to Luke's Gospel: Literary Convention and Social Context in Luke 1.1–4 and Acts 1.1*. Society for New Testament Studies Monograph Series 78. Cambridge: Cambridge University Press, 1993.
Allen, Graham. *Intertextuality*. New Critical Idiom. New York: Routledge, 2011.
Anae, Melani, Falaniko Tominiko, Vavao Fetui, and Ieti Lima. "Transnational Sāmoan Chiefs: Views of the Fa'amatai (Chiefly System)." *Journal of Samoan Studies* 7 (2017) 38–50.
Ashcroft, Bill, Gareth Griffiths, and Helen Tiffin. *The Empire Writes Back: Theory and Practice in Post-Colonial Literatures*. New York: Routledge, 2002.
Bae, Hyunju. "Dancing around Life: An Asian Woman's Perspective." *Ecumenical Review* 56 (2004) 390–403.
Barclay, John M. G. "The Family as the Bearer of Religion in Judaism and Early Christianity." In *Constructing Early Christian Families: Family as Social Reality and Metaphor*, edited by Halvor Moxnes, 66–80. New York: Routledge, 1997.
Bauckham, Richard. "For Whom Were Gospels Written?" In *The Gospels for All Christians: Rethinking the Gospel Audiences*, edited by Richard Bauckham, 9–48. Grand Rapids: Eerdmans, 1998.
———. *Jesus and the Eyewitnesses: The Gospels as Eyewitness Testimony*. Grand Rapids: Eerdmans, 2006.
Beck, Valentin, Henning Hahn, and Robert Lepenies. "Interdisciplinary Perspectives on Poverty Measurement, Epistemic Injustices, and Social Activism." In *Dimensions*

of Poverty: Measurement, Epistemic Injustices, Activism, edited by Valentin Beck et al., 1–20. Philosophy and Poverty. Berlin: Springer, 2020.

Bendor, Jonathan. *Bounded Rationality and Politics*. Aaron Wildavsky Forum for Public Policy 6. Berkeley: University of California Press, 2010.

Berger, Peter L. *The Social Reality of Religion*. London: Faber & Faber, 1969.

Berger, Peter L., and Thomas Luckmann. *The Social Construction of Reality: A Treatise in Sociology of Knowledge*. New York: Penguin, 1966.

Bhabha, Homi K. *The Location of Culture*. New York: Routledge, 1994.

Bock, Darrell L. *A Theology of Luke's Gospel and Acts*. Biblical Theology of the New Testament. Grand Rapids: Zondervan, 2011.

Boer, Roland, and Fernando F. Segovia, eds. *The Future of the Biblical Past: Envisioning Biblical Studies on a Global Key*. Semeia Studies 66. Atlanta: Society of Biblical Literature, 2012.

Botha, Jan. *Subject to Whose Authority? Multiple Readings of Romans 13*. Emory Studies in Early Christianity 4. Atlanta: Scholars, 1994.

Bowman, Alan, and Andrew Wilson. "Quantifying the Roman Economy: Integration, Growth, Decline?" In *Quantifying the Roman Economy: Methods and Problems*. Oxford: Oxford University Press, 2009.

Brawley, Robert L. "Luke." In *Gospels and Acts: Fortress Commentary on the Bible: Study Edition*, edited by Margaret Aymer et al., 217–64. Minneapolis: Fortress, 2016.

Bresson, Alain. *The Making of the Ancient Greek Economy: Institutions, Markets, and Growth in the City-States*. Translated by Steven Rendall. Princeton Scholarship Online. Princeton: Princeton University Press, 2016.

Brousseau, Eric, and Jean-Michel Glachant, eds. *New Institutional Economics: A Guidebook*. New York: Cambridge University Press, 2008.

Burrus, Virginia. "The Gospel of Luke and the Acts of the Apostles." In *A Postcolonial Commentary on the New Testament Writings*, edited by Fernando F. Segovia and R.S. Sugirtharajah, 133–55. Bible and Postcolonialism 13. New York: T. & T. Clark, 2009.

Carr, David M. "The Many Uses of Intertextuality in Biblical Studies: Actual and Potential." In *Congress Volume Helsinki 2010*, edited by Martti Nissinen, 505–35. Vetus Testamentum Supplements 148. Leiden: Brill, 2012.

Carter, Warren. "Between Text and Sermon: Luke 18: 18–27." *Interpretation* 69 (2015) 466–69.

Chancey, Mark A. *Greco-Roman Culture and the Galilee of Jesus*. Society for the Study of the New Testament Monograph Series 134. New York: Cambridge University Press, 2005.

Chang, Steve S.H. "Economic Inequality in the Roman Empire and Paul's Appeal to Isotēs in 2 Corinthians 8:13–15 with Consideration of Inequality in South Korea Today." *Canon & Culture* 12 (2018) 209–34.

Cobb, Christy. *Slavery, Gender, Truth, and Power in Luke–Acts and Other Ancient Narratives*. 1st ed. New York: Springer Science+Business Media, 2019.

Cohick, Lynn H. "Jews and Christians." In *The Routledge Companion to Early Christian Thought*, edited by D. Jeffrey Bingham, 68–86. Routledge Companions. New York: Routledge, 2010.

Coleman, James S., and Thomas J. Fararo, eds. *Rational Choice: Advocacy and Critique*. Key Issues in Sociological Theory 7. Newbury Park, CA: Sage, 1992.

Conzelmann, Hans. *The Theology of St. Luke*. Translated by Geoffrey Buswell. Philadelphia: Fortress, 1961.

Cox, Harvey. "Theology from the Underside." *CrossCurrents* 39 (1989) 385–90.

Craddock, Fred B. *Luke*. Interpretation. Louisville: John Knox, 1990.

Culpepper, R. Alan. "The Gospel of Luke: Introduction, Commentary, and Reflections." In *The New Interpreter's Bible: General Articles & Introduction, Commentary, & Reflections for each Book of the Bible including the Apocryphal/Deuterocanonical Books in Twelve Volumes*, edited by Leander E. Keck. Nashville: Abingdon, 1995.

Culy, Martin M., Mikeal C. Parsons, and Joshua J. Stigall. *Luke: A Handbook on the Greek Text*. Waco, TX: Baylor University Press, 2010.

Dada, Adekunle Oyinloye. "Repositioning Contextual Biblical Hermeneutics in Africa Towards Holistic Empowerment." *Black Theology* 8 (2010) 160–74.

Danker, Frederick William. *A Greek Lexicon of the New Testament and Other Early Christian Literature*. (B.D.A.G.) Revised and Edited by Frederick Danker, Based on Walter Bauer's Sixth German Edition, and on Previous English Editions by W. F. Arndt, F. W. Gingrich, and F. W. Danker. Chicago: University of Chicago Press. Original edition, 1957, 2000.

de Ste Croix, G. E. M. *The Class Struggle in the Ancient Greek World: From the Archaic Age to the Arab Conquests*. Ithaca, NY: Cornell University Press, 1981.

"Deep Sea Mining by 2023 Gets Green Light in Pacific." Radio New Zealand, 2021.

Dicken, Frank. "The Author and Date of Luke–Acts: Exploring the Options." In *Issues in Luke–Acts: Selected Essays*, edited by Sean A. Adams and Michael W. Pahl, 7–26. Piscataway, NJ: Gorgias, 2012.

Didache: The Teaching of the Twelve Apostles. Translated by Clayton N. Jefford. Early Christian Apocrypha 5. Salem, OR: Polebridge, 2013.

Dinkler, Michal Beth. "The Acts of the Apostles." In *The Gospels and Acts: Fortress Commentary on the Bible Study Edition*, edited by Margaret Aymer, Cynthia Briggs Kittredge, and David A. Sánchez, 327–63. Minneapolis: Fortress, 2016.

Draper, Jonathan A. "African Contextual Hermeneutics: Readers, Reading Communities, and Their Options between Text and Context." *Religion & Theology* 22 (2015) 3–22.

Dube, Musa W. *Postcolonial Feminist Interpretation of the Bible*. St. Louis: Chalice, 2000.

Dyck, Bruno. *Management and the Gospel: Luke's Radical Message for the First and Twenty-First Centuries*. New York: Palgrave Macmillan, 2013.

Eagleton, Terry. *The Function of Criticism: From the Spectator to Post-Structuralism*. New York: Verso, 1984.

Edwards, James R. "Parallels and Patterns between Luke and Acts." *Bulletin for Biblical Research* 27 (2017) 485–501.

Ehrensperger, Kathy. *Searching Paul: Conversations with the Jewish Apostle to the Nations, Collected Essay*. Wissenschaftliche Untersuchungen zm Neuen Testament 429. Tübingen: Mohr Siebeck, 2019.

Ehrman, Bart D. *Jesus before the Gospels: How the Earliest Christians Remembered, Changed, and Invented Their Stories of the Savior*. New York: HarperCollins, 2016.

Elliott, John H. "Temple versus Household in Luke–Acts: A Contrast in Social Institutions." In *The Social World of Luke–Acts: Models for Interpretation*, edited by Jerome H. Neyrey, 211–40. Peabody, MA: Hendrickson, 1991.

Elster, Jon, ed. *Rational Choice*. Readings in Social and Political Theory. Washington Square, NY: New York University Press, 1986.

Esler, Philip F. *Community and Gospel in Luke–Acts: The Social and Political Motivations of Lucan Theology*. Society for the Study of the New Testament Monograph Series 57. Cambridge: Cambridge University Press, 1987.

———. "Social-Scientific Approaches." In *Dictionary of Biblical Criticism and Interpretation*, edited by Stanley E. Porter. New York: Routledge, 2007.

Feagaimaali'i, Joyetter. "Church Offerings Increase from $18.3million to $19.4million." *Samoa Observer*, May 23, 2019.

Fetalsana-Apura, Lily. *A Filipino Resistance Reading of Joshua 1:1–9*. International Voices in Biblical Studies 9. Atlanta: SBL Press, 2019.

Field, Michael. *Mau: Samoa's Struggle for Freedom*. Rev. and repr. Auckland, NZ: Polynesian, 1991.

Fiensy, David A. *Christian Origins and the Ancient Economy*. Eugene, OR: Cascade Books, 2014.

———. *Insights from Archaeology*. Insights: Reading the Bible in the 21st Century. Minneapolis: Fortress, 2017.

Finley, M. I. *The Ancient Economy*. 2nd ed. Sather Classical Lectures. Berkeley: University of California Press, 1985.

Fischer, Andrew Martin. *Poverty as Ideology: Rescuing Social Justice from Global Development Agendas*. CROP International Studies in Poverty Research. London: ZED, 2018.

Fish, Stanley. *Is There a Text in This Class?: The Authority of Interpretive Communities*. Cambridge: Harvard University Press, 1980.

Fitzmyer, Joseph A. *The Gospel according to Luke (I-IX)*. Anchor Bible 28. Garden City, NY: Doubleday, 1981.

———. *The Gospel according to Luke (X-XXIV)*. Anchor Bible 28A Garden City, NY: Doubleday, 1985.

Forbes, Greg W. *The God of Old: The Role of the Lukan Parables in the Purpose of Luke's Gospel*. Journal for the Study of the New Testament Supplements 198. Sheffield: Sheffield Academic, 2000.

Forrester, Georgia. "Why Measles Has 'Spread Like Wildfire' in Samoa." *The Sydney Morning Herald*, December 6, 2019.

Fowler, Robert M. *Let the Reader Understand: Reader-Response Criticism and the Gospel of Mark*. Harrisburg, PA: Trinity, 1996.

Freire, Paulo. *Pedagogy of the Oppressed*. Translated by Myra Bergman Ramos with an Introduction by Donaldo Macedo. New York. Continuum, 1970.

Garnsey, Peter et al. *The Roman Empire: Economy, Society and Culture*. 2nd ed. New York: Bloomsbury, 2014.

Gasper, Des. "Interdisciplinarity: Building Bridges and Nurturing a Complex Ecology of Ideas." In *Creative Social Research: Rethinking Theories and Methods*, edited by Ananta Kumar Giri, 308–44. Lanham, MD: Lexington, 2004.

Gillett, Robert. *Fisheries in the Economies of Pacific Island Countries and Territories*. Noumea, New Caledonia: Pacific Community, 2016.

Glass, William. Perceptions of Wealth and Poverty in Samoa. *Independent Study Project (ISP) Collection* 1485, 2012. https://digitalcollections.sit.edu/isp_collection/1485.

Goodnews. "Kolisi I Malua Faauuga", 2001. [Video].

Gootnick, David, and Oliver Richard. *American Samoa: Economic Trends, Status of the Tuna Canning Industry, and Stakeholders' Views on Minimum Wage Increases*. Washington, DC: United States Government Accountability Office, 2020.

Government of Samoa. "Land Titles Registration Act 2008" (2008).
Green, Joel B. *The Gospel of Luke.* New International Commentary on the New Testament. Grand Rapids: Eerdmans, 1997.
———. "The Gospel according to Luke." In *The New Interpreter's Study Bible: New Revised Standard Version with the Apocrypha,* edited by Walter J. Harrelson. Nashville: Abingdon, 2003.
———, ed. *Methods for Luke.* Methods in Biblical Interpretation. New York: Cambridge University Press, 2010.
Gupta, Nijay. "Fasting." In *Dictionary of Jesus and the Gospels,* edited by Joel B. Green et al. Downers Grove, IL: InterVarsity, 2013.
Hardin, Leslie T. 2012. "Searching for a Transformative Hermeneutic." *Journal of Spiritual Formation and Soul Care* 5 (2012) 144–57.
Havea, Jione. *Elusions of Control: Biblical Law on the Words of Women.* Semeia Studies 41. Atlanta: Society of Biblical Literature, 2003.
———. "The Politics of Climate Change." *International Journal of Public Theology: A talanoa from Oceania* 4 (2010) 345–55.
———. "Engaging Scriptures from Oceania." In *Bible, Borders. Belonging(S): Engaging Readings from Oceania,* edited by Jione Havea, David J. Neville, and Elaine M. Wainwright, 3–20. Semeia Studies 75. Atlanta: Society of Biblical Literature, 2014.
———. "Postcolonize Now." In *Postcolonial Voices from Downunder: Indigenous Matters, Confronting Readings,* edited by Jione Havea, 1–16. Eugene, OR: Pickwick Publications, 2017.
Havea, Jione, and Peter H. W. Lau. ———. "Context Matters: Reading from Asia and Pasifika." In *Reading Ecclesiastes from Asia and Pasifika,* edited by Jione Havea and Peter H. W. Lau, 1–12. . International Voices in Biblical Studies 10. Atlanta: SBL Press, 2020a.
———, eds. *Reading Ecclesiastes from Asia and Pasifika.* International Voices in Biblical Studies 10. Atlanta: SBL Press, 2020b.
———. "Reading Ruth Again, in Asia." In *Reading Ruth in Asia,* 1–14. International Voices in Biblical Studies 7. Atlanta: SBL Press, 2015.
Hays, J. Daniel. ""Sell Everything You Have and Give to the Poor": The Old Testament Prophetic Theme of Justice as the Connecting Motif of Luke 18:1—19:10." *Journal of the Evangelical Theological Society* 55 (2012) 43–63.
Hays, Richard B. *Echoes of Scripture in the Gospels.* Waco, TX: Baylor University Press, 2016.
Hedlun, Randy J. "Rethinking Luke's Purpose: The Effect of First-Century Social Conflict " *Journal of Pentecostal Theology* 22 (2013) 226–56.
Hellerman, Joseph H. "Wealth and Sacrifice in Early Christianity: Revisiting Mark's Presentation of Jesus' Encounter with the Rich Young Ruler." *Trinity Journal* 21 (2000) 143–64.
Heschel, Susannah. "Anti-Judaism/Anti-Semitism." In *Dictionary of Feminist Theologies,* edited by Letty M. Russell and J. Shannon Clarkson. Louisville: Westminster John Knox, 1996.
Hezel, Francis X, SJ. "Pacific Island Nations: How Viable Are Their Economies?" East-West Center, 2012.
Holland, Jeremy. *Tools for Institutional, Political, and Social Analysis of Policy Reform: A Sourcebook for Development Practitioners.* Washington, DC: World Bank, 2007.

Hollander, David B. "The Roman Economy in the Early Empire: An Overview." In *Paul and Economics: A Handbook*, edited by Thomas R. Blanton IV and Raymond Pickett, 1–22. Minneapolis: Fortress, 2017.

Holter, Knut. "When Biblical Scholars Talk About "Global" Biblical Interpretation." In *Global Hermeneutics? Reflections and Consequences*, edited by Knut Holter and Louis C. Jonker, 85–93. International Voices in Biblical Studies 1. Atlanta: Society of Biblical Literature, 2010.

Horsley, Richard A. *Jesus and the Politics of Roman Palestine*. Columbia: University of South Carolina Press, 2014.

Howes, Stephen, Beth Orton, and Sherman Surandiran. "In the Pacific, Migration and Population Growth Are Inversely Related." Development Policy Center, 2020. https://devpolicy.org/in-the-pacific-migration-and-population-growth-are-inversely-related-20201106-1/.

Hunkin, Eni Faleomavaega. "Recognizing and Welcoming the Leaders of the Pacific Islands " *Congressional Record* 153 (2007) H4490–H4493.

———. "Sense of the House with Respect to Importance of Diplomatic Relations with Pacific Island Nations." *Congressional Record* 144 (1998) H8491.

Ip, Alex Hon Ho. "An Exploration of Economic Rhetoric in the New Testament in Light of New Institutional Economics." In *Welcoming the Nations: International Sociorhetorical Explorations*, edited by Vernon K. Robbins and Roy R. Jeal. International Voices in Biblical Studies 13. Atlanta: SBL Press, 2020.

Jeffers, James S. *The Greco-Roman World of the New Testament Era: Exploring the Background of Early Christianity*. Downers Grove, IL: InterVarsity, 1991.

Johnson, Luke Timothy. *The Gospel of Luke*. Sacra Pagina. Collegeville, MN: Liturgical, 1991.

Jonge, Jan de. *Rethinking Rational Choice Theory: A Companion on Rational and Moral Action*. New York: Palgrave Macmillan, 2012.

Katovai, Eric, William F. Laurance, and Will Edwards. "Dynamics of Logging in the Solomon Islands: The Need for Restoration and Conservation Alternatives." *Tropical Conservation Science* 8 (2015) 718–31.

Keddie, Anthony. *Class and Power in Roman Palestine: The Socioeconomic Setting of Judaism and Christian Origins*. Cambridge: Cambridge University Press, 2019.

Kim, Seyoon. *Christ and Caesar: The Gospel and the Roman Empire in the Writings of Paul and Luke*. Grand Rapids: Eerdmans, 2008.

Kolohai, Charles Edward. 2013. "Η ΚοινΩνια Τησ Πιωτε Ωσ Σου: A Socio-Rhetorical Interpretation of Paul's Letter to Philemon." PhD diss., Pacific Theological College, Suva, Fiji, 2013.

Kristeva, Julia. 1980. *Desire in Language: A Semiotic Approach to Literature and Art*. Translated by Thomas Cora, Alice Jardine and Leon S. Roudiez. Edited by Leon S. Roudiez. European Perspectives. New York: Columbia University Press, 1980.

Kunukawa, Hisako, ed. *Migration and Diaspora: Exegetical Voices of Women in Northeast Asian Countries*. International Voices in Biblical Studies 6. Atlanta: SBL Press, 2014.

Lampe, Peter. "The Language of Equality in Early Christian House Churches: A Constructivist Approach " In *Early Christian Families in Context: An Interdisciplinary Dialogue*, edited by David L. Balch and Carolyn Osiek, 73–83. Religion, Marriage, and Family Series. Grand Rapids: Eerdmans, 2003.

Lebowitz, Arnold H. "American Samoa: Decline of a Culture." *California Western International Law Journal* 10 (1980) 220-71.

Lefaoseu, Iosefa. "Lalagaga O Le Ola (Weaving Life) with God: Reading the Book of Job as a Tosi-Lasi (Poly-Strandic) Text from a Samoan Relational Perspective: A Contribution to Biblical Hermeneutics in Oceania." PhD diss., Pacific Theological College, Suva, Fiji, 2018.

Leota, Peniamina. "Ethnic Tensions in Persian-Period Yehud: A Samoan Postcolonial Hermeneutic." PhD diss., Melbourne College of Divinity, Melbourne, 2005.

Leshem, Dotan. "From Ecclesiastical to Political Economy: The Rise of the Social." *Journal of Markets and Morality* 19 (2016) 29-39.

Levine, Amy-Jill. "Theological Education, the Bible, and History: Détente in the Culture Wars." In *Early Christian Families in Context: An Interdisciplinary Dialogue*, edited by David L. Balch and Carolyn Osiek, 327-36. Religion, Marriage, and Family Series. Grand Rapids: Eerdmans, 2003.

Liddell, Henry George, et al. *A Greek Lexicon*. Oxford: Clarendon, 1996.

Lioy, Dan. "One Savior and Two Responses: A Comparison and Analysis of Luke 18:18-30 and 19: 1-10." *Conspectus: The Journal of the South African Theological Seminary* 23 (2017) 125-55.

Liu, Jinyu. "Urban Poverty in the Roman Empire: Material Conditions." In *Paul and Economics: A Handbook*, edited by Thomas R. Blanton IV and Raymond Pickett, 23-56. Minneapolis: Fortress, 2017.

Longenecker, Bruce W. "Exposing the Economic Middle: A Revised Economy Scale for the Study of Early Urban Christianity." *Journal for the Study of the New Testament* 31 (2009) 243-78.

———. *In Stone and Story: Early Christianity in the Roman World*. Grand Rapids: Baker Academic, 2020.

Luthuli, Albert J. *Let My People Go: An Autobiography*. New York: McGraw-Hill, 1962.

Lyttkens, Carl Hampus. *Economic Analysis of Institutional Changes in Ancient Greek: Politics, Taxation and Rational Behaviour*. New York: Routledge, 2013.

Ma'ilo, Mosese. *Bible-Ing My Samoan*. Apia, Samoa: Piula Theological College, 2016.

———. "Island Prodigals: Encircling the Void in Luke 15:11-32." In *Sea of Readings: The Bible in the South Pacific*, edited by Jione Havea, 23-36. Semeia Studies 90. Atlanta: SBL Press, 2018.

MacDonald, Margaret Y. "Kinship and Family in the New Testament World." In *Understanding the Social World of the New Testament*, edited by Dietmar Neufeld and Richard E. DeMaris, 28-43. New York: Routledge, 2010.

Maier, Harry O. *New Testament Christianity in the Roman World*. New York: Oxford University Press, 2019.

Malina, Bruce J. *Christian Origins and Cultural Anthropology: Practical Models for Biblical Interpretation*. 1986. Reprint, Eugene, OR: Wipf & Stock, 2010.

———. "Wealth and Poverty in the New Testament and Its World." *Interpretation* 41 (1987) 354-67.

———. *The Social World of Jesus and the Gospels*. New York: Routledge, 1996.

———. "Social-Scientific Methods in Historical Jesus Research." In *The Social Setting of Jesus and the Gospel*, edited by Wolfgang Stegemann, Bruce J. Malina, and Gerd Theissen, 3-26. Minneapolis: Fortress, 2012.

Malina, Bruce J., and Jerome H. Neyrey. 1991a. "First-Century Personality: Dyadic, Not Individual " In *The Social World of Luke–Acts: Models of Interpretation*, edited by Jerome H. Neyrey, 67–96. Peabody, MA: Hendrickson, 1991a.

———. "Honor and Shame in Luke–Acts: Pivotal Values of the Mediterranean World." In *The Social World of Luke–Acts: Models for Interpretation*, edited by Jerome H. Neyrey, 25–65. Peabody, MA: Hendrickson, 1991b.

Marshall, I. Howard. *The Gospel of Luke: A Commentary on the Greek Text*. The New International Greek Testament Commentary. Exeter, UK: Paternoster, 1978.

Mbuvi, Andrew M. "African Biblical Studies: An Introduction to an Emerging Discipline." *Currents in Biblical Research* 15 (2017) 149–78.

McKay, Niall. "Apartheid Resistance and Biblical Interpretation: From Christian Confession to Materialist Analysis." *Politics and Religion* 8 (2015) 358–78.

McKenny, Gerald. "The Rich Young Ruler and Christian Ethics: A Proposal." *Journal of the Society of Christian Ethics* 40 (2020) 59–76.

McLean, B. H. *Biblical Interpretation and Philosophical Hermeneutics*. New York: Cambridge University Press, 2012.

Meeks, Wayne A. *The First Urban Christians: The Social World of the Apostle Paul*. Second. New Haven: Yale University Press, 1983.

Meleisea, Malama. *Lagaga: A Short History of Western Samoa*. Suva, Fiji: University of the South Pacific, 1987a.

———. *The Making of Modern Samoa: Traditional Authority and Colonial Administration in the History of Western Samoa*. Suva, Fiji: Institute of Pacific Studies of the University of the South Pacific, 1987b.

Metzger, James A. *Consumption and Wealth in Luke's Travel Narrative*. Biblical Interpretation Series 88. Leiden: Brill, 2007.

Miller, Amanda C. *Rumors of Resistance: Status Reversals and Hidden Transcripts in the Gospel of Luke*. Emerging Scholars. Minneapolis: Fortress, 2014.

Moessner, David Paul. *Luke the Historian of Israel's Legacy, Theologian of Israel's Christ: A New Reading of the 'Gospel Acts' of Luke*. Beihefte zur Zeitschrift für die neutestamentliche Wissenschaft 182. Berlin: de Gruyter, 2016.

Mofokeng, Takatso. "Black Christians, the Bible, and Liberation." *Journal of Black Theology* 2 (1988) 34–42.

Moraski, Byron J., and Charles R. Shipan. 1999. "The Politics of Supreme Court Nominations: A Theory of Institutional Constraints and Choices." *American Journal of Political Science* 43 (1999) 1069–95.

Morley, Neville. *Theories, Models, and Concepts in Ancient History*. Approaching the Ancient World. New York: Routledge, 2004.

Mosala, Itumeleng J. *Biblical Hermeneutics and Black Theology in South Africa*. Grand Rapids: Eerdmans, 1989.

———. "The Implications of the Text of Esther for African Women's Struggle for Liberation in South Africa." In *The Postcolonial Bible Reader*, edited by R.S. Sugirtharajah, 134–41. Malden, MA: Blackwell, 2006.

Moxnes, Halvor. *The Economy of the Kingdom: Social Conflict and Economic Relations in Luke's Gospels*. Overtures to Biblical Theology. 1988. Reprint, Eugene, OR: Wipf & Stock, 2004.

———. "What Is Family? Problems in Constructing Early Christian Families." In *Constructing Early Christian Families: Family as Social Reality and Metaphor*, edited by Halvor Moxnes, 13–41. New York: Routledge, 1997.

Munro, Alistair. *Bounded Rationality and Public Policy: A Perspective from Behavioural Economics*. New York: Springer, 2009.
Murphy, Edwina. "Sell Your Possessions: Cyprian, Luke and Wealth." *Colloquium: The Australian & New Zealand Theological Review* 49 (2017) 11–23.
Nadella, Raj. *Dialogue not Dogma: Many Voices in the Gospel of Luke*. Library of New Testament Studies. New York: Bloomsbury, 2011.
Nakamura, Robert T., and Thomas W. Church. *Taming Regulation: Superfund and the Challenge of Regulatory Reform*. Washington, DC: Brookings Institution, 2003.
Neufeld, Dietmar, and Richard E. DeMaris. *Understanding the Social World of the New Testament*. New York: Routledge, 2010.
Neyrey, Jerome H., ed. *The Social World of Luke–Acts: Models for Interpretation*. Peabody, MA: Hendrickson, 1991.
Noell, Edd S. 2007. "A "Marketless World"? An Examination of Wealth and Exchange in the Gospels and First-Century Palestine." *Journal of Markets and Morality* 10 (2007) 85–114.
Nofoaiga, Vaitusi. *A Samoan Reading of Discipleship in Matthew*. International Voices in Biblical Studies 8. Atlanta: SBL Press, 2017.
North, Douglass C. *Institutions, Institutional Change and Economic Performance*. New York: Cambridge University Press, 1990.
———. *Understanding the Process of Economic Change*. Princeton: Princeton University Press, 2005.
Oakman, Douglas E. "Execrating? Or Execrable Peasants!" In *The Galilean Economy in the Time of Jesus*, edited by David A. Fiensy and Ralph K. Hawkins, 139–64. Early Christianity and Its Literature 11. Atlanta: Society of Biblical Literature, 2013.
O'Day, Gail R. "The Gospel according to John." In *The New Interpreter's Study Bible: New Revised Standard Version with the Apocrypha*, 1905–52. Nashville: Abingdon, 2003.
Odekon, Mehmet. "Introduction." In *Encyclopedia of World Poverty*, edited by Mehmet Odekon. Thousand Oaks, CA: Sage, 2006.
Oppenheimer, Joe. *Principles of Politics: A Rational Choice Theory Guide to Politics and Social Justice*. New York: Cambridge University Press, 2012.
O'Rourke, Ronald. "U.S.–China Strategic Competition in South and East China Seas: Background and Issues for Congress." Washington, DC: Congressional Research Service, 2021.
Overman, J. Andrew. *Matthew's Gospel and Formative Judaism: The Social World of the Matthean Community*. Minneapolis: Fortress, 1990.
Palu, Ma'afu'otu'itonga. "Pacific Theology: A Re-Consideration of Its Methodology." *Pacific Journal of Theology* 29 (2003) 30–59.
———. "Contextualisation as Bridging the Hermeneutical Gap—Some Biblical Paradigms." *Pacific Journal of Theology* 34 (2005) 22–43.
———. "Contextualisation within the Parameters of the Biblical Narrative 'World': Aids as a Test Case." *Pacific Journal of Theology* 36 (2006) 12–25.
Parc, Elisabeth Du, and Nacanieli Bolo Spieth. "Tropical Cyclone Harold and Covid-19: A Double Blow to the Pacific Islands." Internal Displacement Monitoring Center, 2020. https://www.internal-displacement.org/expert-opinion/tropical-cyclone-harold-and-covid-19-a-double-blow-to-the-pacific-islands.
Park, Rohun. "The Challenge of Economy: A Cultural Interpretation of Luke's *Oikonomia*." PhD diss., Graduate School of Vanderbilt University, 2011.

———. "Whither the Studies of Economy in the Gospel of Luke?: A Critical Review and Search for Methodologies." *Korean Journal of Christian Studies* 84 (2012) 87–103.

Parkins, Helen M. "The 'Consumer City' Domesticated? The Roman City in Élite Economic Strategies." In *Roman Urbanism: Beyond the Consumer City*, edited by Helen M. Parkins, 81–108. New York: Routledge, 1997.

Phillips, Thomas E. 2003. "Reading Recent Readings of Issues of Wealth and Poverty in Luke and Acts." *Currents in Biblical Research* 1 (2003) 231–69.

Piotrowski, Nicholas G. *Matthew's New David at the End of Exile: A Socio-Rhetorical Study of Scriptual Quotations*. Novum Testamentum Supplements 170. Leiden: Brill, 2016.

Polanyi, Karl. *The Great Transformation: The Political and Economic Origins of Our Time; Foreword by Joseph Stiglitz; with New Introduction by Fred Block*. 2nd ed. Boston: Beacon, 2001.

Porter, Stanley E. "Biblical Hermeneutics and Theological Responsibility." In *The Future of Biblical Interpretation: Responsible Plurality in Biblical Hermeneutics*, edited by Stanley E. Porter and Matthew R. Malcolm, 29–50. Downers Grove, IL: InterVarsity, 2013.

Powell, Mark Allan. *What Is Narrative Criticism?* Guides to Biblical Scholarship: New Testament. Minneapolis: Fortress, 1990.

Pratt, George. *Pratt's Grammar Dictionary and Samoan Language*. Apia: Malua, 1911.

Puaina, Seumaninoa. "Beyond Universalism: Unraveling the Anonymous Minor Characters in Matthew 15:21–28". PhD diss., Graduate Theological Union, Berkeley, CA, 2016.

Pui-lan, Kwok. *Introducing Asian Feminist Theology*. Introductions in Feminist Theology 4. Sheffield: Sheffield Academic, 2000.

Putnam, Daniel. "Poverty as a Social Relation." In *Dimensions of Poverty: Measurement, Epistemic Injustices, Activism*, edited by Valentin Beck, Henning Hahn and Robert Lepenies, 41–56. Berlin: Springer, 2020.

Refiti, Albert. "Mavae and Tofiga: Spatial Exposition of the Samoan Cosmogony and Architecture." PhD diss., School of Art & Design, Auckland University of Technology, 2015.

Repschinski, Boris. *The Controversy Stories in the Gospel of Matthew: Their Redaction, Form, and Relevance for the Relationship between the Matthean Community and Formative Judaism*. Forschungen zur Religion und Literatur des Alten und Neuen Testaments 189. Gottingen: Vandenhoeck & Ruprecht, 2000.

Richter, Rudolf. *Essays on New Institutional Economics*. New York: Springer, 2015.

Robbins, Vernon K. *Exploring the Texture of the Texts: A Guide to Socio-Rhetorical Interpretation*. Harrisburg, PA: Trinity, 1996a.

———. *Foundations for Sociorhetorical Exploration: A Rhetoric of Religious Antiquity Reader*. Atlanta: SBL Press, 2016.

———. "The Social Location of the Implied Author of Luke–Acts." In *The Social World of Luke–Acts: Models for Interpretation*, edited by Jerome H. Neyrey, 305–32. Peabody, MA: Hendrickson, 1991.

———. "Socio-Rhetorical Interpretation." In *The Blackwell Companion to the New Testament*, edited by David E. Aune, 192–219. West Sussex, UK: Blackwell, 2010.

———. *Sea Voyages and Beyond: Emerging Strategies in Socio-Rhetorical Interpretation*. Emory Studies in Early Christianity. Atlanta: SBL Press, 2018.

———. *The Tapestry of Early Christian Discourse: Rhetoric, Society, and Ideology.* London: Routledge, 1996.

Robbins, Vernon K., and Roy R. Jeal. *Welcoming the Nations: International Sociorhetorical Explorations.* International Voices in Biblical Interpretation 13. Atlanta: SBL Press, 2020.

Rohrbaugh, Richard L. "The Jesus Tradition: The Gospel Writer's Strategies of Persuasion." In *The Early Christian World*, edited by Philip F. Esler, 169–96. New York: Routledge, 2017.

Rosenfeld, Ben Zion, and Haim Perlmutter. *Social Stratification of the Jewish Population of Roman Palestine in the Period of Mishnah, 70–250 CE.* Brill Reference Library of Judaism 59. Leiden: Brill, 2019.

Runesson, Anna. *Exegesis in the Making: Postcolonialism and New Testament Studies.* Biblical Interpretation Series 103. Leiden: Brill, 2011.

Salamon, Lester M. "The Tools Approach: And the New Governance: Conclusion and Implications." In *The Tools of Government: A Guide to the New Governance*, edited by Lester M. Salamon, 600–610. New York: Oxford University Press, 2002.

Saller, Richard P. "Household and Gender." In *The Cambridge Economic History of the Greco-Roman World*, edited by Walter Scheidel, Ian Morris, and Richard Saller, 87–112. New York: Cambridge University Press, 2008.

Samoa Bureau of Statistics. "Samoa Hardship and Poverty Report: Analysis of the 2013/2014 Household Income and Expenditure Survey." Apia, Samoa: Samoa Bureau of Statistics and UNDP Pacific Center, 2016.

Samoa Law Reform Commission. "Pule a Le Matai Sa'o: Final Report (Fr18/17)." Apia: Government of Samoa: Office of the Prime Minister and Minister for the Samoa Law Reform Commission, 2017.

Sanders, E. P. *Paul: The Apostle's Life, Letters, and Thought.* Minneapolis: Fortress, 2015.

Santandreu, Peter. "Pro-Secular? Luke's Relationship with Roman Imperial System and Culture." *Verbum* 15 (2018). https://fisherpub.sjfc.edu/verbum/vol15/iss1/7

Scheffler, Eben. "Luke's View on Poverty in Its Ancient (Roman) Economic Context: A Challenge for Today." *Scriptura* 106 (2011) 115–35.

Scheidel, Walter. "Population and Demography." *Stanford/Princeton Working Papers in Classics*, 2006. https://www.princeton.edu/~pswpc/pdfs/scheidel/040604.pdf

Scheidel, Walter, and Steven J. Friesen. "The Size of the Economy and the Distribution of Income in the Roman Empire." *Journal of Roman Studies* 99 (2009) 61–91.

Scheidel, Walter, Ian Morris, and Richard P. Saller. *The Cambridge Economic History of the Greco-Roman World.* 1st paperback ed. New York: Cambridge University Press, 2008.

Schottroff, Luise, and Wolfgang Stegemann. *Jesus and the Hope of the Poor.* Translated by Matthew J. O'Connell. 1986. Reprint, Eugene, OR: Wipf & Stock, 2009.

Schweiger, Gottfried, ed. *Poverty, Inequality and the Critical Theory of Recognition.* Salzburg: Springer, 2020.

Segovia, Fernando F. "The Emerging Project of Asian Biblical Hermeneutics: Reading Asian Readers." *Biblical Interpretation* 2 (1994) 371–73.

Shirley, Mary M. *Institutions and Development.* Northampton, MA: Elgar, 2008.

Skinner, Eloise. "Citizens of Two Realms." *Harvard Divinity Bulletin*, Spring/Summer 2021. https://bulletin.hds.harvard.edu/citizens-of-two-realms/.

Smith, Larry. *Six Words Fresh Off the Boat: Stories of Immigration, Identity, and Coming to America.* Glendale, CA: Kingswell, 2017.

Smith, Le Vaotogo Frank. *The Johannine Jesus from a Samoan Perspective: Toward an Intercultural Reading of the Fourth Gospel*. Mauritius: Blessed Hope, 2017.

South Pacific Commission. "Economic Social Impact Indicators," 2020.

Stanley, Alan P. "The Rich Young Ruler and Salvation." *Bibliotheca Sacra* 163 (2006) 46–62.

Stuhlmacher, Peter. *Historical Criticism and Theological Interpretation of Scripture: Toward a Hermeneutics of Consent*. Translated by Roy A. Harrisville. 1977. Reprint, Eugene, OR: Wipf & Stock, 2003.

Sugirtharajah, R. S. *The Bible and Asia: From the Pre-Christian Era to the Postcolonial Age*. Cambridge: Harvard University Press, 2013.

———. *The Bible and the Third World Precolonial, Colonial, and Postcolonial Encounters*. New York: Cambridge University Press, 2001. https://ebookcentral.proquest.com/lib/anu/detail.action?docID=201720.

———. "Introduction and Some Thoughts on Asian Biblical Hermeneutics." *Biblical Interpretation* 2 (1994) 251–63.

———. "Vernacular Resurrections: An Introduction." In *Vernacular Hermeneutics*, 11–19. Bible and Postcolonialism 2. Sheffield: Sheffield Academic, 1999.

———, ed. *Voices from the Margin: Interpreting the Bible in the Third World*—25th Anniversary Edition. Maryknoll, NY: Orbis, 2017.

Talbert, Charles H. "Once Again: Gospel Genre." *Semeia* 43 (1988) 53–73.

———. *Reading Luke–Acts in Its Mediterranean Milieu*. Novum Testamentum Supplements 107. Leiden: Brill, 2003.

Tannehill, Robert C. *The Narrative Unity of Luke–Acts: A Literary Interpretation*. Vol. 1: *The Gospel according to Luke*. Philadelphia: Fortress, 1986.

Tanzer, Sarah J. The Historical Jesus. In *The Jewish Annotated New Testament: New Revised Standard Version Bible Translation*, edited by Amy-Jill Levine and Marc Zvi Brettler. Oxford: Oxford University Press, 2017.

Taper, Bernard. "Mark Twain's San Francisco." *American Heritage*, 1963. https://www.americanheritage.com/mark-twains-san-francisco#.

Temin, Peter. "The Contribution of Economics." In *The Cambridge Companion to the Roman Economy*, edited by Walter Scheidel, 45–70. New York: Cambridge University Press, 2012.

———. *A Market Economy in the Early Roman Empire*. Princeton: Princeton University Press, 2013.

Thiselton, Anthony C. "The Hermeneutical Dynamics of 'Reading Luke' as Interpretation, Reflection, and Formation." In *Reading Luke: Interpretation, Reflection, Formation*, edited by Craig G. Bartholomew, Joel B. Green, and Anthony C. Thiselton, 3–41. Grand Rapids: Zondervan, 2005.

———. *Hermeneutics: An Introduction* Grand Rapids: Eerdmans, 2009.

Thompson, Richard P. "Luke–Acts: The Gospel of Luke and the Acts of the Apostles." In *The Blackwell Companion to the New Testament*, edited by David E. Aune, 319–43. Blackwel Companions to Religion. Malden, MA: Blackwell, 2010.

Tofaeono, Ama'amalele. *Eco-Theology: Aiga—the Household of Life. A Perspective from Living Myths and Traditions of Samoa*: World Mission Scripts, 2000.

Tominiko, Seulupe Falaniko. "Tautua: A Relational Obligation?" In *A Handbook for Translational Samoan Matai (Chiefs)*, edited by Lupematasila Misatauveve Melani Anae and Seugalupemaalii Ingrid Peterson, 113–24. Christchurch, New Zealand: Macmillan Brown Center for Pacific Studies, 2020.

Tool, Marc R., and Paul Dale Bush, eds. *Institutional Analysis and Economic Policy*, 2003.
Trainor, Michael. *About Earth's Child: An Ecological Listening to the Gospel of Luke*. The Earth Bible Commentary. Sheffield: Sheffield Phoenix, 2012.
Tropper, Amram. "The Economics of Jewish Childhood in Late Antiquity." *Hebrew Union College Annual* (2005) 189–233.
Trümper, Monica. "Material and Social Environment of Greco-Roman Households in the East: The Case of Hellenistic Delos " In *Early Christian Families in Context: An Interdisciplinary Dialogue*, edited by David L. Balch and Carolyn Osiek, 19–43. Grand Rapids: Eerdmans, 2003.
Tuigamala, Filemoni. "Soalaupule: A Tool for Christian Leadership Towards Achieving Peace and Justice in Samoa." BD thesis, Malua Theological College, Apia, 2012.
Ukpong, Justin S. "Rereading the Bible with African Eyes: Inculturation and Hermeneutics." *Journal of Theology for Southern Africa* 91 (1995) 3–14.
———. "Reading the Bible in a Global Village: Issues and Challenges from African Readings." In *Reading the Bible in the Global Village: Cape Town*, edited by Justin S. Ukpong et al., 9–40. Global Perspectives on Biblical Scholarship 3. Atlanta: Society of Biblical Literature, 2002.
United Nations. "Transforming Our World: The 2030 Agenda for Sustainable Development," 2015.
Vaka'uta, Nāsili. *Reading Ezra 9–10 Tu'a-Wise: Rethinking Biblical Interpretation in Oceania*. International Voices in Biblical Studies 3. Atlanta: Society of Biblical Literature, 2011.
Wan, Sze-kar. "Does Diaspora Identity Imply Some Sort of Universality? An Asian-American Reading of Galatians." In *Interpreting Beyond Borders*, edited by Fernando F. Segovia, 107–31. Bible and Postcolonialism 3. Sheffield: Sheffield Academic, 2000.
Weingast, Barry R., and Donald A. Wittman. "The Reach of Political Economy." In *The Oxford Handbook of Political Economy*, edited by Barry R. Weingast and Donald A. Wittman, 3–28. Oxford Handbooks of Political Science. New York: Oxford University Press, 2008.
Wenham, David. "The Purpose of Luke–Acts: Israel's Story in the Context of the Roman Empire." In *Reading Luke: Interpretation, Reflection, Formation*, edited by Craig G. Bartholomew, Joel B. Green, and Anthony C. Thiselton, 79–103. Grand Rapids, MI: Zondervan, 2005.
West, Gerald O. *The Academy of the Poor: Towards a Dialogical Reading of the Bible*. Interventions 2. Sheffield: Sheffield Academic, 1999.
———. "Accountable African Biblical Scholarship: Post-Colonial and Tri-Polar." *Canon & Culture* 10 (2016) 35–67.
———. "Locating Contextual Bible Study within Praxis." *Diaconia* 4 (2013) 43–48.
———. *Reading Other-Wise: Socially Engaged Biblical Scholars Reading with Their Local Communities*. Semeia Studies 68. Atlanta: Society of Biblical Literature, 2007.
Wink, Walter. *Naming the Powers: The Language of Power in the New Testament*. Philadelphia: Fortress, 1984.
Wit, Hans de, and Janet Dyk, eds. *Bible and Transformation: The Promise of Intercultural Bible Reading*. Semeia Studies Number 81. Atlanta: SBL Press, 2015.
Wolter, Michael. *The Gospel according to Luke*. Baylor-Mohr Siebeck Studies in Early Christianity. Waco: Baylor University Press, 2016.

World Bank. "Pacific Possible: Long-Term Economic Opportunities and Challenges for Pacific Island Countries." Washington, DC: World Bank, 2017.

———. "East Asia and the Pacific: Macro Poverty Outlook, Country by Country Analysis and Projections for the Developing World." Washington, DC: International Bank for Reconstruction and Development, 2020.

World Council of Churches. Island of Hope—the Pacific Churches' Response on Alternatives to Economic Globalization In *Island of Hope: A Pacific Alternative to Economic Globalization*. Nadi, Fiji: World Council of Churches, 2001.

Wright, N. T. *God and the Pandemic: A Christian Reflection on the Coronavirus and Its Aftermath*. London: Zondervan, 2020.

Wulf, Arthur John. "Was Earth Created Good:? Reappraising Earth in Genesis 1:1—2:4a from a Samoan Gafataulima Perspective". PhD diss., University of Auckland, 2016.

Yee, Gale A. ""She Stood in Tears Amid the Alien Corn": Ruth, the Perpetual Foreigner and Model Minority." In *They Were All Together in One Place? Toward Minority Biblical Criticism*, edited by Randall C. Bailey, Tat-siong Benny Liew, and Fernando F. Segovia, 119–40. Semeia Studies 57. Atlanta: Society of Biblical Literature, 2009.

Yeo, Khiok-Khng. "The Rhetorical Hermeneutic of 1 Corinthians 8 and Chinese Ancestor Worship." In *Exegesis in the Making: Postcolonialism and New Testament Studies*, edited by Anna Runesson, 168–85. Biblical Interpretation Series 103. Leiden: Brill, 2011.

www.ingramcontent.com/pod-product-compliance
Lightning Source LLC
Chambersburg PA
CBHW051053230426
4366TCB00013B/2271